Jaleel

HOUGHTON MIFFLIN

Math
Steps

HOUGHTON MIFFLIN

Boston • Atlanta • Dallas • Denver • Geneva, Illinois • Palo Alto • Princeton

Grateful acknowledgment is given for the contributions of

Student Book

Rosemary Theresa Barry
Karen R. Boyle
Barbara Brozman
Gary S. Bush
John E. Cassidy
Dorothy Kirk

Sharon Ann Kovalcik
Bernice Kubek
Donna Marie Kvasnok
Ann Cherney Markunas
Joanne Marie Mascha
Kathleen Mary Ogrin

Judith Ostrowski
Jeanette Mishic Polomsky
Patricia Stenger
Annabelle L. Higgins Svete

Teacher Book
Contributing Writers

Dr. Judy Curran Buck
Assistant Professor of Mathematics
Plymouth State College
Plymouth, New Hampshire

Dr. Anne M. Raymond
Assistant Professor of Mathematics
Keene State College
Keene, New Hampshire

Michelle Lynn Rock
Elementary Teacher
Oxford School District
Oxford, Mississippi

Dr. Richard Evans
Professor of Mathematics
Plymouth State College
Plymouth, New Hampshire

Stuart P. Robertson, Jr.
Education Consultant
Pelham, New Hampshire

Dr. Jean M. Shaw
Professor of Elementary Education
University of Mississippi
Oxford, Mississippi

Dr. Mary K. Porter
Professor of Mathematics
St. Mary's College
Notre Dame, Indiana

Dr. David Rock
Associate Professor,
Mathematics Education
University of Mississippi
Oxford, Mississippi

ISBN: 0-395-98535-8

9 10 11 12 13 14 15 -PO- 07 06 05

Contents

UNIT 1 • TABLE OF CONTENTS

Place Value

We will be using this vocabulary:

place value the value given to the place, or position, of a digit in a number

round to replace an exact number by another number that is easier to use

compare to decide which number of a group of numbers is greatest or least

order to arrange a group of numbers in a certain way, such as from least to greatest or from greatest to least

Dear Family,

During the next few weeks, our math class will be learning and practicing place value.

You can expect to see homework that provides practice with rounding. Here is a sample you may want to keep handy to give help if needed.

Rounding to the Nearest Hundred

To round a number such as **4,175** to the nearest hundred, first find the digit in the hundreds place.

Hundreds Place
↓

4,175

↑

greater than 5

Next, look at the digit in the place to the right (**7**). If the digit in the place to the right is less than **5**, round down. If it is greater than or equal to **5**, round up.

Since the digit to the right of the hundreds place is greater than **5**, round **4,175** up to **4,200**, the nearest hundred.

During this unit, students will need to continue practicing rounding and other skills related to place value, such as comparing numbers.

Sincerely,

Name _____

You can use a number line to round numbers.

Round **132** to the **nearest ten**.

1. **132** is between **130** and **140**.

2. Since **132** is closer to **130** than to **140**, 132 *rounds down* to **130**.

Round **857** to the **nearest hundred**.

1. **857** is between **800** and **900**.

2. Since **857** is closer to **900** than to **800**, 857 *rounds up* to **900**.

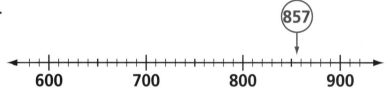

Here's how to round without using a number line.

1. Find the digit in the place to the right of the place you are rounding to.

2. If that digit **is less than 5**, round the number *down* to the place you are rounding to. If that digit **is 5 or greater**, round the number *up* to the place you are rounding to.

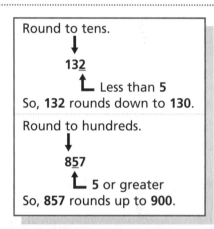

Other Examples

Rounded to the **nearest thousand**, **1,462** rounds *down* to **1,000** because the digit in the place to the right of the thousands place **is less than 5**.

Rounded to the **nearest thousand**, **7,503** rounds *up* to **8,000** because the digit in the place to the right of the thousands place **is 5 or greater**.

Use the number line above to round each number to the nearest ten.

1. 131 _____   136 _____   139 _____   134 _____

2. 137 _____   133 _____   135 _____   138 _____

Use the number line above to round each number to the nearest hundred.

3. 612 _____   850 _____   760 _____   675 _____

4. 820 _____   688 _____   706 _____   815 _____

Round to the nearest ten.

5. 25 _____ 16 _____ 9 _____ 631 _____

6. 35 _____ 55 _____ 24 _____ 358 _____

Round to the nearest hundred.

7. 348 _____ 420 _____ 3,283 _____

8. 580 _____ 940 _____ 5,775 _____

Round to the nearest thousand.

9. 2,500 _____ 6,150 _____ 5,210 _____

10. 3,500 _____ 7,250 _____ 5,795 _____

11. 4,500 _____ 9,350 _____ 7,642 _____

Problem Solving Reasoning Each of the following sentences contains a number. Decide if that number is exact or rounded. Write *rounded number* or *exact number*. Then explain why.

12. The population of Beaumont, California, is about **15,000** people.

_____

_____

13. The basketball team scored **20** points in the first half of the game.

_____

☑ **Quick Check**

Write the value of 7 in each exercise.

14. 64,074 **15.** 107,234 **16.** 575,252

_____ _____ _____

Compare. Write > or <.

17. 9,327 ◯ 9,486 **18.** 27,087 ◯ 27,807

19. 140,265 ◯ 104,265

Round each number to the nearest thousand.

20. 4,509 **21.** 7,353 **22.** 8,099

_____ _____ _____

Work Space.

Name

How deep is the ocean? This bar graph shows the estimated depth of four oceans.

In this lesson, you will use graphs to compare, make estimates, and draw conclusions about the data.

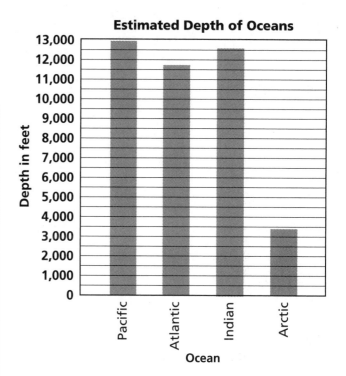

Tips to Remember:

1. Understand	2. Decide	3. Solve	4. Look back

- Ask yourself: Have I solved a problem like this one before? How did I solve it?
- Compare the labels on the graph with the words and numbers in the problem. Find the facts you need from the graph.
- When you can, make a prediction about the answer. Then compare your answer with your prediction.

Solve. Use the bar graph above.

1. What is the estimated depth of the Arctic Ocean to the nearest thousand feet?

   Think: How do you estimate a number using the graph?

   _____

   _____

   _____

   Answer _____

2. Explain whether or not you can use the graph to decide which ocean is the largest ocean.

   Think: What information is given in the graph?

   _____

   Answer _____

   _____

   _____

3. Lake Baikal, the deepest lake in the world, is about **1,800** feet deeper than the Arctic Ocean. Estimate the depth of Lake Baikal.

4. What is the depth of the Atlantic Ocean rounded to the nearest hundred feet?

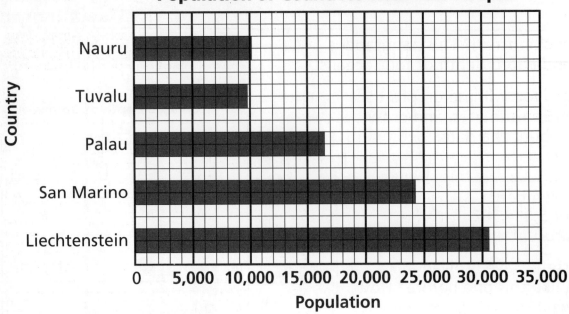

Population of Countries with Few People

Country (vertical axis)

Nauru, Tuvalu, Palau, San Marino, Liechtenstein

Population (horizontal axis): 0, 5,000, 10,000, 15,000, 20,000, 25,000, 30,000, 35,000

Population

Solve. Use the bar graph above.

5. Which country shown in the graph has the greatest population? What is the population to the nearest thousand?

_____

6. Which country has a population about three times the population of Tuvalu?

_____

7. Which two countries on the graph have about the same population?

_____

_____

8. Wichita, Kansas has a population of **304,011**. Does this city have more or fewer people than the countries shown in the graph? Explain.

_____

_____

_____

Extend Your Thinking

9. Can you use the graph to find which country in the *world* has the greatest population in the *world*? Explain.

_____

_____

_____

10. Explain the method you used to solve problem **6.**

_____

_____

_____

_____

Name _____

The period after the thousands period is called the **millions period**.

The **standard form** for the numbers written in this chart is **5,054,782**. To read a number, say the number in each period, beginning with the greatest period, then say the name of each period, except for the ones period.

The number **5,054,782** is read as: five *million*, fifty-four *thousand*, seven hundred eighty-two.

27,001,909

Read: twenty-seven *million*, one *thousand*, nine hundred nine

300,518,040

Read: three hundred *million*, five hundred eighteen *thousand*, forty

Millions Period			Thousands Period			Ones Period		
Hundred millions	Ten millions	Millions	Hundred thousands	Ten thousands	Thousands	Hundreds	Tens	Ones
		5	0	5	4	7	8	2

Place commas in each number. Then write each number in the place-value chart.

1. 1 2 0 0 0 1 7   9 0 5 0 4 6 1   1 7 0 0 5 6 0 5

2. 1 8 4 2 8 0 0 0   1 0 3 6 0 0 3 0 1   4 9 0 2 1 7 0 5 0

Read each number. Then write it in words.

3.   3,782,410   _____

4.   80,050,520   _____

Write each number in standard form. Use commas to separate the periods.

5. eight million, two hundred fifty-one thousand, six hundred ninety-seven

_____

6. three million, one hundred thousand, fifteen

_____

When a number is written using digits, it is written in **standard form**. For example, **24,035,600** is written in standard form.

Write each number in standard form. Use
commas to separate the periods.

7. seventy-one million, three hundred two thousand,
five hundred nine

_____

8. twenty million, eight hundred thirty-seven thousand, four

_____

9. three million, three thousand, two hundred twelve

_____

10. eight million, ninety-one thousand, ten

_____

11. seven hundred million, two thousand,
six hundred

_____

| Problem Solving |
| Reasoning |

Decide if the number is exact or rounded.
Write *exact number* or *rounded number*. Then
explain why.

12. Your computer shows you are the
5,438,891 person to visit a web
site.

_____

_____

13. There are at least **2,700,000** people
living in Chicago, Illinois.

_____

_____

Test Prep ★ Mixed Review

14 Martin says his house address has a
5 in the tens place. Which could be
his address?

A 8056

B 7594

C 5763

D 1507

15 A department store sold 6,009 copies
of the same toy in one month. What
words mean 6,009?

F Sixty thousand nine

G Sixty-nine hundred

H Six thousand nine

J Six hundred nine

Rounding Greater Numbers

You can round greater numbers the same way you round numbers to the nearest ten, hundred, or thousand.

Round **23,977** to the **nearest ten thousand.**

Round to this place ⌐
                    23,977
                    ↑

1. Find the digit to the right of the ten thousands place.

2. If that digit **is less than 5**, round the number **down**. If that digit **is 5 or greater**, round the number **up**.

So, **23,977** rounded to the **nearest ten thousand** is **20,000.**

Example: Round **6,520,099** to the **nearest million.**

Round to this place ⌐
                   6,520,099
                 ↑

1. Find the digit to the right of the millions place.

2. If that digit **is less than 5**, round the number **down**. If that digit **is 5 or greater**, round the number **up**.

So, **6,520,099** rounded to the nearest **million** is **7,000,000**

Round each number to the nearest ten thousand.

1. 19,200 _____   12,400 _____   27,203 _____

2. 123,466 _____   114,937 _____   107,640 _____

Round each number to the nearest hundred thousand.

3. 352,109 _____   467,488 _____   724,607 _____

4. 2,643,000 _____   2,707,480 _____   7,450,620 _____

5. 3,276,407 _____   4,650,171 _____   7,190,404 _____

Round each number to the nearest million.

6. 988,204 _____   1,655,413 _____   3,247,602 _____

7. 5,007,961 _____   3,500,000 _____   6,769,274 _____

Round each number to the nearest ten, hundred, and thousand.

		ten	hundred	thousand
8.	1,719,503	_____	_____	_____
9.	4,220,457	_____	_____	_____
10.	6,871,764	_____	_____	_____
11.	23,305,996	_____	_____	_____
12.	94,558,248	_____	_____	_____
13.	847,356,121	_____	_____	_____

Problem Solving Reasoning Solve.

14. What is the greatest possible number that, when rounded to the nearest million, will become **1,000,000**?

_____

15. What is the least possible number that, when rounded to the nearest million, will become **1,000,000**?

_____

 Quick Check

Write the value of 4 in each number.

16. 4,598,678   **17.** 7,045,369   **18.** 6,409,068

_____   _____   _____

Round each number to the nearest ten thousand.

19. 19,000   **20.** 27,349   **21.** 83,878

_____   _____   _____

Round each number to the nearest hundred thousand.

22. 619,000   **23.** 4,719,000   **24.** 7,435,312

_____   _____   _____

Work Space.

Name _____

In a sequence of numbers, a certain rule determines the order of the numbers.

To find the missing number in a sequence, you can look for a pattern to find the rule.

Problem

What would be the next number in this sequence?
5, 3, 8, 6, 11, 9, 14, ___?___

---

1 **Understand**   As you reread the problem, ask yourself questions.

- What information do you know? _____

  _____

- What do you need to find out? _____

  _____

---

2 **Decide**   Choose a method for solving.

Try the strategy Find a Pattern.

- Think about what you must do to the first number to get the second number. What must you do to the second number to get the third number?

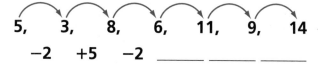

5,   3,   8,   6,   11,   9,   14

−2   +5   −2   _____ _____ _____

---

3 **Solve**   Decide how to describe the pattern.

Subtract **2**, add **5**, _____, and so on.

Use the pattern to find the missing number.

I _____ to get 14. So I _____
from **14** to find the next number in the sequence.

_____

---

4 **Look back**   Check your answer. Write the answer. **Answer** _____

- Why was it important to look at all the numbers before deciding on the pattern?

  _____

  _____

Solve. Use the Find a Pattern Strategy or any other strategy you have learned.

1. What is the next number in this sequence?

Think: What can I do to the **4** to get **8**? _____

4, 8, 12, 16, 20, _____

2. What is the next number in this sequence?

Think: What can I do to the **7** to get **10** and with **10** to get **9**?

_____

7, 10, 9, 12, 11, _____

3. Draw the next figure in this sequence.

 _____

4. Draw the next figure in this sequence.

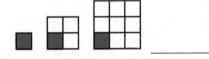 _____

5. What is the greatest 3-digit number whose digits have a sum of **12**?

_____

6. When you round this number to the nearest ten, you get **310**. The sum of the digits is **6**. What is the number?

_____

7. **1, 5, 9, 13, 17,** _____, _____, _____

What will be the eighth number in this sequence?

_____

8. What will be the next letter in this sequence?

A, C, E, G, I

_____

9. Use the clues to find the **7**-digit mystery number.

- It is between **1** and **2** million.
- The first three digits are the same.
- The least possible digit is in the thousands place.
- The greatest possible digit is in the ones place.
- The hundreds digit is **1** more than the tens digit.
- The sum of the digits is **21**.

_____

10. Use the clues to find another **7**-digit mystery number.

- It is between **7** and **8** million.
- It contains all of the digits greater than **1** and less than **8**.
- The hundred thousands digit is **3**.
- The ten thousands digit and the thousands digit are the same. Their sum is the ones digit.
- The tens digit is greater than the hundreds digit.

_____

Name _____

Write each number in standard form.

1. three thousand, five hundred thirty-nine _____

2. seventy-two thousand, one hundred four _____

3. six hundred fifty-three thousand, twenty _____

4. nine million, four hundred thousand, two _____

5. two hundred sixty million, twenty-five thousand, four hundred sixteen _____

6. thirty-one million, one hundred six thousand, seven hundred fifty-three _____

Write <, >, or =.

7. 567 ◯ 547   8. 3,209 ◯ 3,290   9. 9,900 ◯ 9,899

10. 13,000 ◯ 13,100   11. 89,745 ◯ 89,745   12. 750,221 ◯ 705,221

Round to the nearest hundred.

13. 449 _____   14. 850 _____   15. 44,061 _____   16. 178,888 _____

Round to the nearest ten thousand.

17. 75,503 _____   18. 549,840 _____   19. 1,427,607 _____

Round to the nearest hundred thousand.

20. 1,750,621 _____   21. 7,247,063 _____

The bar graph shows the number of hours a figure skater practices each day. Use the graph to solve each problem.

22. Look for a pattern in the number of hours the skater practices each day. Describe the pattern.

_____

23. Use the pattern to predict the number of hours the skater will practice on Saturday. _____

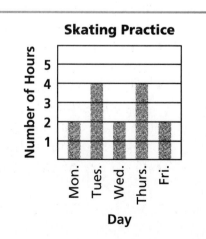

Skating Practice

Name _____

1 A teacher has 42 sheets of paper for 7 students. If he divides the sheets of paper equally, how many sheets of paper will each student get?

A 9   C 7

B 8   D 6

2 The chart shows the population of four California cities.

California Cities	Population
Laguna Beach	23,170
Montclair	28,434
San Marcos	38,974
Monterey	31,954

Which shows the cities in order of population size, from *greatest* to *least*?

F San Marcos, Monterey, Laguna Beach, Montclair

G Laguna Beach, Monterey, San Marcos, Montclair

H Laguna Beach, Montclair, Monterey, San Marcos

J San Marcos, Monterey, Montclair, Laguna Beach

3 Which group of number sentences belong to the same family of facts as $8 \times 9 = 72$?

A $3 \times 3 = 9; 4 \times 2 = 8; 9 \div 3 = 3$

B $9 \times 8 = 72, 72 \div 8 = 9; 72 \div 9 = 8$

C $8 \times 8 = 64; 64 \div 8 = 8$

D $9 \times 6 = 63; 63 \div 9 = 6; 63 \div 6 = 9$

4 Linda's horse weighs 1,234 pounds. What is the number rounded to the nearest hundred?

F 1,200   H 1,300   K NH

G 1,240   J 1,400

5 Mrs. Mulligan pays 4 friends $9 each to work in her yard. How much money does she pay them in all?

A $18   C $32

B $27   D $36

6 Which group of number sentences belong to the same family of facts as $63 \div 9 = 7$?

F $9 \times 7 = 63; 7 \times 9 = 63; 63 \div 7 = 9$

G $3 \times 3 = 9; 7 \times 1 = 7; 9 \div 3 = 3$

H $7 \times 9 = 56; 56 \div 7 = 9; 9 \times 7 = 56$

J $63 \div 3 = 21; 21 \times 3 = 63$

7 A candy company gave away 70,065 samples of its new chocolate bar. What words mean 70,065?

A seventy-six thousand, sixty-five

B seventy thousand, six hundred fifty

C seventy thousand, six hundred five

D seventy thousand, sixty-five

UNIT 2 • TABLE OF CONTENTS

Addition and Subtraction of Whole Numbers

Dear Family,

During the next few weeks, our math class will be learning and practicing addition and subtraction of whole numbers.

You can expect to see homework that provides practice with estimating sums. Here is a sample you may want to keep handy to give help if needed.

Estimating Sums

An estimate is a way to check an exact answer; it can be compared to an exact answer to help decide if that answer is reasonable.

Add:
$$\begin{array}{r} 6,379 \\ + 1,658 \\ \hline 8,057 \end{array}$$

To decide if this answer is reasonable, estimate by rounding each number to its greatest place. The greatest place in both **6,379** and **1,658** is thousands.

Estimate by rounding each number:

$$\begin{array}{rcr} 6,379 & \rightarrow & 6,000 \\ + 1,658 & \rightarrow & + 2,000 \\ \hline & & 8,000 \end{array}$$

An estimate of the exact answer is **8,000**. If the exact answer is close to **8,000**, it is a reasonable answer. If the exact answer is not close to **8,000**, the problem should be worked a second time.

During this unit, students will need to continue practicing addition and subtraction facts.

Sincerely,

Name _____

An addition problem of two addends can be written in horizontal or vertical form.

$5 + 3 = 8$ ← sum

↑ ↑

addend   addend

5 ← addend
$\underline{+\,3}$ ← addend
8 ← sum

If you change the order of the addends, the sum does not change.
This is called the **Commutative Property of Addition**.

$1 + 6 = 7$ $6 + 1 = 7$

$1 + 6 = 6 + 1$

2
$\underline{+\,9}$
11

9
$\underline{+\,2}$
11

If zero is added to any number, the sum is that number.
This is called the **Property of Zero for Addition**.

$8 + 0 = 8$ $0 + 3 = 3$ $84 + 0 = 84$

Use the commutative property to complete.

1. $5 + 4 = 4 + \underline{}$ $6 + 7 = \underline{} + 6$ $\underline{} + 9 = 9 + 0$

2. $7 + \underline{} = 2 + 7$ $8 + 4 = 4 + \underline{}$ $6 + 3 = \underline{} + \underline{}$

3.
$\begin{array}{r} 4 \\ \underline{+\,6} \end{array}$
$\begin{array}{r} 6 \\ \underline{+\,4} \end{array}$
$\begin{array}{r} 8 \\ \underline{+\,7} \end{array}$
$\begin{array}{r} \underline{} \\ \underline{+\,8} \end{array}$
$\begin{array}{r} 9 \\ \underline{+\,4} \end{array}$
$\begin{array}{r} \underline{} \\ \underline{+\,9} \end{array}$

Add or subtract.

4.
$\begin{array}{r} 2 \\ \underline{+\,0} \end{array}$
$\begin{array}{r} 9 \\ \underline{+\,0} \end{array}$
$\begin{array}{r} 0 \\ \underline{+\,5} \end{array}$
$\begin{array}{r} 32 \\ \underline{+\,0} \end{array}$
$\begin{array}{r} 0 \\ \underline{+\,6} \end{array}$
$\begin{array}{r} 4 \\ \underline{+\,0} \end{array}$
$\begin{array}{r} 19 \\ \underline{+\,0} \end{array}$
$\begin{array}{r} 0 \\ \underline{+\,7} \end{array}$

5.
$\begin{array}{r} 1 \\ \underline{+\,0} \end{array}$
$\begin{array}{r} 18 \\ \underline{+\,0} \end{array}$
$\begin{array}{r} 0 \\ \underline{+\,3} \end{array}$
$\begin{array}{r} 18 \\ \underline{+\,0} \end{array}$
$\begin{array}{r} 0 \\ \underline{+\,0} \end{array}$
$\begin{array}{r} 0 \\ \underline{+\,8} \end{array}$
$\begin{array}{r} 41 \\ \underline{+\,0} \end{array}$
$\begin{array}{r} 0 \\ \underline{+\,7} \end{array}$

Name the property that the addition sentence shows.

6. $18 + 0 = 18$ _____

7. $23 + 16 = 16 + 23$ _____

The way in which addends are grouped does not change the sum. This is called the **Associative Property of Addition**.

$$(3 + 4) + 2 = 3 + (4 + 2)$$
$$7 + 2 = 3 + 6$$
$$9 = 9$$

Use the associative property to complete each equation. Find each sum in parentheses first.

8. $(6 + 2) + 8$ _____ + __8__ = _____ $8 + (2 + 4)$ __8__ + _____ = _____

   $6 + (2 + 8)$ __6__ + _____ = _____ $(8 + 2) + 4$ _____ + __4__ = _____

9. $(4 + 3) + 7$ _____ + _____ = _____ $(3 + 4) + 6$ _____ + _____ = _____

   $4 + (3 + 7)$ _____ + _____ = _____ $3 + (4 + 6)$ _____ + _____ = _____

10. $(6 + 3) + 7$ _____ + _____ = _____ $(9 + 1) + 8$ _____ + _____ = _____

   $6 + (3 + 7)$ _____ + _____ = _____ $9 + (1 + 8)$ _____ + _____ = _____

11. $5 + (2 + 7)$ _____ + _____ = _____ $3 + (9 + 2)$ _____ + _____ = _____

   $(5 + 2) + 7$ _____ + _____ = _____ $(3 + 9) + 2$ _____ + _____ = _____

Problem Solving Reasoning Solve.

12. Write a number sentence that has three addends and shows that the commutative property of addition is true for three addends.

_____

Test Prep ★ Mixed Review

13 What number is equal to 70,000 + 600 + 30 + 4?

   A 76,340

   B 76,034

   C 70,634

   D 7,634

14 Which number could go in the ☐ to make the number sentence true?

$4 + \boxed{} < 12$

   F 10   H 8

   G 9   J 7

Name _____   **Inverse Operations**

The number line shows:

$$4 + 3 = 7$$
$$7 - 3 = 4$$

The number line also shows:

Subtraction is the **inverse**, or opposite, of addition.
Addition is the **inverse**, or opposite, of subtraction.

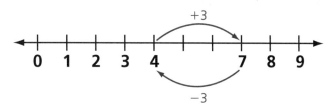

Since addition and subtraction are inverse operations, you can write a **fact family** using **4, 3,** and **7.**

$$4 + 3 = 7 \qquad 3 + 4 = 7$$
$$7 - 3 = 4 \qquad 7 - 4 = 3$$

Find each sum or difference. Write the number sentence that shows the inverse operation.

1. $7 + 3 =$ ___10___ $8 - 3 =$ _____ $9 + 3 =$ _____

$10 - 3 =$ ___7___   _____   _____

2. $17 - 9 =$ _____ $10 - 1 =$ _____ $2 + 3 =$ _____

_____   _____   _____

Write a fact family for each group of numbers.

3.   3, 7, 10   2, 11, 9

_____   _____

_____   _____

Make each number sentence true. Write + or −. Then write a number sentence you could use to check your answer.

4. $15 \bigcirc 5 = 10$ $5 \bigcirc 9 = 14$ $13 \bigcirc 9 = 4$

_____   _____   _____

5. $9 \bigcirc 9 = 18$ $9 \bigcirc 8 = 1$ $8 \bigcirc 5 = 13$

_____   _____   _____

Complete each table.

6.

■	■ + 4
8	
7	
2	
6	
5	
9	
3	
4	

■	■ − 10
18	
23	
46	
35	
14	
29	
10	
47	

■	■ − 1
24	
	18
33	
	29
13	
	42
	17
25	

■	■ + 6
	22
17	
	36
11	
	19
10	
23	
	15

■	■ + 11
17	
12	
	11
26	
	49
	20
47	
28	

Problem Solving
Reasoning

7. Write the numbers **2** and **3** in the table so that the sum of each row, column, and diagonal is the same. (**6, 5,** and **4** are on a diagonal.)

8		4
1	5	9
6	7	

8. Write the numbers **2, 5,** and **9** in the table so that the sum of each row, column, and diagonal is the same.

3	8	7
10	6	
	4	

Test Prep ★ Mixed Review

9 What number is equal to
2,000,000 + 30,000 + 7,000?

A 2,037,000

B 2,003,700

C 2,000,370

D 2,000,037

10 In one month, 702,650 cars used a single exit off the interstate highway. What words mean 702,650?

F Seven hundred twenty thousand, six hundred fifty

G Seven hundred two thousand, six hundred fifty

H Seven hundred two thousand, six hundred five

J Seventy-two thousand, six hundred fifty

Number sentences contain numbers operations, and an equal sign.

Examples:
$$3 + 2 = 5$$
$$5 - 2 = 3$$

$$1 + 7 = 8$$
$$8 - 7 = 1$$

$$6 + 4 = 10$$
$$10 - 4 = 6$$

In algebra, letters called **variables** are used to represent unknown numbers.

Examples:
$$n + 3 = 5$$
$$5 - 3 = n$$

$$x + 7 = 8$$
$$8 - 7 = x$$

$$n + 4 = 10$$
$$10 - 4 = n$$

Number sentences with variables are called **open sentences**.

You can use a related number sentence to make an open number sentence true.

Find n in the number sentence $n + 5 = 11$.

1. Use a related number sentence.

   $n + 5 = 11$ Think: $11 - 5 = 6$, so $n = 6$.

2. Check your work. Replace n with **6** in the open sentence!

   > Decide if the number sentence is true.

   $$n + 5 = 11$$
   $$\downarrow$$
   $$6 + 5 = 11 \quad \textbf{True}$$

$7 + 3 = 10$ is a **True Sentence**.
$n + 3 = 10$ is an **Open Sentence**.
$7 + 3 = 12$ is a **False Sentence**.

Label each number sentence True, False, or Open.

1. $7 - 3 = 4$ _____ $12 + 2 = 10$ _____ $x - 1 = 5$ _____ $11 + 4 = 15$ _____

Use a related number sentence to find the value of n.

2. $n + 2 = 7$ $n + 9 = 15$ $n + 8 = 10$ $n + 3 = 6$

  $n =$ _____ $n =$ _____ $n =$ _____ $n =$ _____

3. $n + 6 = 8$ $n + 1 = 5$ $n + 7 = 11$ $n + 5 = 6$

  $n =$ _____ $n =$ _____ $n =$ _____ $n =$ _____

4. $n + 3 = 10$ $n + 4 = 9$ $n + 9 = 17$ $n + 8 = 15$

  $n =$ _____ $n =$ _____ $n =$ _____ $n =$ _____

Subtraction rules can sometimes be used to find the
value of a variable in an open sentence.

What is the value of *n* in the number sentence *n* − 0 = 9?

Rule: When you subtract zero from a
number, the answer is that number.

So: If *n* − 0 = 9,
then *n* = 9.

What is the value of *x* in the number sentence 5 − 5 = *x*?

Rule: Any number subtracted from
itself equals **0**.

So: If 5 − 5 = *x*,
then *x* = 0.

Write the value of *x*.

5. 8 − 8 = *x*   4 − 0 = *x*   7 − 2 = *x*   10 − 0 = *x*

   x = _____   *x* = _____   *x* = _____   *x* = _____

6. 3 − 3 = *x*   12 − 5 = *x*   16 − 7 = *x*   11 − 11 = *x*

   x = _____   *x* = _____   *x* = _____   *x* = _____

| **Problem Solving** |
| **Reasoning** |

Each number sentence below is false. Change one number in
each sentence to make it a true number sentence.

7. 10 − 5 = 12 − 9   15 − 8 = 7 − 6   4 − 4 = 9 − 3

 Quick Check

Solve.

8. 9 + 6 = 6 + ☐   **9.** (3 + 4) + 1 = 3 + (4 + ☐)

10. 7 + 6 = (3 + ☐) + 6

Work Space.

Write the number sentence that shows the
inverse operation.

11. 13 − 6 = 7   **12.** 18 + 6 = 24   **13.** 17 − 6 = 11

_____   _____   _____

Use related number sentences to find the value of *n*.

14. 8 + *n* = 17 *n* = _____   **15.** 5 + *n* = 13 *n* = _____

16. *n* − 12 = 7 *n* = _____   **17.** 15 − *n* = 4 *n* = _____

Name _____

One way to estimate a sum or difference is to round each number to its greatest place value. The greatest place value of any number is the place farthest to the left.

Estimate the sum. *Tens* is the greatest place value of the addends.

58	Round to nearest **10** →	60
+ 29	Round to nearest **10** →	+ 30
		90

A good estimate of the sum is
58 + 29 is **90**.

Estimate the difference. *Hundreds* is the greatest place value of the addends.

742	Round to nearest **100** →	700
−388	Round to nearest **100** →	−400
		300

A good estimate of the difference is
742 − 388 is **300**.

Estimate each sum or difference by rounding to the greatest place value.

1. 62 → 60   87 →   42 →   45 →
       + 39 → + 40   + 46 → + ___   + 37 → + ___   + 35 → + ___

2. 64 →   51 →   83 →   94 →
       − 27 → − ___   − 39 → − ___   − 74 → − ___   − 68 → − ___

3. 184 →   671 →   465 →   555 →
       + 453 → + ___   − 305 → − ___   + 275 → + ___   − 250 → − ___

4. 776 →   168 →   627 →   814 →
       − 519 → − ___   + 384 → + ___   − 179 → − ___   − 116 → − ___

5. 5,368 →   4,543 →   7,538 →
       − 2,154 → − ___   + 3,568 → + ___   + 1,524 → + ___

6. 4,762 →   6,151 →   1,805 →
       − 2,813 → − ___   + 2,183 → + ___   − 1,372 → − ___

Solve.

Read each situation. Round the numbers to the greatest place value. Then use those numbers to write an estimated answer.

7. On their trip through Canada, Tom's family drove **206** kilometers one day and **98** the next. About how many kilometers did they drive in two days?

_____

8. In the auditorium, **735** chairs were set up. The audience used only **568**. About how many chairs were not used?

_____

9. A school parking lot has enough space for **275** cars. During the school play, **157** cars were parked in the parking lot. About how many spaces were not used?

_____

10. In Jane's school there are **917** pupils. There are **489** boys. About how many girls are there?

_____

11. Suppose you were asked this question: "How many people live in the city or town where you live?" To answer the question, would you give an estimate or an exact answer? Tell why.

_____

Test Prep ★ Mixed Review

12 What number should go in the ☐ to make the number sentence true?

$$(4 + 7) + 6 = 4 + (\boxed{} + 6)$$

A 4

B 6

C 7

D 9

13 The zoo had 127,678 visitors in July and August. What is this number rounded to the nearest ten thousand?

F 120,000

G 125,000

H 130,000

J 135,000

Adding Whole Numbers

Sometimes you may need to regroup when you add.

Add: 315 + 607.

1. Add ones. Regroup **10** ones as **1** ten.

H	T	O
	1	
3	1	5
+ 6	0	7
		2

2. Add tens.

H	T	O
	1	
3	1	5
+ 6	0	7
	2	2

3. Add hundreds.

H	T	O
	1	
3	1	5
+ 6	0	7
9	2	2

Add.

1.

H	T	O
	5	1
+	4	3

H	T	O
	1	7
+	8	9

H	T	O
	7	3
+	2	6

H	T	O
	6	4
+	9	6

H	T	O
	8	8
+	4	7

2.

H	T	O
5	4	8
+ 3	8	9

H	T	O
2	7	5
+ 1	9	9

H	T	O
7	4	6
+ 1	5	9

H	T	O
7	6	7
+ 1	5	3

H	T	O
2	3	9
+ 1	7	8

3.
```
  27        43        72        81        93        65
+ 31      + 19      + 36      + 14      + 50      + 25
```

4.
```
  12        26        70        34        51        48
+ 39      + 124     + 46      + 202     + 41      + 396
```

5.
```
 543       648       456       564       249       376
+ 189     + 275     + 266     + 268     + 395     + 487
```

6.
```
 543       716       324       327       186       561
+ 178     + 97      + 397     + 198     + 89      + 239
```

To find each sum, begin with the ones place. Regroup when necessary.

Add: **4,678 + 4,783.**

$$\begin{array}{r} \overset{1\ 1\ 1}{4{,}678} \\ +\ 4{,}783 \\ \hline 9{,}461 \end{array}$$

Add: **20,413 + 31,750.**

$$\begin{array}{r} \overset{1}{20{,}413} \\ +\ 31{,}750 \\ \hline 52{,}163 \end{array}$$

Add: **671 + 280 + 206.**

$$\begin{array}{r} \overset{1}{671} \\ 280 \\ +\ 206 \\ \hline 1{,}157 \end{array}$$

Add.

7.

2,639	6,181	4,107	5,728	57,240
+ 3,574	+ 1,498	+ 3,895	+ 2,748	+ 31,175

8.

12,743	26,604	46,367	948	646
+ 56,155	+ 22,581	+ 19,066	160	129
			+ 788	+ 936

Problem Solving
Reasoning

Solve.

9. Find the greatest possible sum of two **3**-digit numbers that use the digits **1, 2, 3, 4, 5, 6** only once.

_____

10. Find the least possible sum of two **3**-digit numbers that use the digits **1, 2, 3, 4, 5, 6** only once.

_____

✓ **Quick Check**

Estimate the sum or difference. Then find the exact answer.

Work Space.

11. 543 + 167   **12.** 927 − 465   **13.** 4,657 − 2,453

_____   _____

Add.

14.

3,479
+ 4,319

15.

5,587
+ 3,291

16.

2,477
+ 2,396

17.

177
564
+ 196

18.

477
673
+ 826

19.

369
208
+ 184

Subtracting Whole Numbers

Sometimes when you subtract you must regroup.

Subtract: **832 − 478.**

1. Not enough ones. Regroup **1** ten as **10** ones. Subtract ones.

$$
\begin{array}{c|c|c}
\text{H} & \text{T} & \text{O} \\
\hline
8 & \overset{2}{\cancel{3}} & \overset{12}{\cancel{2}} \\
-4 & 7 & 8 \\
\end{array}
$$

2. Not enough tens. Regroup **1** hundred as **10** tens. Subtract tens.

$$
\begin{array}{c|c|c}
\text{H} & \text{T} & \text{O} \\
\hline
\overset{7}{\cancel{8}} & \overset{12}{\cancel{3}} & \overset{12}{\cancel{2}} \\
-4 & 7 & 8 \\
\hline
 & 5 & 4 \\
\end{array}
$$

3. Subtract hundreds.

$$
\begin{array}{c|c|c}
\text{H} & \text{T} & \text{O} \\
\hline
\overset{7}{\cancel{8}} & \overset{12}{\cancel{3}} & \overset{12}{\cancel{2}} \\
-4 & 7 & 8 \\
\hline
3 & 5 & 4 \\
\end{array}
$$

Subtract.

1.

T	O
2	8
−1	5

T	O
5	1
−3	9

T	O
7	7
−4	8

T	O
6	2
−3	0

T	O
5	6
−1	8

2.

H	T	O
3	1	4
−2	0	3

H	T	O
6	7	5
−4	8	1

H	T	O
5	2	6
−1	1	9

H	T	O
9	4	9
−8	5	2

H	T	O
7	2	1
−4	6	5

3.

617	592	474	819	726	531
− 11	− 136	− 90	− 356	− 88	− 34

4.

432	384	452	925	824	341
− 235	− 198	− 378	− 257	− 267	− 162

5.

521	258	179	932	879	623
− 198	− 187	− 96	− 876	− 159	− 197

To find each difference, begin with the ones place
and regroup when necessary. Then subtract.

Subtract: 6,431 − 5,117

$$\begin{array}{r} 6,4\overset{2}{\cancel{3}}\overset{11}{\cancel{1}} \\ -\ 5,117 \\ \hline 1,314 \end{array}$$

Subtract: 94,727 − 36,180

$$\begin{array}{r} \overset{8}{\cancel{9}}\overset{14}{\cancel{4}},\overset{6}{\cancel{7}}\overset{12}{\cancel{2}}7 \\ -\ 36,180 \\ \hline 58,547 \end{array}$$

Subtract.

6.

4,715	9,411	7,332	3,625	5,282
− 3,602	− 4,103	− 2,721	− 1,014	− 2,550

7.

82,613	71,195	24,381	39,837	54,923
− 41,501	− 28,040	− 15,129	− 33,225	− 36,044

Problem Solving Reasoning   Solve.

8. Each time you subtract two numbers, you find a
difference. Is there a way to check if the
difference you find is correct? Explain.

_____

_____

9. Find the least possible difference
of two **2**-digit numbers that use
the digits **2, 4, 6,** and **8** only once
in each number.

_____

10. Find the greatest possible
difference of two **3**-digit numbers
that use the digits **3, 5, 7,** and **9**
only once in each number.

_____

Test Prep ★ Mixed Review

11 What number should go in the ☐ to
make the number sentence true?

$$8 + (9 + 4) = \boxed{} + (8 + 9)$$

A 9   **C** 4

B 8   **D** 2

12 Jason's parents bought him a bicycle
for $127 and a helmet for $25,
including tax. How much money did
they spend all together?

F $102   **H** $142

G $132   **J** $152

These are some coins and bills we use.

twenty-dollar bill	ten-dollar bill	five-dollar bill

$20 or **$20.00**	**$10** or **$10.00**	**$5** or **$5.00**

one-dollar bill	half-dollar	quarter

$1 or **$1.00**	**50¢** or **$.50**	**25¢** or **$.25**

dime	nickel	penny
10¢ or **$.10**	**5¢** or **$.05**	**1¢** or **$.01**

Write the amounts. Then circle the amount that is greater.

1.

_____   _____

Write the amounts. Then circle the amount that is less.

2.

_____

_____

3.

_____

_____

| Problem Solving Reasoning | Complete each sentence. |

4. One dollar is the same as _____ pennies, _____ half-dollars, or _____ quarters.

5. Fifty cents is the same as _____ nickels, _____ quarters, or _____ dimes.

Test Prep ★ Mixed Review

6 What number should go in the ☐ to make the number sentence true?

$$(3 + 8) + 9 = \boxed{} + (8 + 9)$$

A 9   **C** 3

B 7   **D** 0

7 Melissa bought a jacket for $64.79 and a pair of shoes for $32.54. How much more money did she spend on the jacket than on the shoes?

F $31.25   **H** $32.54

G $32.25   **J** $33.54

Cashiers use a cash register to find the total cost of your purchases. The cash register then subtracts the total from the amount of money that you give the cashier.
The cashier "counts out" the change to you.
Here is a way to check the amount of change you receive.

Thomas bought a yo-yo for **$1.39**.
He gave the clerk a **5**-dollar bill.
Thomas' change was **$3.61**.

The clerk gave Thomas his change by counting this way:

Draw your change. Use the fewest coins and bills.

	You have	You spend	
1.	$10.00	$6.25	
2.	$6.00	$5.19	
3.	$20.00	$4.39	
4.	$1.00	$.43	

Except for a dollar sign and a decimal point, adding and subtracting money is like adding and subtracting whole numbers.

Add: **$1.25 + $3.80**

Line up the decimal points. Then add as you would with whole numbers.

$$\begin{array}{r} \overset{1}{\$1.25} \\ + \$3.80 \\ \hline \$5.05 \end{array}$$

Subtract: **$2.94 − $1.78**

Line up the decimal points. Then subtract as you would with whole numbers.

$$\begin{array}{r} \$2.\overset{8\ 14}{\cancel{9}\cancel{4}} \\ - \$1.78 \\ \hline \$1.16 \end{array}$$

Remember to use a decimal point and a dollar sign when you write your sum or difference.

Add or subtract.

5.
$$\begin{array}{r} \$2.00 \\ + \$7.00 \\ \hline \end{array}$$
$$\begin{array}{r} \$6.50 \\ - \$1.50 \\ \hline \end{array}$$
$$\begin{array}{r} \$3.10 \\ - \$2.00 \\ \hline \end{array}$$
$$\begin{array}{r} \$8.45 \\ - \$6.10 \\ \hline \end{array}$$
$$\begin{array}{r} \$4.45 \\ - \$1.25 \\ \hline \end{array}$$

6.
$$\begin{array}{r} \$8.00 \\ - \$5.00 \\ \hline \end{array}$$
$$\begin{array}{r} \$9.30 \\ + \$\ .20 \\ \hline \end{array}$$
$$\begin{array}{r} \$7.12 \\ + \$3.55 \\ \hline \end{array}$$
$$\begin{array}{r} \$4.10 \\ - \$\ .05 \\ \hline \end{array}$$
$$\begin{array}{r} \$1.19 \\ + \$2.49 \\ \hline \end{array}$$

 Quick Check

Write the amount of money.

Work Space.

7. 4 dollar bills, 1 quarter, 2 dimes, 1 nickel, 3 pennies _____

8. 1 ten dollar bill, 1 five dollar bill, 2 quarters, 3 pennies _____

Compare. Write > or <.

9. 3 quarters ◯ 7 nickels

10. 2 quarters ◯ 6 dimes

Write the amount you would receive in change.

11. Cost: $2.28
Cash given: $5.00
_____

12. Cost: $6.65
Cash given: $10.00
_____

13. Cost: $13.47
Cash given: $20.00
_____

14. Cost: $19.25
Cash given: $20.00
_____

Name _____

Complete.

1. $2 + 9 = 9 +$ _____

2. $7 + 6 =$ _____ $+ 7$

3. _____ $+ 4 = 4 + 8$

4. $0 + 12 =$ _____

5. $9 + 0 =$ _____

6. $0 + 0 =$ _____

7. $(5 + 3) + 7 =$ _____ $+$ _____ $=$ _____

8. $5 + (3 + 7) =$ _____ $+$ _____ $=$ _____

Find each sum or difference. Write the number sentence that shows the inverse operation.

9. $7 + 3 =$ _____

10. $12 - 3 =$ _____

11. $15 - 9 =$ _____

_____

_____

_____

Estimate each sum or difference by rounding to the greatest place value.

12. $37 \rightarrow$
$+ 19 \rightarrow +$
_____ _____

_____

13. $723 \rightarrow$
$- 199 \rightarrow -$
_____ _____

_____

14. $6,555 \rightarrow$
$+ 8,299 \rightarrow +$
_____ _____

_____

Add or subtract.

15. 572
$+ 635$

16. $\$36.04$
$- \$4.75$

17. $34,570$
$+ 5,299$

18. $29,400$
$- 7,566$

Write each amount. Then draw your change. Use the fewest coins and bills.

19. You have

You spend

Your change

_____

_____

_____

Solve.

20. Michelle bought a book for **$4.50** and a magazine for **$1.95**. Write a number sentence that shows how much she spent.

_____

21. Roger wants to buy a hat for **$8.99** and a shirt for **$9.99**. How much change will he get back if he pays with a **$20** bill?

_____

1 The population of San Diego is shown in the box.

Population of San Diego	1,148,851

What words mean 1,148,851?

A one hundred forty-eight thousand, eight hundred fifty-one

B one million, forty-eight thousand, eight hundred fifty-one

C one million, one hundred forty-eight thousand, eight hundred fifty-one

D one hundred forty-eight million, eight hundred fifty-one thousand

2 Look at the box in question 1. What is the population of San Diego rounded to the nearest hundred thousand?

F 1,000,000   H 1,150,000   K NH

G 1,100,000   J 1,200,000

3 On Saturday, three groups toured the exhibits at the zoo. The table shows the number of people in each group.

Zoo Tours on Saturday	
Morning	62
Afternoon	127
Evening	68

How many people were in these groups in all?

A 121   C 227   E NH

B 211   D 257

4 Ms. Richards drove from McFarland to Cambria and then to San Jose along the road shown.

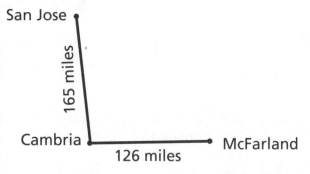

About how many miles did he drive?

F 200   H 400

G 300   J 600

5 The table below shows four items and their prices at a local store.

Item	Price
ice cream	$3.29
dog food	$9.67
flowers	$6.97
cereal	$2.75

Which shows the items in order of price from *least* to *greatest*?

A ice cream, cereal, flowers, dog food

B cereal, dog food, ice cream, flowers

C dog food, flowers, ice cream, cereal

D cereal, ice cream, flowers, dog food

UNIT 3 • TABLE OF CONTENTS

Multiplication of Whole Numbers

We will be using this vocabulary:

factors numbers used in a multiplication problem

product the answer to a multiplication problem

graph a picture used to show some information; a graph can be a bar graph, a pictograph, a circle graph, or a line graph.

Dear Family,

During the next few weeks, our math class will be learning and practicing multiplication of whole numbers.

You can expect to see homework that provides practice with multiplying 4-digit numbers by 1-digit numbers. Here is a sample you may want to keep handy to give help if needed.

Multiplying 4-Digit Numbers by 1-Digit Numbers

To multiply **2,734** by **3**, first write the numbers in vertical form. Then multiply the digits in each place.

1. Multiply ones. Regroup to tens.	2. Multiply tens. Add the regrouped tens. Regroup to hundreds.	3. Multiply hundreds. Add the regrouped hundreds. Regroup to thousands.	4. Multiply thousands. Add the regrouped thousands.
$\begin{array}{r} 1 \\ 2{,}734 \\ \times\ 3 \\ \hline 2 \end{array}$	$\begin{array}{r} 1\ 1 \\ 2{,}734 \\ \times\ 3 \\ \hline 02 \end{array}$	$\begin{array}{r} 2\ 1\ 1 \\ 2{,}734 \\ \times\ 3 \\ \hline 202 \end{array}$	$\begin{array}{r} 2\ 1\ 1 \\ 2{,}734 \\ \times\ 3 \\ \hline 8{,}202 \end{array}$

Here is a short way to record multiplication.

$$\begin{array}{r} 2\ 2 \\ 8{,}165 \\ \times\ 4 \\ \hline 32{,}660 \end{array}$$

During this unit, students will need to continue practicing multiplication and addition facts.

Sincerely,

Name _____ **Multiplying with Regrouping**

To find the total number of blocks you can multiply.

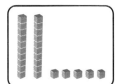 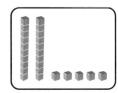 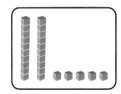

25 ← blocks in each group
$\times\ 3$ ← number of groups
$?$ ← total number of blocks

1. Multiply the ones.

2. Regroup ones as tens and ones. Write the ones digit.

3. Multiply the tens. Then add the regrouped tens. Write the tens digit.

3×5 ones $= 15$ ones

$$\begin{array}{r} 25 \\ \times\ \ 3 \end{array}$$

15 ones $= 1$ ten and 5 ones

$$\begin{array}{r} 25 \\ \times\ \ 3 \\ \hline 5 \end{array}$$

$3 \times 2 = 6$ tens

6 tens $+ 1$ ten $= 7$ tens

$$\begin{array}{r} \overset{1}{2}5 \\ \times\ \ 3 \\ \hline 75 \end{array}$$

Multiply.

1.
$$\begin{array}{r} 11 \\ \times\ 5 \end{array}$$
$$\begin{array}{r} 21 \\ \times\ 3 \end{array}$$
$$\begin{array}{r} 33 \\ \times\ 2 \end{array}$$
$$\begin{array}{r} 42 \\ \times\ 2 \end{array}$$
$$\begin{array}{r} 32 \\ \times\ 3 \end{array}$$
$$\begin{array}{r} 22 \\ \times\ 4 \end{array}$$
$$\begin{array}{r} 11 \\ \times\ 7 \end{array}$$

2.
$$\begin{array}{r} 20 \\ \times\ 6 \end{array}$$
$$\begin{array}{r} 54 \\ \times\ 2 \end{array}$$
$$\begin{array}{r} 74 \\ \times\ 2 \end{array}$$
$$\begin{array}{r} 41 \\ \times\ 4 \end{array}$$
$$\begin{array}{r} 81 \\ \times\ 3 \end{array}$$
$$\begin{array}{r} 63 \\ \times\ 3 \end{array}$$
$$\begin{array}{r} 73 \\ \times\ 2 \end{array}$$

3.
$$\begin{array}{r} 16 \\ \times\ 5 \end{array}$$
$$\begin{array}{r} 13 \\ \times\ 7 \end{array}$$
$$\begin{array}{r} 26 \\ \times\ 3 \end{array}$$
$$\begin{array}{r} 12 \\ \times\ 6 \end{array}$$
$$\begin{array}{r} 17 \\ \times\ 2 \end{array}$$
$$\begin{array}{r} 15 \\ \times\ 6 \end{array}$$
$$\begin{array}{r} 36 \\ \times\ 2 \end{array}$$

4.
$$\begin{array}{r} 16 \\ \times\ 4 \end{array}$$
$$\begin{array}{r} 18 \\ \times\ 3 \end{array}$$
$$\begin{array}{r} 26 \\ \times\ 2 \end{array}$$
$$\begin{array}{r} 16 \\ \times\ 3 \end{array}$$
$$\begin{array}{r} 19 \\ \times\ 2 \end{array}$$
$$\begin{array}{r} 27 \\ \times\ 3 \end{array}$$
$$\begin{array}{r} 12 \\ \times\ 7 \end{array}$$

5.
$$\begin{array}{r} 14 \\ \times\ 6 \end{array}$$
$$\begin{array}{r} 19 \\ \times\ 3 \end{array}$$
$$\begin{array}{r} 16 \\ \times\ 2 \end{array}$$
$$\begin{array}{r} 37 \\ \times\ 2 \end{array}$$
$$\begin{array}{r} 13 \\ \times\ 4 \end{array}$$
$$\begin{array}{r} 47 \\ \times\ 2 \end{array}$$
$$\begin{array}{r} 14 \\ \times\ 3 \end{array}$$

6.
$$\begin{array}{r} 15 \\ \times\ 4 \end{array}$$
$$\begin{array}{r} 17 \\ \times\ 4 \end{array}$$
$$\begin{array}{r} 46 \\ \times\ 2 \end{array}$$
$$\begin{array}{r} 15 \\ \times\ 3 \end{array}$$
$$\begin{array}{r} 25 \\ \times\ 3 \end{array}$$
$$\begin{array}{r} 18 \\ \times\ 5 \end{array}$$
$$\begin{array}{r} 24 \\ \times\ 4 \end{array}$$

Multiply.

8.
$$999 \times 2$$
$$894 \times 4$$
$$971 \times 4$$
$$406 \times 5$$
$$670 \times 3$$
$$550 \times 6$$

9.
$$745 \times 3$$
$$968 \times 4$$
$$914 \times 4$$
$$870 \times 5$$
$$695 \times 4$$
$$783 \times 9$$

| Problem Solving Reasoning | **Solve.** |

10. The student price for a ticket to the museum is **$4**. How much will it cost for **234** students to go to the museum?

_____

11. By noon, **598** spaces in a parking lot were filled. By **5** P.M., **3** times as many spaces were filled. How many spaces were filled by **5** P.M.?

_____

12. There are **137** strawberry plants in one row of a farm. If there are **8** rows, how many plants are there in all?

_____

13. Jason sold **175** raffle tickets. Mary Beth sold twice as many. How many tickets did they sell together?

_____

✓ Quick Check

Complete to make the sentence true.   **Work Space.**

14. $7 \times 8 = \boxed{} \times 7$ 15. $9 = 1 \times (3 \times \boxed{})$

16. $(7 \times 12) \times 3 = \boxed{} \times (12 \times 3)$

Multiply.

17.
$$223 \times 3$$
18.
$$103 \times 7$$
19.
$$218 \times 4$$

20.
$$256 \times 3$$
21.
$$304 \times 6$$
22.
$$516 \times 4$$

You can use what you know about multiplying with **3**-digit numbers to multiply with **4**-digit numbers.

1. Multiply ones. Regroup to tens.	**2.** Multiply tens. Add regrouped tens. Then regroup to hundreds.	**3.** Multiply hundreds. Add regrouped hundreds. Regroup to thousands.	**4.** Multiply thousands. Add regrouped thousands.
$\overset{4}{7{,}318}$ $\times \quad 6$ $\overline{8}$	$\overset{1\ 4}{7{,}318}$ $\times \quad 6$ $\overline{08}$	$\overset{1\ 1\ 4}{7{,}318}$ $\times \quad 6$ $\overline{908}$	$\overset{1\ 1\ 4}{7{,}318}$ $\times \quad 6$ $\overline{43{,}908}$

Multiply.

1.   3,421   7,614   2,835   6,024   5,106
      ×   5   ×   3   ×   6   ×   4   ×   2

2.   4,425   3,781   9,065   4,235   9,142
      ×   5   ×   3   ×   2   ×   5   ×   4

3.   4,126   4,562   8,395   9,517   3,084
      ×   6   ×   7   ×   2   ×   8   ×   3

4. $61.25 $45.37 $37.86 $16.04 $80.31
      ×   4   ×   7   ×   6   ×   5   ×   8

5. $71.36 $53.47 $90.06 $67.16 $13.95
      ×   7   ×   3   ×   8   ×   4   ×   9

6. $21.15 $44.18 $82.13 $75.16 $13.25
      ×   3   ×   5   ×   9   ×   8   ×   4

7.   5,623   3,412   6,222   1,919   2,617
      ×   7   ×   9   ×   8   ×   5   ×   8

When you multiply with zero, you may need to write zeros in the product.

1. Multiply ones. Regroup to tens.

$$\overset{4}{7{,}009} \times 5 \over 5$$

5×9 ones = 45 ones

2. Multiply tens. Add regrouped tens.

$$\overset{4}{7{,}009} \times 5 \over 45$$

5×0 tens = 0 tens
0 tens + 4 tens = 4 tens

3. Multiply hundreds. There are no regrouped tens. Write 0 in the hundreds place.

$$\overset{4}{7{,}009} \times 5 \over 045$$

5×0 hundreds = 0 hundreds

4. Multiply thousands.

$$\overset{4}{7{,}009} \times 5 \over 35{,}045$$

5×7 thousands = 35 thousands

Multiply.

8.   602 × 3   801 × 6   603 × 2   510 × 4   304 × 2

9.   5,113 × 3   8,014 × 2   9,001 × 6   8,100 × 7   8,011 × 6

10. $511 \times 9 =$ _____ $901 \times 8 =$ _____ $610 \times 7 =$ _____

11. $6{,}102 \times 4 =$ _____ $5{,}001 \times 9 =$ _____ $9{,}111 \times 6 =$ _____

Problem Solving Reasoning   Solve.

12. There are **1,250** pushpins in each box. How many pushpins are in **5** boxes?

_____

13. There are **3,435** visitors to a web site every day. How many visitors are there each week?

_____

Test Prep ★ Mixed Review

14 What words mean 520,335?

   A five hundred thousand, two hundred thirty-five

   B five hundred two thousand, three hundred thirty-five

   C five hundred twenty thousand, three hundred thirty-five

   D five hundred thirty thousand, two hundred thirty-five

15 What number is equal to 6,000 + 400 + 70?

   F 647

   G 6,407

   H 6,470

   J 6,740

Name _____

To solve a problem, you may need to begin with a **conjecture** about the answer.

When you make a conjecture, you make a "first guess" about the answer. Then you **verify** or check to see if it is correct.

Problem

The school store sells erasers and pencils. Zoe bought one of each. The total cost was **$.36**. The pencil cost twice as much as the eraser. What was the cost of each?

....

❶ Understand   As you reread, ask yourself questions.

 • What do you know about the cost of the items?

   The total cost is **$.36**. The cost of the pencil is **2** times the cost of the eraser.

 • What do you need to find out?

   _____

....

❷ Decide   Choose a method for solving.

Try the strategy Conjecture and Verify.

 • What will your first guess be?

   Eraser: **$.10**   Pencil: **$.20**

 • Is the cost of the pencil twice as much as the

   cost of the eraser? _____

....

❸ Solve   Verify your conjecture. Try again if you need to.

First guess	Try Again	Try Again
Eraser: **$.10**	_____	_____
Pencil: **$.20**	_____	_____
Total: **$.30**	_____	_____

....

❹ Look back   Check your answer. Write the answer below.

Answer _____

 • How did your first guess help you try again?

   _____

Solve. Use the Conjecture and Verify strategy or
any other strategy you have learned.

PEANUT BUTTER $1.99

WHOLE WHEAT BREAD $2.39

COTTAGE CHEESE $1.79

EGGS $1.49

APPLE PIE $3.59

YOGURT LEMON $.99

1. Lorinda bought **2** items. She spent **$4.18**. Which items did she buy?

Think: Can one apple pie be paired with any item to equal **$4.18**?

_____

Answer _____

2. Carley bought **2** items. She spent **$5.98**. Which items did she buy?

Think: Do you need to find an exact answer or estimate to answer the question?

_____

Answer _____

3. Jake bought **3** items. He spent **$4.77**. Which items did he buy?

_____

_____

4. Christopher bought **3** items. He spent **$7.97**. Which items did he buy?

_____

_____

5. As part of their grand opening, a new store is giving out prizes. The prizes will be given out according to a pattern. The store gives the **9th, 18th, 27th**, and **36th** customers each a prize. Which customer will get the next prize?

_____

6. Yosemite National Park in California covers **761,236** acres. Crater Lake National Park in Oregon covers **183,224** acres. How much larger is Yosemite National Park than Crater Lake National Park?

_____

7. Benjamin says "I am thinking of a number. If you triple my number and add **18**, you get **438**." What number is Benjamin thinking of?

_____

8. Samina has some dimes and quarters in her pocket. She has **7** coins in all and the total amount is **$1.15**. How many quarters does she have? How many dimes does she have?

_____

Mental Math: Multiplying with 10 and 100

When you multiply a number by **10** or by **100**, the number of zeros in both the factors is equal to the number of zeros in the product.

$$
\begin{array}{r}
25 \\
\times\ 10 \leftarrow \text{one zero} \\
\hline
250 \leftarrow \text{one zero}
\end{array}
\qquad
\begin{array}{r}
35 \\
\times\ 100 \leftarrow \text{two zeros} \\
\hline
3{,}500 \leftarrow \text{two zeros}
\end{array}
$$

When a multiple of **10** is multiplied by **10** or **100**, the number of zeros in the product is equal to the total number of zeros in the factors.

$$
\begin{array}{r}
40 \leftarrow \text{one zero} \\
\times\ 10 \leftarrow \text{one zero} \\
\hline
400 \leftarrow \text{two zeros}
\end{array}
\qquad
\begin{array}{r}
60 \leftarrow \text{one zero} \\
\times\ 100 \leftarrow \text{two zeros} \\
\hline
6{,}000 \leftarrow \text{three zeros}
\end{array}
$$

Write the number of zeros in each product.

1. 12×10 _____ 40×10 _____ 10×100 _____

2. 650×10 _____ 85×10 _____ 720×100 _____

3. 80×10 _____ 20×100 _____ 24×10 _____

4. 99×10 _____ 140×10 _____ 50×10 _____

5. 30×100 _____ 270×100 _____ 810×10 _____

Multiply.

6.
$$
\begin{array}{r} 462 \\ \times\ 10 \\ \hline \end{array}
\qquad
\begin{array}{r} 691 \\ \times\ 10 \\ \hline \end{array}
\qquad
\begin{array}{r} 57 \\ \times\ 10 \\ \hline \end{array}
\qquad
\begin{array}{r} 83 \\ \times\ 10 \\ \hline \end{array}
\qquad
\begin{array}{r} 739 \\ \times\ 10 \\ \hline \end{array}
$$

7.
$$
\begin{array}{r} 94 \\ \times\ 100 \\ \hline \end{array}
\qquad
\begin{array}{r} 804 \\ \times\ 100 \\ \hline \end{array}
\qquad
\begin{array}{r} 530 \\ \times\ 100 \\ \hline \end{array}
\qquad
\begin{array}{r} 60 \\ \times\ 100 \\ \hline \end{array}
\qquad
\begin{array}{r} 400 \\ \times\ 100 \\ \hline \end{array}
$$

8. $10 \times 72 =$ _____ $100 \times 72 =$ _____

9. $10 \times 84 =$ _____ $100 \times 84 =$ _____

10. $10 \times 59 =$ _____ $100 \times 59 =$ _____

11. $10 \times 65 =$ _____ $100 \times 65 =$ _____

Multiply.

12. $10 \times 319 = $ _____ $\qquad$ $100 \times 319 = $ _____

13. $10 \times 783 = $ _____ $\qquad$ $100 \times 783 = $ _____

14. $10 \times 561 = $ _____ $\qquad$ $100 \times 561 = $ _____

Problem Solving Reasoning | **Solve.**

15. There are **12** months in a year. How many months are there in **10** years? In **100** years?

_____

16. Suppose your heart beats **72** times in **1** minute. How many times will it beat in **10** minutes? In **100** minutes?

_____

_____

17. Elliott weighed **80** pounds last year. He gained **10** pounds. How much does he weigh now?

_____

18. Gerry walks to and from school **23** times a month. How many times does she walk to and from school in **10** months?

_____

_____

☑ **Quick Check**

Multiply.

				Work Space.
19. $\begin{array}{r} \$.34 \\ \times\ \ 2 \\ \hline \end{array}$	**20.** $\begin{array}{r} \$1.43 \\ \times\ \ \ 3 \\ \hline \end{array}$	**21.** $\begin{array}{r} \$3.61 \\ \times\ \ \ 5 \\ \hline \end{array}$		
22. $\begin{array}{r} 2{,}313 \\ \times\ \ \ 3 \\ \hline \end{array}$	**23.** $\begin{array}{r} 4{,}142 \\ \times\ \ \ 4 \\ \hline \end{array}$	**24.** $\begin{array}{r} 3{,}305 \\ \times\ \ \ 5 \\ \hline \end{array}$		
25. $\begin{array}{r} 29 \\ \times\ 10 \\ \hline \end{array}$	**26.** $\begin{array}{r} 33 \\ \times\ 100 \\ \hline \end{array}$	**27.** $\begin{array}{r} 210 \\ \times\ 100 \\ \hline \end{array}$		

Estimating Products

You can estimate products. Round the factors.
Then multiply.

$$\begin{array}{r} 62 \\ \times\, 45 \end{array} \xrightarrow[\text{round up}]{\text{round down}} \begin{array}{r} 60 \\ \times\, 50 \\ \hline 3{,}000 \end{array}$$

$$\begin{array}{r} 97 \\ \times\, 76 \end{array} \xrightarrow[\text{round up}]{\text{round up}} \begin{array}{r} 100 \\ \times\, 80 \\ \hline 8{,}000 \end{array}$$

> **Rounding to the Nearest Ten**
> - If the ones digit is **5** or greater, round up to the next higher multiple of **10**.
> - If the ones digit is less than **5**, round down to the next lower multiple of **10**.

Round to the nearest ten.

1. 62 → _____   **2.** 39 → _____   **3.** 45 → _____   **4.** 75 → _____

   58 → _____   21 → _____   83 → _____   99 → _____

Round each of the factors to the nearest ten. Find the estimated product by multiplying the rounded factors.

5.   32 → 30   48 → _____   26 → _____
    × 44 → × 40   × 89 → × _____   × 72 → × _____

6.   75 → _____   56 → _____   35 → _____
    × 38 → × _____   × 63 → × _____   × 65 → × _____

7.   17 → _____   46 → _____   30 → _____
    × 80 → × _____   × 83 → × _____   × 92 → × _____

8.   36 → _____   67 → _____   81 → _____
    × 24 → × _____   × 31 → × _____   × 55 → × _____

9.   45 → _____   33 → _____   46 → _____
    × 65 → × _____   × 75 → × _____   × 42 → × _____

Estimate each product. Round each of the factors to the nearest ten.

10.
$$63 \times 25 \qquad 75 \times 35 \qquad 38 \times 71 \qquad 44 \times 12 \qquad 55 \times 55 \qquad 23 \times 36$$

11.
$$13 \times 29 \qquad 61 \times 36 \qquad 80 \times 45 \qquad 15 \times 15 \qquad 25 \times 30 \qquad 95 \times 10$$

12.
$$18 \times 41 \qquad 64 \times 81 \qquad 67 \times 40 \qquad 78 \times 52 \qquad 92 \times 56 \qquad 10 \times 87$$

Problem Solving Reasoning | **Decide whether you need an exact answer or an estimated answer. Then solve the problem.**

13. Mr. Mason bought **30** boxes of pencils for the office. There are **12** pencils in each box. Does he have more than **400** pencils?

_____

14. Emily bought **2** notebooks for school. They each cost **$3.79**. How much change did she receive from a ten-dollar bill?

_____

15. Mrs. Benson bought **36** bags of apples for the school fair. Each bag holds **18** apples. If she sells each apple for **5¢**, about how much money could she make from the fair?

_____

16. Hassan made **15** quarts of lemonade. Each quart contains **4** cups of lemonade. Will he be able to sell at least **50** cups of lemonade?

_____

Test Prep ★ Mixed Review

17 Which problem has the same product as $13 \times (17 \times 19)$?

A 221×247

B $3 \times 7 \times 9$

C $13 \times (17 \times 19) \times 0$

D $(13 \times 17) \times 19$

18 Marla filled 57 bags with apples. She put 8 apples in each bag. How many apples did she use in all?

F 406

G 456

H 469

J 496

Name _____

Multiplying by 2-Digit Numbers

You know how to multiply by **1**-digit numbers.
Now you can multiply by **2**-digit numbers.

Find: **36 × 24.**

1. Multiply 24 by 6 ones.

$$\begin{array}{r} \overset{2}{24} \\ \times\, 36 \\ \hline \end{array}$$

$6 \times 24 \rightarrow \quad 144$

2. Multiply 24 by 3 tens.

$$\begin{array}{r} \overset{1}{\underset{}{\overset{2}{2}}4} \\ \times\, 36 \\ \hline 144 \end{array}$$

$30 \times 24 \rightarrow \quad 720$

3. Add the products.

$$\begin{array}{r} 24 \\ \times\, 36 \\ \hline 144 \\ +\, 720 \\ \hline 864 \end{array}$$

4. Estimate to decide if the product is reasonable.
You can see that **864** is close to **800.** So the
product is reasonable.

$$\begin{array}{r} 24 \\ \times\, 36 \end{array} \rightarrow \begin{array}{r} 20 \\ \times\, 40 \\ \hline 800 \end{array}$$

**Multiply. Estimate to decide if the product
is reasonable.**

1.
$\begin{array}{r} 24 \\ \times\, 15 \\ \hline \end{array}$
$\begin{array}{r} 36 \\ \times\, 21 \\ \hline \end{array}$
$\begin{array}{r} 48 \\ \times\, 34 \\ \hline \end{array}$
$\begin{array}{r} 18 \\ \times\, 56 \\ \hline \end{array}$
$\begin{array}{r} 75 \\ \times\, 67 \\ \hline \end{array}$

2.
$\begin{array}{r} 27 \\ \times\, 28 \\ \hline \end{array}$
$\begin{array}{r} 76 \\ \times\, 34 \\ \hline \end{array}$
$\begin{array}{r} \$.42 \\ \times\quad 36 \\ \hline \end{array}$
$\begin{array}{r} \$.94 \\ \times\quad 22 \\ \hline \end{array}$
$\begin{array}{r} 32 \\ \times\, 47 \\ \hline \end{array}$

3.
$\begin{array}{r} 52 \\ \times\, 23 \\ \hline \end{array}$
$\begin{array}{r} 57 \\ \times\, 34 \\ \hline \end{array}$
$\begin{array}{r} 43 \\ \times\, 58 \\ \hline \end{array}$
$\begin{array}{r} 68 \\ \times\, 36 \\ \hline \end{array}$
$\begin{array}{r} \$.69 \\ \times\quad 76 \\ \hline \end{array}$

4.
$\begin{array}{r} 26 \\ \times\, 89 \\ \hline \end{array}$
$\begin{array}{r} 89 \\ \times\, 26 \\ \hline \end{array}$
$\begin{array}{r} 75 \\ \times\, 92 \\ \hline \end{array}$
$\begin{array}{r} 92 \\ \times\, 75 \\ \hline \end{array}$
$\begin{array}{r} \$.83 \\ \times\quad 43 \\ \hline \end{array}$

Copyright © Houghton Mifflin Company. All rights reserved.

Unit 3 Lesson 10   **65**

Multiply.

5.
$$\begin{array}{r} 47 \\ \times\ 19 \\ \hline \end{array}$$
$$\begin{array}{r} 39 \\ \times\ 54 \\ \hline \end{array}$$
$$\begin{array}{r} 56 \\ \times\ 77 \\ \hline \end{array}$$
$$\begin{array}{r} 32 \\ \times\ 24 \\ \hline \end{array}$$
$$\begin{array}{r} 56 \\ \times\ 38 \\ \hline \end{array}$$

6.
$$\begin{array}{r} 40 \\ \times\ 29 \\ \hline \end{array}$$
$$\begin{array}{r} 83 \\ \times\ 43 \\ \hline \end{array}$$
$$\begin{array}{r} 29 \\ \times\ 62 \\ \hline \end{array}$$
$$\begin{array}{r} 98 \\ \times\ 27 \\ \hline \end{array}$$
$$\begin{array}{r} 59 \\ \times\ 56 \\ \hline \end{array}$$

| Problem Solving |
| Reasoning |

Solve.

7. There are **24** stamps on each page of Lester's stamp album. There are **18** pages in his album. How many stamps are in Lester's collection?

8. Sue Lynn collects coins. There are **52** coins in each of **15** boxes. Does Sue Lynn have more than **1,000** coins? Explain.

9. Mrs. Washington has **35** each of **22** different beads. How many beads does she have?

10. Leonard has **10** times as many sports trading cards as his sister. His sister has **84**. How many does Leonard have?

Test Prep ★ Mixed Review

11 What number could go in the ☐ to make the number sentence true?

$$5 \times \boxed{} < 25$$

A 7

B 6

C 5

D 4

12 What number should go in the ☐ to make the number sentence true?

$$3 \times \boxed{} = 3$$

F 0

G 1

H 3

J 6

Name _____

You can multiply with **3**-digit numbers the same way you multiply with **2**-digit numbers.

Find: 86 × 347.

1. Multiply **347** by **6** ones.

$$
\begin{array}{r}
347 \\
\times\ 86 \\
\hline
6 \times 347 \rightarrow 2{,}082
\end{array}
$$

2. Multiply **347** by **8** tens.

$$
\begin{array}{r}
347 \\
\times\ 86 \\
\hline
2{,}082 \\
80 \times 347 \rightarrow 27{,}760
\end{array}
$$

3. Add the products.

$$
\begin{array}{r}
347 \\
\times\ 86 \\
\hline
2\ 082 \\
+\ 27\ 76 \\
\hline
29{,}842
\end{array}
$$

4. Estimate to decide if your answer is reasonable.

$$90 \times 300 = 27{,}000$$

$$
\begin{array}{r}
347 \rightarrow \quad 300 \\
\times\ 86 \rightarrow \quad \times\ 90 \\
\hline
27{,}000
\end{array}
$$

You can see that **29,842** is close to **27,000**. So the product is reasonable.

Multiply. Estimate to decide if your answer is reasonable.

1.

$$
\begin{array}{r} 396 \\ \times\ 38 \\ \hline \end{array}
\qquad
\begin{array}{r} 197 \\ \times\ 29 \\ \hline \end{array}
\qquad
\begin{array}{r} 418 \\ \times\ 67 \\ \hline \end{array}
\qquad
\begin{array}{r} 269 \\ \times\ 46 \\ \hline \end{array}
\qquad
\begin{array}{r} 375 \\ \times\ 57 \\ \hline \end{array}
$$

2.

$$
\begin{array}{r} 656 \\ \times\ 23 \\ \hline \end{array}
\qquad
\begin{array}{r} 390 \\ \times\ 48 \\ \hline \end{array}
\qquad
\begin{array}{r} 507 \\ \times\ 54 \\ \hline \end{array}
\qquad
\begin{array}{r} 378 \\ \times\ 76 \\ \hline \end{array}
\qquad
\begin{array}{r} 476 \\ \times\ 93 \\ \hline \end{array}
$$

3.

$$
\begin{array}{r} 547 \\ \times\ 73 \\ \hline \end{array}
\qquad
\begin{array}{r} 406 \\ \times\ 32 \\ \hline \end{array}
\qquad
\begin{array}{r} 327 \\ \times\ 44 \\ \hline \end{array}
\qquad
\begin{array}{r} 215 \\ \times\ 58 \\ \hline \end{array}
\qquad
\begin{array}{r} 108 \\ \times\ 92 \\ \hline \end{array}
$$

Multiply.

4.

48	109	55	212	498	290
× 13	× 24	× 55	× 29	× 84	× 30

5.

239	87	523	860	753	47
× 19	× 24	× 17	× 62	× 71	× 30

Problem Solving Reasoning Solve.

6. a. Teachers bought **6** pizzas for students who are on a field trip. Each pizza has **8** slices. If each student gets one slice, how many students will be served?

_____

b. Each pizza costs **$6.95**. How much did **6** cost? _____

7. a. The pizza restaurant sells single slices of pizza. Each slice is **$.95**. If **48** students each bought one slice, how much would they pay altogether?

_____

b. Is it cheaper to buy **6** pizzas or **48** single slices? What is the difference in cost?

_____

 Quick Check

Multiply.

Work Space.

8.	67	9.	32	10.	83
	× 25		× 46		× 62

11.	417	12.	208	13.	457
	× 22		× 37		× 43

Name _____

Use properties to solve.

1. (3 × **4**) × 2 = 24   **2.** 4 × 0 = **0**   **3.** 1 × 9 = **9**

Multiply.

4. 53
   × 7
   371

5. 81
   × 5
   405

6. 301
   × 9
   2,709

7. 7,326
   × 6
   33,950

8. 1,205
   × 2
   3410

9. 15 × 10
   150

10. 290 × 100
   229

11. 60 × 40
   240

12. 70 × 70
   7,900

13. $2.76
   × 4
   11,04

14. $17.25
   × 5
   86.25

15. 26
   × 16
   416

16. 66 **24**
   × 34
   2041

17. 125 **48**
   × 28
   280

Use rounding to estimate the product.

18. 65 → **60**
   × 4 → × **1**
   60

19. 71 → **70**
   × 17 → × **20**
   140

20. $6.29 → **630**
   × 32 → × **30**
   646

Solve.

21. Jennifer bought **2** notebooks and a pencil. One notebook cost twice as much as the other. The pencil cost **$.30**. She spent **$6.75**. How much did each notebook cost?

_____

22. Which school has the most runners? How many runners in total are at all three schools?

   welington
   school

Number of Runners at Three Schools

Fairfield School	
Litchfield School	
Wellington School	
Key	● = 6 Runners

1 On one day of their vacation, the Rodríquez family spent $26 for breakfast, $38 for lunch, and $79 for dinner. How much did they spend in all for these meals?

A $133

B $143

C $152

D $1223

E NH

2 A machine uses 27 gallons to paint the lines on 1 mile of highway. How many gallons will the machine need to paint the lines on 35 miles of highway?

F 655

G 745

H 945

J 965

K NH

3 A window washer finishes 1 window in 4 minutes. There are 76 windows on the building. *About* how many minutes will it take him to wash all the windows?

A 240

B 280

C 320

D 3200

E NH

4 A plane is flying from San Diego, California, to Seattle, Washington. The distance between these cities is 1,270 miles. If the plane has flown 396 miles, how many more miles are left?

F 1666   J 874

G 984   K NH

H 884

5 A total of 15,472 runners entered a road race. What is this number rounded to the nearest hundred?

A 15,000   D 16,500

B 15,400   E NH

C 16,000

6 What number is four hundred seventy thousand, nine in standard form?

F 47,009

G 407,009

H 470,009

J 470,090

7 Which problem has the same product as 217×3?

A $(200 \times 3) + (10 \times 3) + (7 \times 3)$

B $(200 \times 17) + (10 \times 17) + (3 \times 17)$

C $(200 \times 3) + (10 \times 3)$

D $(200 \times 19) + (10 \times 7) + (7 \times 3)$

E NH

UNIT 4 • TABLE OF CONTENTS

Division with 1-Digit Divisors

Dear Family,

During the next few weeks, our math class will be learning and practicing division of whole numbers.

You can expect to see homework that provides practice with finding averages. Here is a sample you may want to keep handy to give help if needed.

Finding an Average

During the first **5** soccer games of the year, the Parkside Elementary School soccer team scored **3, 0, 1, 6,** and **0** goals.

To find the average number of goals the team scored in each game, first add to find the total number of goals scored.

$$3 + 0 + 1 + 6 + 0 = 10$$ The team scored a total of **10** goals.

Then divide the total number of goals scored by the number of games the team played.

$$
\begin{array}{r}
2 \\
5\overline{)10} \\
-10 \\
\hline
0
\end{array}
$$

During the first five games, the team scored an average of **2** goals per game.

During this unit, students will need to continue practicing addition, subtraction, multiplication, and division facts.

Sincerely,

Missing Factors and Division

Multiplication and division are **inverse operations**. You can use a related division fact to find a missing factor.

> **Inverse** means opposite.

factor × factor = product

$? \times 6 = 48$

$48 \div 6 = ?$

$48 \div 6 = 8$, so $8 \times 6 = 48$

You can use a related number sentence to find the value of n.

Find n in the number sentence $n \times 5 = 30$.

1. Use a related number sentence.

   $n \times 5 = 30$
   Think: $n = 30 \div 5$
   $n = 6$

   > Division is the inverse of multiplication.
   >
   > **Think: 30** divided by **5** is what number?

2. Check your work.

   Is the number sentence $n \times 5 = 30$ **true** when $n = 6$?

   $n \times 5 = 30$

   $6 \times 5 = 30$ **Yes, it is true.**

Use related number sentences to find the value of n.

1. $n \times 2 = 18$

Think: $n = 18 \div$ _____

$n =$ _____

$n \times 9 = 63$

Think: $n = 63 \div$ _____

$n =$ _____

$n \times 8 = 64$

Think: $n =$ _____ $\div 8$

$n =$ _____

2. $n \times 6 = 36$

Think: $n = 36 \div$ _____

$n =$ _____

$n \times 1 = 40$

Think: $n =$ _____ $\div 1$

$n =$ _____

$n \times 7 = 28$

Think: $n =$ _____ $\div 7$

$n =$ _____

3. $4 \times n = 28$

Think: $n =$ _____ $\div 4$

$n =$ _____

$6 \times n = 54$

Think: $n =$ _____ $\div 6$

$n =$ _____

$7 \times n = 56$

Think: $n = 56 \div$ _____

$n =$ _____

Division rules can sometimes be used to find the value of a variable.

What is the value of *n* in the number sentence $0 \div 5 = n$?

When you divide zero by any number, the answer is zero.

If $0 \div 5 = n$, then $n = 0$.

Remember, you can never divide by zero.

What is the value of *n* in the number sentence $5 \div 5 = n$?

Any number divided by itself equals **1**.

If $5 \div 5 = n$, then $n = 1$.

What is the value of *n* in the number sentence $5 \div 1 = n$?

Any number divided by **1** is that number.

If $5 \div 1 = n$, then $n = 5$.

Find the value of *n*.

4. $8 \div 8 = n$ $0 \div 4 = n$ $18 \div 2 = n$ $1 \times 5 = n$

$n =$ _____ $n =$ _____ $n =$ _____ $n =$ _____

Problem Solving Reasoning — **Complete each table. Think about multiplication facts to help you divide.**

5.

Divide by 4	
16	
36	
24	
12	

6.

Divide by 7	
21	
56	
49	
28	

7.

Divide by 9	
45	
27	
63	
81	

Test Prep ★ Mixed Review

8 What number should go in the ☐ to make the number sentence true?

$$(11 + 21) + 8 = \boxed{} + (11 + 8)$$

A 21   C 8

B 11   D 7

9 What number should go in the ☐ to make the number sentence true?

$$(3 \times 2) \times 10 = 3 \times \boxed{}$$

F 20   H 3

G 10   J 2

A mathematical **expression** contains numbers and operation signs. Some expressions may also contain letters that stand for numbers. These are all expressions:

$$2 \times 3 \qquad n + 1 \qquad 3 \div n \qquad 9 + 4$$

Sometimes an expression contains more than one operation. The **order of operations** is a set of rules that tells you which operation to do first.

$4 + 6 \times 2$ Multiply first,
then add.
↓
$4 + \;\; 12$
↓
16 There is only one correct value for this expression.

Order of Operations
1. Do the operation in the parentheses first.
2. Multiply and divide from left to right.
3. Add and subtract from left to right.

Parentheses are grouping symbols that tell you what to do first. When an expression contains parentheses, do the operation inside the parentheses first.

$12 \div (6 - 2)$
↓
$12 \div \;\; 4$
↓
3

$(12 \div 6) - 2$
↓
$2 - 2$
↓
0

The values of the expressions are different.

Use the order of operations. Find the value of each expression.

1. $3 + 6 \times 2$ $14 \div 2 + 3$ $4 \div 2 \times 3$

2. $5 - 4 \div 2$ $7 \times 3 - 3$ $14 - 6 + 11$

3. $16 + 8 \div 4$ $4 \times 3 - 2$ $11 + 9 \div 3$

4. $8 + 6 \times 3$ $16 - 10 \div 2$ $16 \div 4 \times 8$

5. $24 \div 3 + 3$ $30 - 5 \times 4$ $21 - 3 \times 7$

6. $36 - 9 \times 4$ $27 \div 3 + 6$ $64 - 18 + 4$

7. $12 \times 3 - 1$ $9 \div 9 \times 9$ $64 + 16 \times 4$

8. $22 \times 4 - 1$ $29 - 13 \times 2$ $18 \div 6 \times 3$

9. $16 + 8 \div 4$ $50 \times 4 \div 2$ $27 - 9 \div 3$

10. $42 \div 6 \times 7$ $30 + 5 - 4$ $36 \div 3 \times 3$

Use the order of operations. Find the value of each expression.

11. $(56 - 6) \div 5$ _____ $(48 \div 6) \times 3$ _____ $(32 \div 8) + 5$ _____

12. $5 \times (4 + 7)$ _____ $4 \times (8 - 2)$ _____ $6 \times (9 \div 3)$ _____

13. $(4 \times 7) + 3$ _____ $(5 \times 6) \div 10$ _____ $(7 \times 7) \div 7$ _____

Draw parentheses to make each number sentence true.

14. $9 + 3 \times 2 = 24$ $4 \times 9 - 4 = 32$

15. $42 \div 2 \times 3 = 7$ $5 \times 3 + 3 = 30$

16. $7 - 28 \div 4 = 0$ $5 + 2 \times 4 = 13$

17. $15 - 4 \times 3 = 33$ $9 + 9 \div 6 = 3$

Problem Solving Reasoning   Use parentheses and the numbers 2, 3, and 4 to make each number sentence true.

18. ☐ × ☐ − ☐ = 5   ☐ + ☐ ÷ ☐ = 5

19. ☐ + ☐ × ☐ = 10   ☐ × ☐ ÷ ☐ = 6

20. ☐ ÷ ☐ + ☐ = 5   ☐ + ☐ × ☐ = 14

Test Prep ★ Mixed Review

21 Which number could go in the ☐ to make the number sentence true?

$$24 + \boxed{} > 36$$

A 13

B 12

C 10

D 9

22 Anthony practices golf at a driving range. He goes to the range 15 times and hits exactly 55 balls each time. How many balls does he hit in all?

F 575

G 805

H 825

J 3,075

Division with Remainders

Suppose you had **21** marbles and wanted to put **4** marbles in each group. How many groups would you have?

You can show this with division:

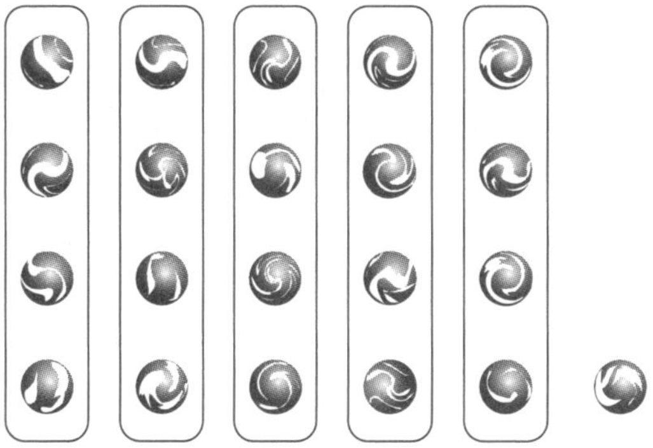

$$\begin{array}{r} 5 \leftarrow \text{quotient} \\ \text{divisor} \rightarrow 4\overline{)21} \leftarrow \text{dividend} \\ -20 \\ \hline 1 \leftarrow \text{remainder} \end{array}$$

You have **5** groups of **4** with **1** marble left over.

The **1** left over is called the remainder. You write the answer as **5 R1**.

Other Examples:

$$\begin{array}{r} 6\ R2 \\ 4\overline{)26} \\ -24 \\ \hline 2 \end{array} \qquad \begin{array}{r} 4\ R5 \\ 7\overline{)33} \\ -28 \\ \hline 5 \end{array} \qquad \begin{array}{r} 8\ R8 \\ 9\overline{)80} \\ -72 \\ \hline 8 \end{array}$$

> The remainder is always less than the divisor!

Complete. Make groups if you need to.

1. 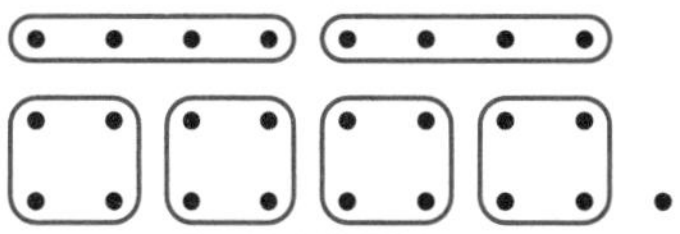
$$\begin{array}{r} 6 \\ 4\overline{)25} \end{array}$$

2. 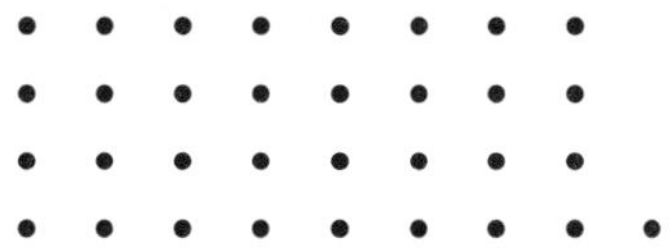
$$8\overline{)33}$$

3. 
$$5\overline{)17}$$

4. 
$$6\overline{)13}$$

5. 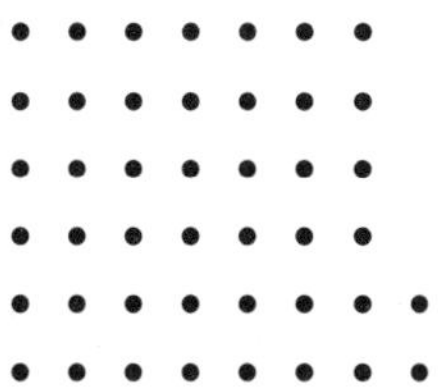
$$7\overline{)44}$$

6. 
$$3\overline{)26}$$

Divide.

7. $4\overline{)17}$ $5\overline{)19}$ $8\overline{)41}$ $3\overline{)29}$ $7\overline{)38}$ $4\overline{)31}$

8. $3\overline{)26}$ $9\overline{)20}$ $6\overline{)52}$ $5\overline{)47}$ $9\overline{)73}$ $6\overline{)22}$

Problem Solving Reasoning   Solve.

9. $(6 \times 7) + 2 =$ _____ $36 = ($ _____ $\times 5) + 1$ $42 = (8 \times 5) +$ _____

10. $($ _____ $\times 5) + 3 = 23$ _____ $= (4 \times 5) + 1$ $(7 \times 6) + 3 =$ _____

11. $(7 \times$ _____ $) + 0 = 56$ _____ $= (4 \times 8) + 2$ $(6 \times 8) + 7 =$ _____

 Quick Check

Write the number that completes the number sentence.

12. $7 \times \boxed{} = 56$ **13.** $8 \times \boxed{} = 72$ **14.** $27 \div \boxed{} = 1$

Work Space.

Use the order of operations to find the value of each expression.

15. $4 + (17 - 2)$ **16.** $(2 \times 6) \div 3$ **17.** $(3 \times 5) + 2$

_____   _____   _____

Divide. Write the remainder if there is one.

18. $8\overline{)37}$ **19.** $4\overline{)27}$ **20.** $7\overline{)54}$

80   Unit 4 Lesson 3

So far with your work in division, you have found one-digit quotients. Sometimes when you divide, the quotient has more digits.

Divide 48 blocks into 4 groups.

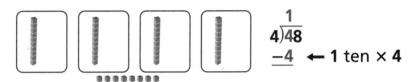

1. Divide the tens. Put **1** ten in each group.

$$
\begin{array}{r}
1 \\
4\overline{)48} \\
-4 \quad \leftarrow \textbf{1 ten} \times \textbf{4}
\end{array}
$$

2. Divide the ones. Put **2** ones in each group.

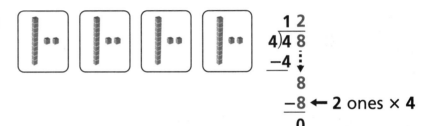

$$
\begin{array}{r}
1\ 2 \\
4\overline{)4\ 8} \\
-4 \\
\hline
8 \\
-8 \quad \leftarrow \textbf{2 ones} \times \textbf{4} \\
\hline
0
\end{array}
$$

Answer: **12** blocks in each group

Divide.

1.

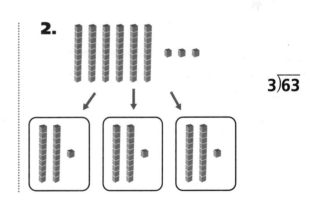

$2\overline{)28}$

2.

$3\overline{)63}$

Divide.

3. $2\overline{)84}$ $5\overline{)55}$ $3\overline{)39}$ $4\overline{)88}$ $3\overline{)96}$ $6\overline{)66}$ $2\overline{)68}$

Sometimes you need to regroup.

Divide **53** blocks into **4** groups.

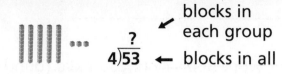

blocks in
each group

$4\overline{)53}$ ← blocks in all

1. Divide the tens.

Put **1** ten
in each group.

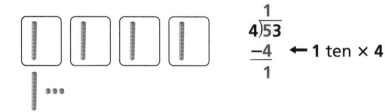

$$\begin{array}{r} 1 \\ 4\overline{)53} \\ -4 \\ \hline 1 \end{array}$$ ← **1** ten × **4**

2. Regroup **1** ten as **10** ones.
1 ten + **3** ones = **13** ones

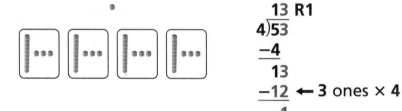

$$\begin{array}{r} 1 \\ 4\overline{)5\,3} \\ -4\!\downarrow \\ \hline 1\,3 \end{array}$$

3. Divide the ones.
Put **3** ones
in each group.
13 ones ÷ **4** = **3** ones **R1**

Answer: **13 R1**

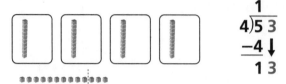

$$\begin{array}{r} 13 \text{ R1} \\ 4\overline{)53} \\ -4 \\ \hline 13 \\ -12 \\ \hline 1 \end{array}$$ ← **3** ones × **4**

Divide.

4.

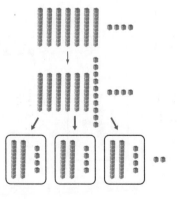

$3\overline{)74}$

5.

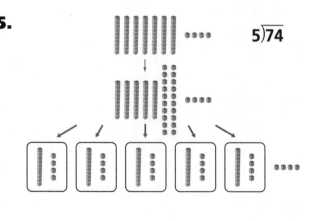

$5\overline{)74}$

Divide.

6. $8\overline{)97}$ $3\overline{)77}$ $4\overline{)93}$ $7\overline{)88}$ $5\overline{)84}$

Name _____

Follow these steps to divide without blocks.

Find $3\overline{)79}^{?}$

1. Divide tens.	**2. Multiply and subtract.**	**3. Bring down the next digit. Regroup.**	**4. Divide ones.**	**5. Multiply and subtract.**

1. Divide tens.

Think: $3\overline{)7}^{? \text{ tens}}$ tens

2 tens

$3\overline{)79}^{2}$

2. Multiply and subtract.

$$\begin{array}{r} 2 \\ 3\overline{)79} \\ -6 \leftarrow 2\text{ tens}\times 3 \\ \hline 1 \end{array}$$

3. Bring down the next digit. Regroup.

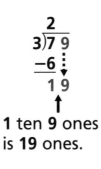

$$\begin{array}{r} 2 \\ 3\overline{)7\,9} \\ -6 \\ \hline 1\,9 \end{array}$$

1 ten 9 ones is 19 ones.

4. Divide ones.

Think: 19 ones ÷ 3 6 ones

$$\begin{array}{r} 26 \\ 3\overline{)79} \\ -6 \\ \hline 19 \end{array}$$

5. Multiply and subtract.

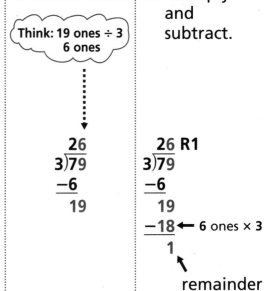

$$\begin{array}{r} 26 \text{ R1} \\ 3\overline{)79} \\ -6 \\ \hline 19 \\ -18 \leftarrow 6\text{ ones}\times 3 \\ \hline 1 \end{array}$$

remainder

6. Check your work.

Multiply the quotient by the divisor. Then add the remainder.

26 × 3 + 1 = 78 + 1 or 79

The result is the dividend, so this answer is correct.

Complete each division.

7.

$$\begin{array}{r} 1 \\ 3\overline{)4\,7} \\ -3 \\ \hline 1\,7 \end{array}$$

$$\begin{array}{r} 1 \\ 6\overline{)8\,4} \\ -6 \\ \hline 2\,4 \end{array}$$

$$\begin{array}{r} 2 \\ 4\overline{)93} \\ -8 \\ \hline 13 \end{array}$$

$$\begin{array}{r} 3 \\ 2\overline{)71} \\ -6 \\ \hline 11 \end{array}$$

$$\begin{array}{r} 1 \\ 7\overline{)92} \\ -7 \\ \hline 22 \end{array}$$

8.

$$\begin{array}{r} 1 \\ 5\overline{)85} \end{array}$$

$$\begin{array}{r} 2 \\ 2\overline{)47} \end{array}$$

$$3\overline{)82}$$

$$7\overline{)95}$$

$$8\overline{)95}$$

Divide.

9. $6\overline{)87}$ $2\overline{)93}$ $4\overline{)78}$ $5\overline{)78}$ $3\overline{)92}$

10. $3\overline{)55}$ $6\overline{)78}$ $4\overline{)67}$ $7\overline{)73}$ $2\overline{)91}$

11. $3\overline{)97}$ $4\overline{)84}$ $6\overline{)61}$ $4\overline{)87}$ $7\overline{)90}$

12. $2\overline{)59}$ $8\overline{)84}$ $5\overline{)67}$ $6\overline{)67}$ $3\overline{)65}$

Problem Solving Reasoning   Solve.

13. Three boys divided **84** pennies equally among themselves. How many pennies did each boy get?

_____

14. Four girls played a game with **52** number cards. They divided the whole deck equally. How many cards did each girl get?

_____

Test Prep ★ Mixed Review

15 The population of the town of Carmichael, California, is 48,702. The population of the town of Fair Oaks is 26,867. What is the combined population of these two towns?

A 741,569

B 75,669

C 75,569

D 65,569

E NH

16 The store sold 67 T-shirts each hour. *About* how many T-shirts did it sell in 12 hours?

F 800

G 700

H 600

J 500

Name _____

3-Digit Quotients

Working with 3-digit quotients is like working
with 2-digit quotients.

Example: $3\overline{)875}$

1. Divide hundreds.

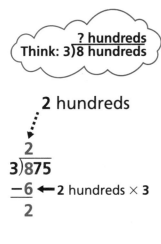

Think: $3\overline{)8\text{ hundreds}}$? hundreds

2 hundreds

$$
\begin{array}{r}
2 \\
3\overline{)875} \\
-6 \leftarrow \text{2 hundreds} \times 3 \\
\hline
2
\end{array}
$$

2. Bring down the next digit.

$$
\begin{array}{r}
2 \\
3\overline{)8\,7\,5} \\
-6 \\
\hline
2\,7
\end{array}
$$

2 hundreds 7 tens is 27 tens

3. Divide tens.

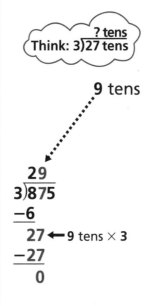

Think: $3\overline{)27\text{ tens}}$? tens

9 tens

$$
\begin{array}{r}
29 \\
3\overline{)875} \\
-6 \\
\hline
27 \leftarrow \text{9 tens} \times 3 \\
-27 \\
\hline
0
\end{array}
$$

4. Bring down the next digit. Divide ones.

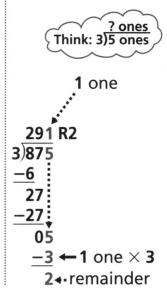

Think: $3\overline{)5\text{ ones}}$? ones

1 one

$$
\begin{array}{r}
291\ \text{R2} \\
3\overline{)875} \\
-6 \\
\hline
27 \\
-27 \\
\hline
05 \\
-3 \leftarrow \text{1 one} \times 3 \\
\hline
2 \leftarrow \text{remainder}
\end{array}
$$

5. Check your work.

Multiply the quotient by the divisor. Then add the remainder.

291 × 3 = 873 + 2 or 875

The result is the dividend, so the answer is correct.

Divide.

1.

$$
\begin{array}{r}
1 \\
4\overline{)759} \\
-4 \\
\hline
35
\end{array}
\qquad
\begin{array}{r}
2 \\
4\overline{)923} \\
-8 \\
\hline
12
\end{array}
\qquad
\begin{array}{r}
1 \\
6\overline{)824} \\
-6 \\
\hline
22
\end{array}
\qquad
\begin{array}{r}
4 \\
2\overline{)971} \\
-8 \\
\hline
17
\end{array}
\qquad
\begin{array}{r}
1 \\
5\overline{)814} \\
-5 \\
\hline
31
\end{array}
$$

2.

$$
\begin{array}{r}
2 \\
3\overline{)762}
\end{array}
\qquad
\begin{array}{r}
1 \\
5\overline{)913}
\end{array}
\qquad
\begin{array}{r}
2 \\
4\overline{)882}
\end{array}
\qquad
\begin{array}{r}
2 \\
3\overline{)806}
\end{array}
\qquad
\begin{array}{r}
1 \\
7\overline{)932}
\end{array}
$$

Copyright © Houghton Mifflin Company. All rights reserved.

Unit 4 Lesson 5 **85**

Divide. Then check your work.

3. $6\overline{)718}$ Check: $4\overline{)805}$ Check: $2\overline{)953}$ Check:

4. $3\overline{)517}$ Check: $5\overline{)891}$ Check: $6\overline{)903}$ Check:

5. $7\overline{)856}$ Check: $4\overline{)735}$ Check: $3\overline{)572}$ Check:

| Problem Solving |
| Reasoning |

Solve.

6. Eric has **532** marbles and **5** marble bags. He wants each bag to contain the same number of marbles. How many marbles should he put in each bag?

7. How many marbles does Eric need to add to his collection in order to have exactly **110** marbles in each of his **5** bags?

Test Prep ★ Mixed Review

8 Andrea's heart beat 93 times a minute while she was running. She ran for 15 minutes. How many times did her heart beat during this run?

A   558

B 1,385

C 1,395

D 5,445

9 Eight friends share $96.00 equally. How much money does each friend get?

F $10.00

G $11.00

H $12.00

J $13.00

Sometimes, when you divide with a 3-digit dividend, the quotient has 2 digits.

Find: 237 ÷ 5.

1. Divide hundreds.

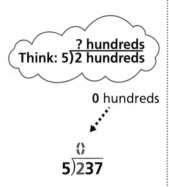

Think: 5)2 hundreds **? hundreds**

0 hundreds

$$0 \atop 5)\overline{237}$$

Not enough hundreds. Regroup as tens.

2. Divide tens.

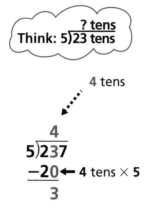

Think: 5)23 tens **? tens**

4 tens

$$4 \atop 5)\overline{237}$$
$$-20 \leftarrow 4 \text{ tens} \times 5$$
$$3$$

3. Regroup as ones. Then divide ones.

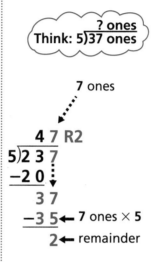

Think: 5)37 ones **? ones**

7 ones

$$4\ 7 \text{ R2} \atop 5)\overline{2\ 3\ 7}$$
$$-2\ 0$$
$$3\ 7$$
$$-3\ 5 \leftarrow 7 \text{ ones} \times 5$$
$$2 \leftarrow \text{remainder}$$

Be sure to write the remainder.

4. Check.

$$\begin{array}{r} 47 \\ \times\ \ 5 \\ \hline 235 \\ +\ \ \ 2 \\ \hline 237 \end{array}$$

The result, **237**, checks with the dividend, so the answer is correct.

Complete each division.

1.
$$\begin{array}{r} 6 \\ 3)\overline{194} \\ -18 \\ \hline 14 \end{array}$$

$$\begin{array}{r} 3 \\ 4)\overline{147} \\ -12 \\ \hline 27 \end{array}$$

$$\begin{array}{r} 7 \\ 5)\overline{381} \\ -35 \\ \hline 31 \end{array}$$

$$\begin{array}{r} 4 \\ 6)\overline{297} \\ -24 \\ \hline 57 \end{array}$$

2.
$$\begin{array}{r} 4 \\ 5)\overline{237} \\ -20 \end{array}$$

$$\begin{array}{r} 4 \\ 3)\overline{128} \\ -12 \end{array}$$

$$\begin{array}{r} 8 \\ 6)\overline{492} \\ -48 \end{array}$$

$$\begin{array}{r} 7 \\ 7)\overline{539} \\ -49 \end{array}$$

Divide.

3. 4)315   6)416   8)592   7)394

Divide.

4. $6\overline{)178}$ $8\overline{)196}$ $5\overline{)185}$ $7\overline{)196}$

5. $5\overline{)283}$ $4\overline{)195}$ $5\overline{)387}$ $6\overline{)389}$

| Problem Solving Reasoning | **Solve.** |

6. Tony needs **252** tiles to cover a wall. He needs the same number of red, green, and yellow tiles. How many of each color should he buy?

_____

7. Ann put **365** tokens in **5** equal groups. How many tokens are in each group?

_____

✔ Quick Check

Solve.

8. $4\overline{)95}$ **9.** $7\overline{)87}$ **10.** $2\overline{)73}$

11. $6\overline{)773}$ **12.** $4\overline{)523}$ **13.** $8\overline{)899}$

14. $8\overline{)733}$ **15.** $6\overline{)469}$ **16.** $5\overline{)407}$

Work Space.

Name _____

Zeros in the Quotient

Sometimes a quotient contains one or more zeros.

Example: $4\overline{)825}^{\;?}$

1. Divide hundreds.	**2. Bring down the 2. Divide tens.**	**3. Bring down the 5. Divide ones.**	**4. Check.**
Think: $4\overline{)8}$ **? hundreds / 8 hundreds**	Think: $4\overline{)2}$ **? tens / 2 tens**	Think: $4\overline{)25}$ **? ones / 25 ones**	$\begin{array}{r} 206 \\ \times\ \ 4 \\ \hline 824 \\ +\ \ \ 1 \\ \hline 825 \end{array}$
$\begin{array}{r} 2\ \ \ \ \\ 4\overline{)825} \\ -8\ \ \ \ \\ \hline 0\ \ \ \ \end{array}$	$\begin{array}{r} 2\ 0\ \ \\ 4\overline{)8\ 2\ 5} \\ -8\ \ \ \ \\ \hline 0\ 2\ \end{array}$	$\begin{array}{r} 2\ 0\ 6\ \text{R1} \\ 4\overline{)8\ 2\ 5} \\ -8\ \ \ \ \ \\ \hline 2\ 5 \\ -2\ 4 \\ \hline 1 \end{array}$	The result, **825**, is the dividend. So the answer is correct.
	Not enough tens. Write a **0** in the tens place in the quotient.		

Divide. Then check.

1. $6\overline{)645}$ $2\overline{)609}$ $3\overline{)302}$

2. $2\overline{)815}$ $8\overline{)565}$ $2\overline{)613}$

3. $4\overline{)438}$ $7\overline{)761}$ $6\overline{)364}$

4. $3\overline{)721}$ $4\overline{)827}$ $9\overline{)919}$

Write the greatest multiple of 100 that will make
each sentence true.

5. $3 \times$ __300__ < 945 $5 \times$ _____ < 800 _____ $\times 9 < 1{,}900$

6. $2 \times$ _____ < 530 $6 \times$ _____ $< 1{,}300$ _____ $\times 6 < 2{,}300$

Circle the greatest number that makes the
sentence true.

7. $5 \times \blacksquare < 98$ $8 \times \blacksquare < 769$ $2 \times \blacksquare < 721$

        1   2   10   20   80   90   800   900   30   40   300   400

Write the first digit of each quotient. Use your
answers in Row 7 to help you.

8. $5\overline{)98}$ $8\overline{)769}$ $2\overline{)721}$

Divide and check.

9. $5\overline{)98}$ $8\overline{)769}$ $2\overline{)721}$

| Problem Solving |
| Reasoning |

Solve.

10. Does a zero in the ones place of a quotient mean
there is never a remainder? Explain.

_____

_____

Test Prep ★ Mixed Review

11 What number should go in the ☐ to
make the number sentence
true?

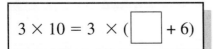

A 2

B 4

C 6

D 8

12 Six friends divide 22 tennis balls
evenly. How many balls are left over?

F 6

G 4

H 3

J 2

Name ____________________

Dividing Money

You can divide money just as you would divide whole numbers.

Example: $4\overline{)\$5.40}$

1. Divide as if you were dividing whole numbers.

$$\begin{array}{r} 1\ 35 \\ 4\overline{)\$5.40} \\ -4 \\ \hline 14 \\ -12 \\ \hline 20 \\ -20 \\ \hline 0 \end{array}$$

2. Write the dollar sign and decimal point in the quotient.

$$\begin{array}{r} \$1.35 \\ 4\overline{)\$5.40} \\ -4 \\ \hline 14 \\ -12 \\ \hline 20 \\ -20 \\ \hline 0 \end{array}$$

Align the decimal point in the quotient with the decimal point in the dividend.

Divide. Remember to write the dollar sign and decimal point in the quotient when you need to.

1. $7\overline{)84¢}$ $7\overline{)\$.84}$ $9\overline{)\$6.48}$ $8\overline{)\$6.48}$

2. $2\overline{)\$6.24}$ $3\overline{)\$4.26}$ $3\overline{)\$2.76}$ $4\overline{)\$.88}$

3. $8\overline{)\$5.76}$ $9\overline{)\$8.10}$ $3\overline{)\$9.03}$ $5\overline{)\$9.75}$

4. $9\overline{)\$3.78}$ $6\overline{)\$.84}$ $7\overline{)91¢}$ $6\overline{)\$8.64}$

You can buy **6** balloons for **$10.20**. How much does **1** balloon cost?

To find out how much one item costs when all the items cost the same, divide the total amount by the number in the group.

$$\begin{array}{r} \$\ 1.70 \\ 6\overline{)\$10.20} \\ -6 \\ \hline 42 \\ -42 \\ \hline 0 \end{array}$$

Always remember to include the dollar sign and decimal point in your answer.

Find the cost of one item.

5. Two burgers cost **$7.80**.

One burger costs _____ .

6. Four cups of jello cost **$3.00**.

One jello costs _____ .

7. Five glasses of juice cost **$6.75**.

One juice costs _____ .

8. Six small salads cost **$9.00**.

One salad costs _____ .

| Problem Solving |
| Reasoning |

Decide whether you need an exact answer or an estimated answer. Then solve the problem.

9. At the fair, Mrs. Washington gave her **4** children **$30.00**. She said they should share the money equally. How much did each child get?

_____

10. The school pageant had an attendance of **126** people on Monday and **214** people on Tuesday. It cost **$1.00** to attend. Did the school collect at least **$400.00**?

_____

Test Prep ★ Mixed Review

11 One pad of colored paper has 85 sheets of paper. How many sheets of paper do 12 pads have?

A 245

B 255

C 1,010

D 1,020

12 Howard is placing photographs in an album. He can fit 4 photographs on a page. How many pages will he need for 172 photographs?

F 40

G 43

H 430

J 688

Name _____

To solve problems, you need to decide whether to add, subtract, multiply, or divide. To choose the correct operation, think about how each operation can be used.

- Both **addition** and **multiplication** can be used to find a total.

- **Subtraction** can be used to find out how many are left, to compare two numbers, or to find a missing addend.

- **Division** can be used to find the number in each group or the number of groups.

Tips to Remember:

| 1. Understand | 2. Decide | 3. Solve | 4. Look back |

- Read the problem carefully. Ask yourself questions about any part that does not make sense. Reread to find answers.
- Find the action in the problem. Which operation shows the action best: addition, subtraction, multiplication, or division?
- Predict the answer. Then solve the problem. Compare your answer with your prediction.

Solve.

1. There are **108** students in the fourth grade at Eastbrook School. There are **4** fourth grade classes. Each class is the same size. How many students are in each class?

Think: How does the question help you decide what operation to use?

_____

_____

_____

Answer _____

2. Mrs. Chang bought a flannel shirt for each of her sons, Mike and Russell. Each shirt cost **$16.98**. What was the total cost?

Think: What operations can you use to find a total? What two methods could you use to solve this problem?

_____

_____

_____

Answer _____

Solve.

3. A total of **72** girls signed up to play in a soccer league. The league organized them into **6** teams, all with the same number of players. How many girls were on each team?

_____

4. On Wednesday, **288** students in a school ordered pizza for lunch. Nine students ordered fish. How many more students ordered pizza than ordered fish?

_____

5. Chairs were set up in the gym for a school play. There were **24** rows with **12** chairs in each row. How many chairs were there in all?

_____

6. Andrew saw a pair of rollerblades for **$69.95** in one store. He saw the same rollerblades in another store for **$57.99**. What was the difference in price?

_____

7. Alexandra earns money babysitting. During one weekend, she earned a total of **$36**. She earned **$15.50** of this total on Friday and **$10.50** on Saturday. How much did she earn on Sunday?

_____

8. Three brothers shared the cost of flowers for their mother. The flowers cost **$12.42**. If each boy paid the same amount, how much did each pay?

_____

9. There were **56** people on a bus— both students and teachers. There are **3** times as many students as teachers. How many teachers are on the bus?

_____

10. Everytime Jenna loses a tooth, **50¢** is added to her piggy bank. How many teeth does Jenna need to lose to make **$5.00**?

_____

Extend Your Thinking

11. Go back to problem 4. Compare the two numbers in a different way. Find the missing number in this sentence: The number of students who ordered pizza was ? times the number of students who ordered fish.

_____

12. Explain the method you used to solve problem 7. Did you use more than one operation?

_____

_____

_____

Divisibility

A number is divisible by another whole number when it can be divided by that number and there is no remainder.

Example: 21 is divisible by **3** but not by **5**.

$$21 \div 3 = 7 \text{ (no remainder)}$$
$$21 \div 5 = 4 \text{ R1}$$

Use these rules to help you decide if a number is divisible by **2, 5,** or **10.**

A number is divisible by **2** if the ones digit is **0, 2, 4, 6, 8.**	A number is divisible by **5** if the ones digit is **0** or **5.**	A number is divisible by **10** if the ones digit is **0.**
Examples: 30, 42, 54, 86, 128, 508, 724	**Examples: 20, 35, 15, 100, 240, 365, 890**	**Examples: 30, 80, 90, 120, 230, 350, 810**

Numbers that are **divisible by 2** are called **even** numbers.

Even Numbers
2, 4, 6, 8, 10, 12, 14, 16 . . .

Numbers that are **not divisible by 2** are called **odd** numbers.

Odd Numbers
1, 3, 5, 7, 9, 11, 13, 15 . . .

**Circle the numbers that are divisible by 2.
Use the rule shown above.**

1. 30	42	27	63	74	92	140	271
2. 225	306	708	232	473	891	726	982

**Circle the numbers that are divisible by 5.
Use the rule shown above.**

3. 20	37	65	42	55	74	125	102
4. 615	431	336	510	705	600	345	924

**Circle the numbers that are divisible by 10.
Use the rule shown above.**

5. 36	47	60	52	76	40	130	408
6. 330	501	216	460	607	728	930	825

Use these rules to help you decide if a number is
divisible by **3** or **9**.

A number is divisible by **3** if the sum of
its digits is divisible by **3**. **27** is divisible
by **3** since **2 + 7**, or **9**, is divisible by **3**.

Examples: 30, 42, 54, 87, 138, 507, 735

A number is divisible by **9** if the sum of
its digits is divisible by **9**. **36** is divisible
by **9** since **3 + 6**, or **9**, is divisible by **9**.

Examples: 18, 72, 99, 108, 216, 594, 864

**Circle the numbers that are divisible by 3.
Use the rule shown above.**

7. 15   24   36   45   90   122   35   606

8. 28   447   813   40   69   72   55   33

**Circle the numbers that are divisible by 9.
Use the rule shown above.**

9. 15   24   36   45   90   22   435   603

10. 28   147   81   240   69   72   855   33

Circle all the even numbers that are divisible by 3.

11. 18   27   36   42   45   54   63   75

 Quick Check

Solve.

Work Space.

12. 2)615

13. 5)533

14. 4)818

15. 9)$2.16

16. 5)$6.75

17. 7)$9.31

18. Circle the numbers that are divisible by both 3 and 2.

   9   12   15   18   21   24

19. Circle all the odd numbers that are divisible by 9.

   27   36   54   63   81   99

Name ______________________________

Factors: Prime and Composite Numbers

A number is a **factor** of another number if it divides that number with no remainder.

factors of 24

1, 2, 3, 4, 6, 8, 12, 24

A factor of a number is also a **divisor** of that number.

24 = 3 × 8
24 ÷ 8 = 3
24 ÷ 3 = 8
3 and **8** are divisors of **24**.

If a number greater than **1** has **exactly two factors, 1** and the number itself, it is called a **prime number**. A number having **more than two factors** is called a **composite number**.

The number 1 is neither a prime number nor a composite number. It has only one factor, itself.

Complete by writing each product with as many different pairs of factors as possible. Circle the prime numbers.

1.

1	2	3	4	5
1 × 1				

2.

6	7	8	9	10
1 × 6				
2 × 3				

3.

11	12	13	14	15

4.

16	17	18	19	20

Complete by writing each product with as many different pairs of factors as possible. Circle the prime numbers.

5.

21	23	25	27	29

6.

31	33	35	37	39

7.

41	43	45	47	49

Problem Solving Reasoning Solve.

8. Are all prime numbers odd numbers? Explain.

_____

_____

Test Prep ★ Mixed Review

9 What number should go in the ☐ to make the number sentence true?

$5 \times 36 = 5 \times (30 + \boxed{})$

  A 180   **C** 6

  B 30   **D** 5

10 A school fair has a throwing contest. Each student throws 3 balls to hit a target. If 167 students play, how many balls are thrown in all?

  F 321   **H** 501

  G 381   **J** 521

Name _____

When you divide with a **4**-digit number, use the same steps you use for dividing **3**-digit numbers.

Example: $6\overline{)3,587}$

1. Decide if there are enough thousands to divide. If not, regroup and divide hundreds.

   Continue dividing, following the steps you have learned.

   $$
   \begin{array}{r}
   597 \text{ R5} \\
   6\overline{)3,587} \\
   -3\,0 \\
   \hline
   58 \\
   -54 \\
   \hline
   47 \\
   -42 \\
   \hline
   5
   \end{array}
   $$

2. With greater numbers, it is important to check your answer.

   Check:
   $$
   \begin{array}{r}
   597 \\
   \times\ \ \ 6 \\
   \hline
   3,582 \\
   +\ \ \ 5 \\
   \hline
   3,587
   \end{array}
   $$
   ← This is the dividend. So the answer is correct.

Divide. Then check.

1. $7\overline{)1,492}$ $6\overline{)4,985}$ $6\overline{)1,305}$

2. $8\overline{)2,870}$ $7\overline{)5,672}$ $7\overline{)6,390}$

Divide and check.

3. 8)5,892   9)8,489   8)5,049

4. 7)2,960   4)2,601   2)1,634

 Problem Solving Reasoning   **Solve.**

5. Leslie has **547** tomato plants. She wants to plant them in **5** equal rows. How many plants can she put in each row? How many plants will be left over?

6. A poultry farm produced **2,364** eggs. The eggs are put in packages of **6**. How many packages can they fill? How many eggs will be left over?

✓ **Quick Check**

Solve.   **Work Space.**

7. Find all the factors of 12. _____

8. Find all the factors of 16. _____

9. Circle the prime numbers.

   13   24   33   41   45

10. Circle all the composite numbers that are also odd numbers.

   7   15   21   29   35   41

11. 8)3,752   **12.** 4)2,902   **13.** 6)4,285

Name _____

Some problems can be solved by working backward.

When working backward, you can often use opposite, or inverse, operations.

Adding and subtracting are inverse operations. Multiplying and dividing are inverse operations.

Problem

On Tuesday, Lauren rode her bike **3 miles** more than on Monday. On Wednesday, she rode **4 miles** less than on Tuesday. On Thursday, she rode twice as far as on the day before. On Friday, she rode **27 miles**. This was **5 miles** more than on Thursday. How far did she ride on Monday?

① Understand   As you reread, organize the information.

Miles Lauren Rode

Mon.	Tues.	Wed.	Thurs.	Fri.
?	**3** miles more than Mon.	____ miles less than Tues.	**2** times as many miles as Wed.	____ miles more than Thurs. or **27**

② Decide   Choose a method for solving.

Try the strategy Work Backward.

- Show the operations in the order they are given in the problem.

| ? | → | +3 | → | −4 | → | ___ | → | ___ | → | 27 |

③ Solve   Work backward, using inverse operations.

| 27 | → | −5 | → | ÷2 | → | ___ | → | ___ | → | ? ___ |

④ Look back   Check your answer. Write the answer below.

Answer _____

- Why is it important to go back to the problem to check your answer?

_____

Solve. Use the Work Backward strategy or any other strategy you have learned.

1. A class had a can drive. Cara collected **6** more cans than Diane. Cam collected **8** more cans than Cara. Maria collected twice as many cans as Cam. If Maria collected **76** cans, how many cans did Diane collect?

Think: What information will you start with? Explain.

_____

_____

Answer _____

2. Christina opened a savings account by depositing a check from her aunt. Ten days later, she put in **$12** more. A week later, she took out **$7**. She then had **$45** in her account. What was the amount of the check from Christina's aunt?

Think: What information will you start with? Explain.

_____

_____

Answer _____

3. Draw the missing figure in this sequence.

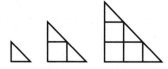

_____

4. Akil is thinking of a mystery number. If he divides his number by **4** and then multiplies it by **5**, the result is **135**. What is Akil's mystery number?

_____

5. On Monday, Mr. Riccio filled up his tank with gasoline. He then used up **6** gallons. On Tuesday, he used up **3** more gallons. On Wednesday, he put in **7** gallons. He then had **10** gallons of gasoline in the tank. How many gallons does the tank hold?

_____

6. A store owner had a large supply of purple shoes. The owner made the price **$5** less. There were still many pairs left. The store then sold them for half of the lower price. The new price was **$14**. What was the original price of the shoes?

_____

7. Look at the numbers in this sequence. What is the next number?

8,000, 4,000, 2,000, 1,000

_____

8. Lucy buys jeans and a shirt. The shirt costs half as much as the jeans. The total cost is **$36**. How much do the jeans cost?

_____

Suppose you went on a three-day hike. You walked **15** miles the first day, **21** miles the second day, and **12** miles the third day. You want to know the average number of miles you walked each day.

An **average** is a special way of describing a group of numbers. Here's one way to think about it.

1. Make **3** stacks of counters to show the number of miles you walked each of **3** days.	**2.** Put the stacks of counters together in one group.	**3.** Divide the group of counters into **3** equal stacks—one stack for each day.

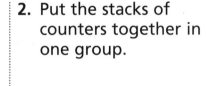

Record the number of counters in each stack.	Find the total number of counters.	Find the number in each stack.
15, 21, 12	**15 + 21 + 12 = 48**	**48 ÷ 3 = 16**

You walked an average of **16** miles each day.

To find an average:

1. Add the given numbers.

2. Count the addends.

3. Divide the sum by the number of addends.

Write the number you divide by to find the average. Then find the average.

1. 2, 5, 4, 12, 7

Divide by _____ Average _____

2. 25, 38, 42

Divide by _____ Average _____

Write the number you divide by to find the average. Then find the average.

3. 76, 125, 117, 86

Divide by _____. Average _____

4. 132, 129, 138

Divide by _____. Average _____

Find the average.

5. 10, 8, 6

6. 9, 14, 7

7. 15, 10, 11

8. 68¢ 82¢, 96¢

9. 68, 93, 46

10. 98, 85, 75

Problem Solving
Reasoning

Solve.

11. Mario's class collected cans for recycling. They collected **76** cans the first day, **64** cans the second day, **116** cans the third day, and **92** cans the fourth day. What was the average number of cans they collected a day?

_____

12. Diane bowled **3** games. She knocked down **93** pins in the first game, **84** pins in the second, and **114** in the third. What was the average number of pins she knocked down in each game?

_____

13. Do you need to add and divide to find the average of these numbers: **45, 45, 45**? Explain.

_____

_____

14. List three numbers that have an average of **125**. Explain how you chose the three numbers.

_____

_____

Test Prep ★ Mixed Review

15 Which of the following is a prime number?

A 15

B 28

C 37

D 42

16 Which group of numbers shows all the factors of 15?

F 1, 3, 5, 15

G 1, 2, 3, 7, 15

H 1, 5, 15

J 15, 30, 45

Sometimes, when you divide greater numbers, the
quotient will have four digits.

Long Division   Short Division | Long Division   Short Division

```
   1,0 9 5              1, 0 9 5    |      8,701 R1          8, 701 R1
8)8, 7 6 0           8)8, 7 7 6 4 0 | 2)17,403            2)17,¹403
 −8                                 |   −16
   7 6                              |     1 4
  −7 2                              |    −1 4
     4 0                            |      03
    −4 0                            |     − 2
      0                             |      1
```

Think: Regoup
7 hundred 6 tens
as 76 tens

Think:
17 thousands − 16 thousands = 1 thousand.
Regroup 1 thousand 4 hundred as 14 hundreds.

Divide. Use long division.

1.
$$\begin{array}{r} 3, \\ 2\overline{)7,395} \end{array}$$
$$\begin{array}{r} 4, \\ 3\overline{)14,276} \end{array}$$
$$\begin{array}{r} 1, \\ 4\overline{)7,053} \end{array}$$
$$\begin{array}{r} 2, \\ 5\overline{)12,607} \end{array}$$

2. $6\overline{)19,490}$ $\qquad$ $6\overline{)7,156}$ $\qquad$ $7\overline{)52,613}$ $\qquad$ $7\overline{)9,273}$

3. $3\overline{)7,164}$ $\qquad$ $3\overline{)23,075}$ $\qquad$ $9\overline{)26,183}$ $\qquad$ $2\overline{)7,161}$

4. $6\overline{)10,538}$ $\qquad$ $3\overline{)1,538}$ $\qquad$ $5\overline{)3,932}$ $\qquad$ $4\overline{)9,387}$

Divide. Use short division. Check your work.

5. 8)8,402   5)4,407   7)5,675   7)756

6. 4)8,023   6)6,125   5)5,042   2)3,873

Solve.

7. A total of **5,130** fans watched the first **6** soccer games of the season. What was the average number of fans for each game?

_____

8. Lisa's family is driving **2,569** miles in **7** days. If they want to drive the same distance every day, how many miles should they drive each day?

_____

 Quick Check

Find the average for each set of numbers.   **Work Space.**

9. 12, 13, 14   **10.** 17, 28, 36   **11.** 65, 68, 69, 74

_____   _____   _____

Divide.

12. 6)7,759   **13.** 8)9,606   **14.** 4)18,238

Name _____

Use the order of operations to find the value of
each expression.

1. $4 \times (6 + 3)$ **2.** $30 - 5 \times 5$ **3.** $4 + 9 \div 3$ **4.** $8 \times (4 \div 2)$

Divide.

5. $9\overline{)39}$ **6.** $3\overline{)262}$ **7.** $6\overline{)\$6.24}$ **8.** $7\overline{)2,447}$

Use divisibility rule to solve.

9. Circle the numbers that are divisible by both **5** and **2**.

   25   40   55   70   80   95

10. Circle the numbers that are divisible by both **2** and **3**.

   20   36   42   45   50   78

Complete by writing the products with as many
different pairs of factors as possible. Circle the
prime numbers.

11. 24   **12.** 28   **13.** 67   **14.** 42

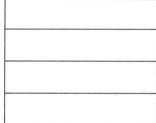

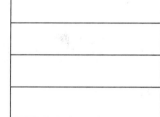

Find the average of each set of numbers.

15. 3, 7, 2, 8, 10   **16.** 21, 34, 53   **17.** 49¢, 18¢, 27¢, 14¢

Solve.

18. The clerk gave Tanya **$4.50** in change when she
bought **3** notebooks for **$3.50** each, including tax.
How much money did Tanya give the clerk?

   _____

19. Terry paid **$1.35**, including tax, for **3** pens. Each pen
was the same price. What was the price of each pen?

   _____

1 The Levitt family drove from San Francisco to Kansas City, Missouri. They drove the distances shown.

Cities	Distances
From San Francisco, California to Reno, Nevada	**215** miles
From Reno, Nevada to to Aspen, Colorado	**940** miles
From Aspen, Colorado to Kansas City, Missouri	**804** miles

How far did they drive in all?

A 1,959 miles   D 1,859 miles

B 1,949 miles   E NH

C 1,895 miles

2 Angela is counting telephone poles from the window of a moving train. She counts 12 poles in 1 minute. *About* how many will she count in 1 hour?

F 500   H 5,000   K NH

G 600   J 6,000

3 Which group of numbers shows all the factors of 16?

A 1, 2, 3, 6, 16   C 1, 3, 9, 15, 16

B 1, 2, 4, 8, 16   D 1, 7, 8, 16

4 An airplane trip from Los Angeles to San Francisco and back again is 688 miles. Ms. Lee flies this distance 21 times in a year. How many miles has she flown all together?

F 17,248   H 14,248   K NH

G 14,448   J 2,354

5 Mr. Ivanson drove from Stockton, California, to Portland, Oregon, along the road shown.

About how many miles did he drive?

A 400   C 800

B 600   D 1,000

6 The chart shows the number of students in 4 different schools.

School	Number of Students
School A	705
School B	457
School C	962
School D	926

Which shows the number of students in order from *greatest* to *least*?

F School D, School C, School A, School B

G School C, School A, School D, School B

H School C, School D, School A, School B

J School B, School A, School D, School C

UNIT 5 • TABLE OF CONTENTS

Fractions and Mixed Numbers

Dear Family,

During the next few weeks, our math class will be learning about fractions and mixed numbers.

You can expect to see homework that provides practice with writing equivalent fractions. Here is a sample you may want to keep handy to give help if needed.

Writing Equivalent Fractions

For any given fraction, you can use multiplication or division to write equivalent fractions.

Example: Write three equivalent fractions for $\frac{3}{4}$.

Multiply the numerator (top number) and denominator (bottom number) of the fraction $\frac{3}{4}$ by the same number.

$$\frac{3 \times 2}{4 \times 2} = \frac{6}{8} \qquad \frac{3 \times 5}{4 \times 5} = \frac{15}{20} \qquad \frac{3 \times 10}{4 \times 10} = \frac{30}{40}$$

The fractions $\frac{6}{8}$, $\frac{15}{20}$, and $\frac{30}{40}$ are equivalent fractions for $\frac{3}{4}$.

Example: Write three equivalent fractions for $\frac{32}{48}$.

Divide the numerator (top number) and denominator (bottom number) of the fraction $\frac{32}{48}$ by the same number.

$$\frac{32 \div 2}{48 \div 2} = \frac{16}{24} \qquad \frac{32 \div 4}{48 \div 4} = \frac{8}{12} \qquad \frac{32 \div 16}{48 \div 16} = \frac{2}{3}$$

The fractions $\frac{16}{24}$, $\frac{8}{12}$, and $\frac{2}{3}$ are equivalent fractions for $\frac{32}{48}$.

During this unit, students will need to continue practicing multiplication and division facts.

Sincerely,

A **multiple** is the product of a number and another whole number. The number line shows some multiples of **3**.

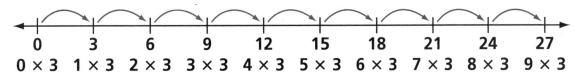

0	3	6	9	12	15	18	21	24	27
0 × 3	1 × 3	2 × 3	3 × 3	4 × 3	5 × 3	6 × 3	7 × 3	8 × 3	9 × 3

> A number that is a multiple of another number is also divisible by the first number.

21 is a multiple of **3**.
21 is also divisible by **3** and the remainder is **0**.

$$\begin{array}{r} 7\,R\,0 \\ 3\overline{)21} \end{array}$$

16 is *not* a multiple of **3**.
16 is also *not* divisible by **3**.

$$\begin{array}{r} 5\,R\,1 \\ 3\overline{)16} \end{array}$$ ← The remainder is not zero.

Complete the list of all the multiples shown on each number line.

1. Multiples of 4

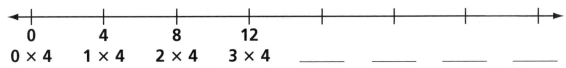

0	4	8	12
0 × 4	1 × 4	2 × 4	3 × 4	____	____	____

2. Multiples of 7

0	7	14
0 × 7	1 × 7	2 × 7	____	____	____	____

3. Multiples of 8

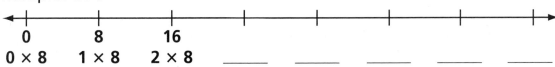

0	8	16
0 × 8	1 × 8	2 × 8	____	____	____	____

4. Multiples of 9

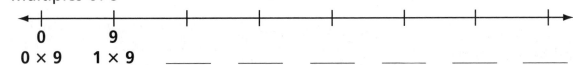

0	9
0 × 9	1 × 9	____	____	____	____

5. Multiples of 5

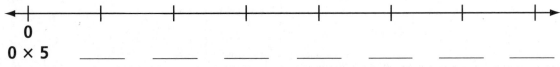

0
0 × 5	____	____	____	____	____

A multiple that is the same for two or more numbers is called a **common multiple**.

To find some common multiples of **3** and **5**, first list some of the multiples of each number. Then circle the multiples that are the same in both lists.

Multiples of 3: **3, 6, 9, 12, (15), 18, 21, 24, 27, (30),** . . .
Multiples of 5: **5, 10, (15), 20, 25, (30), 35, 40, 45,** . . .

So, **15** and **30** are common multiples of both **3** and **5**.

Complete the lists of multiples. Circle the common multiples.

6. Multiples of 2: **26, 28,** _____, _____, _____, _____, **38,** _____

Multiples of 5: **25,** _____, _____, _____, **45**

---

7. Multiples of 3: **30, 33,** _____, _____, _____, _____, **48,** _____, _____

Multiples of 4: **28,** _____, **36,** _____, _____, _____, _____, _____

---

8. Multiples of 6: _____, _____, _____, **54,** _____, _____, _____, **78,** _____, _____

Multiples of 9: _____, _____, **45,** _____, _____, _____, _____, _____, **99**

| Problem Solving |
| Reasoning |

Find multiples and common multiples to solve each problem.

9. Are all multiples of **9** also multiples of **3**? Explain.

_____

10. What are the first three common multiples of **5** and **6**?

_____

Test Prep ★ Mixed Review

11 An athlete runs around a track. Each complete trip around is 422 yards. He runs around the track 4 times. About how many yards does he run?

A 1,200   **C** 1,800

B 1,600   **D** 2,400

12 Which group of numbers shows all the factors of 36?

F 1, 2, 3, 4, 6, 9, 12, 18, 36

G 1, 3, 8, 10, 21, 36

H 1, 2, 5, 7, 13, 36

J 1, 2, 4, 8, 16, 36

Fractions that name the same number are called **equivalent fractions**. You can use number lines to find equivalent fractions.

The fraction $\frac{1}{2}$ is halfway between **0** and **1**.

The fractions $\frac{2}{4}$ and $\frac{4}{8}$ are also halfway between **0** and **1**.

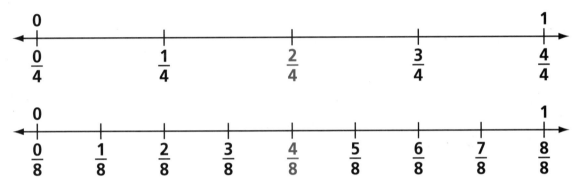

So, $\frac{1}{2}$, $\frac{2}{4}$, and $\frac{4}{8}$ are equivalent fractions.

Complete using the number lines above.

1. Write one equivalent fraction for $\frac{3}{4}$. _____

2. Write one equivalent fraction for $\frac{1}{4}$. _____

3. Write two equivalent fractions for $\frac{8}{8}$. _____, _____

4. Write two equivalent fractions for $\frac{1}{2}$. _____, _____

5. Write three equivalent fractions for **0**. _____, _____, _____

6. Write three equivalent fractions for **1**. _____, _____, _____

You can also use fraction models to find equivalent fractions.

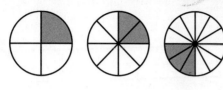

$$\frac{1}{4} = \frac{2}{8} \quad \text{or} \quad \frac{1}{4} = \frac{3}{12}$$

$$\frac{3}{4} = \frac{6}{8} \quad \text{or} \quad \frac{3}{4} = \frac{9}{12}$$

Write a pair of equivalent fractions for each picture.

7.

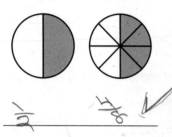

$$\frac{1}{2} \qquad \frac{4}{8} \checkmark$$

8.

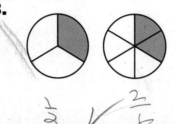

$$\frac{1}{3} \checkmark \qquad \frac{2}{6} \checkmark$$

9.

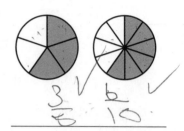

$$\frac{3}{5} \checkmark \qquad \frac{6}{10} \checkmark$$

10.

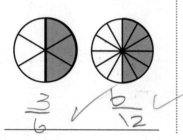

$$\frac{3}{6} \checkmark \qquad \frac{6}{12} \checkmark$$

11.

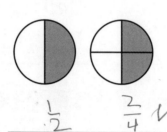

$$\frac{1}{2} \qquad \frac{2}{4} \checkmark$$

12.

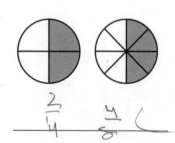

$$\frac{3}{4} \qquad \frac{4}{8} \checkmark$$

Problem Solving Reasoning Solve. Which fraction comes next in the pattern?

13. $\dfrac{1}{2}, \dfrac{1}{4}, \dfrac{1}{6}, \dfrac{1}{8}, \dfrac{1}{10},$ _____

14. $\dfrac{1}{3}, \dfrac{3}{9}, \dfrac{9}{27}, \dfrac{27}{81},$ _____

Test Prep ★ Mixed Review

15 What number should go in the ☐ to make the number sentence true?

$$(5 \times 2) \times 4 = \boxed{} \times (2 \times 4)$$

A 5

B 4

C 2

D 1

16 A factory makes and ships 1,120 model airplane kits in one day. One shipping carton holds 8 model kits. How many shipping cartons does the factory use in one day?

F 139

G 140

H 141

J 142

Name_____

You can use a number line to compare and order fractions.

Compare $\frac{3}{4}$ (?) $\frac{2}{4}$.

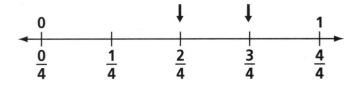

Find each fraction on the number line.

$\frac{3}{4}$ is to the right of $\frac{2}{4}$ $\frac{3}{4}$ is greater than $\frac{2}{4}$ $\frac{3}{4}$ (>) $\frac{2}{4}$

....

Order $\frac{2}{8}$, $\frac{7}{8}$, and $\frac{5}{8}$ **from least to greatest.**

Find each fraction on the number line.

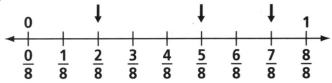

- $\frac{2}{8}$ is to the left of both $\frac{7}{8}$ and $\frac{5}{8}$.

  $\frac{2}{8}$ is the least fraction.

- $\frac{7}{8}$ is to the right of both $\frac{2}{8}$ and $\frac{5}{8}$.

  $\frac{7}{8}$ is the greatest fraction.

Ordered from least to greatest: $\frac{2}{8}$ $\frac{5}{8}$ $\frac{7}{8}$

....

If two fractions have like denominators, you can compare the number of equal parts or numerators.

Compare $\frac{5}{12}$ (?) $\frac{7}{12}$.

$\frac{5}{12}$ and $\frac{7}{12}$ have the same denominator.

Since **7** is greater than **5**, then:

$\frac{7}{12}$ (>) $\frac{5}{12}$

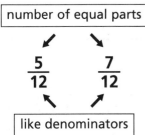

_____

Use the number lines to compare the fractions. Write <, >, or =.

1. $\frac{1}{4}$ ◯ $\frac{3}{4}$ $\frac{2}{4}$ ◯ $\frac{1}{4}$ $\frac{7}{8}$ ◯ $\frac{5}{8}$ $\frac{3}{8}$ ◯ $\frac{7}{8}$

_____

Write the following in order from the least to the greatest.

2. $\frac{1}{8}$, $\frac{3}{8}$, $\frac{5}{8}$, $\frac{4}{8}$, $\frac{0}{8}$, $\frac{7}{8}$ _____, _____, _____, _____, _____, _____

You can also compare and order fractions that have unlike denominators.

Compare $\frac{3}{5}$ ⃝? $\frac{7}{10}$.

1. Write both fractions with like denominators. Find an equivalent fraction.

$$\frac{3 \times 2}{5 \times 2} = \frac{6}{10} \rightarrow \frac{6}{10} \;?\; \frac{7}{10}$$

2. Compare the numerators. Since **7** is greater than **6** then:

$$\frac{6}{10} < \frac{7}{10}. \text{ So, } \frac{3}{5} < \frac{7}{10}$$

Compare each pair of fractions. Write <, >, or =.

3. $\frac{2}{3} \bigcirc \frac{1}{6}$ $\frac{3}{8} \bigcirc \frac{3}{4}$ $\frac{1}{5} \bigcirc \frac{1}{10}$ $\frac{1}{3} \bigcirc \frac{2}{9}$

4. $\frac{3}{8} \bigcirc \frac{1}{4}$ $\frac{1}{3} \bigcirc \frac{5}{9}$ $\frac{5}{6} \bigcirc \frac{1}{2}$ $\frac{4}{6} \bigcirc \frac{2}{3}$

Write the fractions in order from the least to the greatest.

5. $\frac{1}{2}, \frac{1}{4}, \frac{0}{2}, \frac{4}{4}, \frac{7}{8}$ _____, _____, _____, _____, _____

6. $\frac{1}{3}, \frac{2}{6}, \frac{1}{2}$ _____, _____, _____, _____, _____

Problem Solving
Reasoning Solve.

7. Compare $\frac{1}{2}$ or $\frac{1}{15}$ without finding equivalent fractions.
Explain how you know which fraction is greater.

_____

_____

Test Prep ★ Mixed Review

8 What number is the common factor of both 14 and 28?

   A 3   C 7

   B 4   D 8

9 Which fraction represents the shaded portion of the model?

   F $\frac{1}{3}$ H $\frac{1}{2}$

   G $\frac{3}{6}$ J $\frac{4}{6}$

You can estimate where to place fractions
on a number line.

Place $\frac{4}{6}$ between **0** and **1** on a
number line.

1. Divide the number line into
six equal parts.

2. Then count to $\frac{4}{6}$.

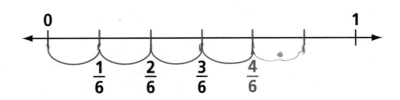

Estimate. Place the fractions on the number line.

1. $\frac{1}{4}$ $\frac{2}{4}$ $\frac{3}{4}$

2. $\frac{2}{5}$ $\frac{3}{5}$ $\frac{4}{5}$

3. $\frac{1}{8}$ $\frac{4}{8}$ $\frac{7}{8}$

4. $\frac{1}{6}$ $\frac{5}{6}$ $\frac{3}{6}$

5. $\frac{3}{8}$ $\frac{2}{8}$ $\frac{5}{8}$

6. $\frac{1}{10}$ $\frac{4}{10}$ $\frac{7}{10}$

Where would you place $\frac{1}{4}$ on this number line?

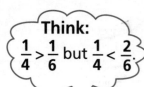

Think:
$\frac{1}{4} > \frac{1}{6}$ but $\frac{1}{4} < \frac{2}{6}$.

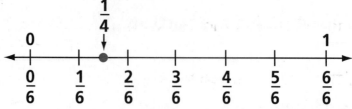

$\frac{1}{4}$

| 0 | | | | | | 1 |

$\frac{0}{6}$ $\frac{1}{6}$ $\frac{2}{6}$ $\frac{3}{6}$ $\frac{4}{6}$ $\frac{5}{6}$ $\frac{6}{6}$

Estimate. Place the fractions on the number line.

7. $\frac{1}{4}$ $\frac{5}{6}$ $\frac{3}{8}$

0 —————————————————— 1

8. $\frac{3}{4}$ $\frac{1}{3}$ $\frac{5}{8}$

0 —————————————————— 1

Place each fraction on the number line. Then explain.

9. $\frac{1}{3}$

0 —|————|————|————|—— 1
    $\frac{1}{4}$ $\frac{2}{4}$ $\frac{3}{4}$

_____

10. $\frac{1}{4}$

0 —|————|————|————|————|—— 1
    $\frac{1}{5}$ $\frac{2}{5}$ $\frac{3}{5}$ $\frac{4}{5}$

_____

✓ **Quick Check**

Write >, <, or =.

11. $\frac{1}{3} \bigcirc \frac{1}{4}$ **12.** $\frac{2}{5} \bigcirc \frac{4}{10}$ **13.** $\frac{3}{4} \bigcirc \frac{5}{8}$

Work Space.

Write the letter of the point that shows the position of each fraction on the number line.

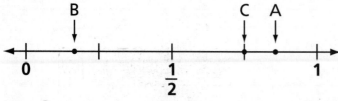

14. $\frac{3}{4}$ _____   **15.** $\frac{5}{6}$ _____   **16.** $\frac{1}{5}$ _____

Name_____

You can use models to add fractions with like denominators.

In the figure, the region shaded red represents the fraction $\frac{1}{4}$. The region shaded gray represents the fraction $\frac{2}{4}$. The total shaded region is $\frac{3}{4}$.

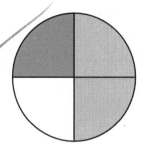

$$\frac{1}{4} + \frac{2}{4} = \frac{3}{4}$$

Use one color to shade the first addend and another color for the second addend. Then find each sum.

1.

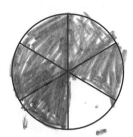

$$\frac{2}{6} + \frac{3}{6} = \underline{\frac{5}{6}}$$

2.

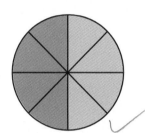

$$\frac{4}{8} + \frac{4}{8} = \underline{\frac{8}{8}}$$

3.

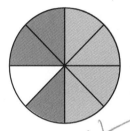

$$\frac{2}{8} + \frac{5}{8} = \underline{\frac{7}{8}}$$

4.

$$\frac{1}{6} + \frac{5}{6} = \underline{\frac{6}{6} + 1}$$

5.

$$\frac{2}{5} + \frac{2}{5} = \underline{\frac{4}{5}}$$

6.

$$\frac{1}{3} + \frac{1}{3} = \underline{\frac{3}{3}}$$

7.

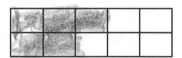

$$\frac{2}{10} + \frac{3}{10} = \underline{\frac{5}{10}}$$

8.

$$\frac{1}{2} + \frac{1}{2} = \underline{\frac{3}{2} = 1}$$

9.

$$\frac{2}{8} + \frac{5}{8} = \underline{\frac{7}{6}}$$

can help you find a missing addend or sum.

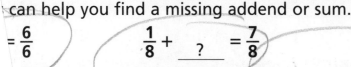

$$= \frac{6}{6}$$

$$\frac{1}{8} + \underline{\ ?\ } = \frac{7}{8}$$

$$\frac{3}{10} + \frac{4}{10} = \underline{\ ?\ }$$

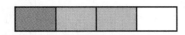

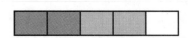

$$\frac{2}{6} + \frac{4}{6} = \frac{6}{6}$$

$$\frac{1}{8} + \frac{6}{8} = \frac{7}{8}$$

$$\frac{3}{10} + \frac{4}{10} = \frac{7}{10}$$

Find the missing addend.

10.

$$\frac{1}{4} + \underline{\frac{3}{4}} = \frac{3}{4}$$

11.

$$\frac{2}{5} + \underline{\frac{3}{5}} = \frac{4}{5}$$

Find the missing addend or sum.

12. $\frac{1}{6} + \frac{3}{6} = \underline{\frac{4}{6}}$ $\quad \frac{1}{4} + \underline{\frac{3}{4}} = \frac{4}{4}$ $\quad \frac{3}{8} + \frac{4}{8} = \underline{\frac{7}{8}}$ $\quad \frac{3}{10} + \underline{\frac{5}{10}} = \frac{8}{10}$

| Problem Solving |
| Reasoning |

Solve. Draw a picture if you need to.

13. Mike walked $\frac{3}{16}$ mile to one store. Then he walked $\frac{4}{16}$ mile to another store. How far did he walk altogether? $\underline{\frac{7}{16}}$

14. Kim lives between Rick and Peter. She lives $\frac{3}{8}$ mile from Rick and $\frac{2}{8}$ mile from Peter. How far does Rick live from Peter? $\underline{\frac{5}{8}}$

Test Prep ★ Mixed Review

15 Which group of numbers shows all the factors of 18?

A 1, 2, 3, 6, 9, 18

B 1, 2, 4, 8, 18

C 2, 8, 9, 10, 16

D 1, 2, 3, 8, 16, 18

16 Which fraction is equivalent to $\frac{4}{12}$?

F $\frac{1}{8}$

G $\frac{1}{4}$

H $\frac{2}{6}$

J $\frac{1}{2}$

Name _____

You can use models to subtract fractions.

Find $\frac{6}{9} - \frac{4}{9}$.

$$\frac{6}{9} - \frac{4}{9} = \frac{2}{9}$$

6 shaded   cross out   **2** shaded
figures   **4** shaded   figures left
              figures

Find $\frac{5}{8} - \frac{2}{8}$.

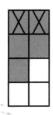

$$\frac{5}{8} - \frac{2}{8} = \frac{3}{8}$$

5 shaded   cross out   **3** shaded
parts   **2** shaded   parts left
              parts

Find each difference.

1.

$$\frac{4}{5} - \frac{1}{5} = \frac{3}{5}$$

$$\frac{4}{7} - \frac{3}{7} = \frac{1}{7}$$

$$\frac{5}{10} - \frac{5}{10} = \frac{0}{10}$$

2.

$$\frac{4}{6} - \frac{2}{6} = \frac{2}{6}$$

$$\frac{5}{6} - \frac{2}{6} = \frac{3}{6}$$

$$\frac{6}{8} - \frac{4}{8} = \frac{2}{8}$$

$$\frac{2}{3} - \frac{1}{3} = \frac{1}{3}$$

Subtract.

3. $\frac{8}{8} - \frac{7}{8} = \frac{1}{8}$ $\frac{4}{5} - \frac{3}{5} = \frac{1}{5}$ $\frac{5}{6} - \frac{3}{6} = \frac{2}{6}$ $\frac{3}{7} - \frac{2}{7} = \frac{1}{7}$

4. $\frac{1}{3} - \frac{1}{3} = \frac{0}{3}$ $\frac{3}{4} - \frac{2}{4} = \frac{1}{4}$ $\frac{6}{6} - \frac{1}{6} = \frac{5}{6}$ $\frac{4}{8} - \frac{1}{8} = \frac{3}{8}$

Subtract.

5. $\frac{4}{9} - \frac{3}{9} =$ _$\frac{1}{9}$_ $\frac{6}{8} - \frac{1}{8} =$ _$\frac{5}{8}$_ $\frac{3}{4} - \frac{1}{4} =$ _$\frac{2}{4}$_ $\frac{2}{2} - \frac{1}{2} =$ _$\frac{1}{2}$_

6. $\frac{5}{8} - \frac{4}{8} =$ _$\frac{1}{8}$_ $\frac{3}{5} - \frac{1}{5} =$ _$\frac{2}{5}$_ $\frac{7}{9} - \frac{5}{9} =$ _$\frac{2}{9}$_ $\frac{3}{4} - \frac{3}{4} =$ _$\frac{0}{4}$_

Add or subtract.

7. $\frac{0}{4} + \frac{3}{4} =$ _$\frac{3}{4}$_ $\frac{3}{9} - \frac{1}{9} =$ _$\frac{2}{9}$_ $\frac{2}{7} + \frac{4}{7} =$ _$\frac{6}{7}$_ $\frac{5}{8} - \frac{2}{8} =$ _$\frac{3}{8}$_

8. $\frac{2}{4} - \frac{2}{4} =$ _$\frac{0}{4}$_ $\frac{3}{12} + \frac{2}{12} =$ _$\frac{1}{12}$_ $\frac{2}{9} + \frac{3}{9} =$ _$\frac{5}{9}$_ $\frac{4}{15} + \frac{7}{15} =$ _$\frac{11}{15}$_

Problem Solving Reasoning

Solve.

9. Eddie was making cookies. The recipe called for $\frac{3}{4}$ cup milk and $\frac{1}{4}$ cup honey. How much more milk than honey did Eddie add?

$\frac{3}{4} + \frac{1}{4} = \frac{4}{4} = 1$ whole

10. The sum of two fractions is $\frac{7}{12}$. There difference is $\frac{1}{12}$. They have the same denominator. What are the two fractions?

$\frac{8}{12}$ because

$7 + \frac{1}{12} = \frac{8}{12}$

12

✓ Quick Check

Solve.

11. $\frac{1}{3} + \frac{1}{3}$ _$\frac{2}{3}$_

12. $\frac{6}{8} + \frac{1}{8}$ _$\frac{7}{8}$_

13. $\frac{3}{6} + \frac{2}{6}$ _$\frac{5}{6}$_

14. $\frac{4}{7} + \frac{2}{7}$ _$\frac{6}{7}$_

15. $\frac{2}{3} - \frac{1}{3}$ _$\frac{1}{3}$_

16. $\frac{7}{8} - \frac{6}{8}$ _$\frac{1}{8}$_

17. $\frac{5}{6} - \frac{1}{6}$ _$\frac{4}{6}$_

18. $\frac{8}{9} - \frac{3}{9}$ _$\frac{5}{9}$_

Work Space.

Some fractions name numbers between **0** and **1**. Other fractions name numbers equal to or greater than **1**.

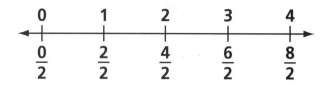

Some fractions name whole numbers. This number line is labeled with whole numbers and fractions.

To show **2** halves in **1**, write $\frac{2}{2} = 1$.   To show **8** halves in **4**, write $\frac{8}{2} = 4$.

Some fractions name numbers between whole numbers.

The number halfway between **1** and **2** is **3** halves or $\frac{3}{2}$.

Mixed numbers are another way of writing fractions greater than **1**. A **mixed number** has a whole number part and a fraction part. This number line is labeled with whole numbers, fractions, and mixed numbers.

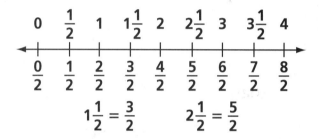

$1\frac{1}{2} = \frac{3}{2}$ $2\frac{1}{2} = \frac{5}{2}$

Write the missing whole numbers, fractions, and mixed numbers.

1.

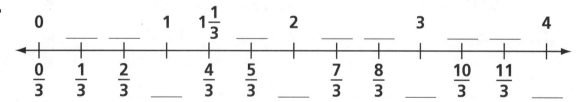

Write mixed numbers for the shaded regions.

2.

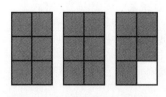

_____ wholes and _____ sixths

_____

3.

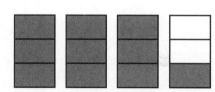

_____ wholes and _____ third

_____

Write a mixed number and a fraction for the shaded parts.

4.

_____ _____

5.

_____ _____

6.

_____ _____

7.

_____ _____

Write a mixed number for the fraction.

8. $\frac{9}{4}$ _____ $\frac{14}{6}$ _____ $\frac{11}{2}$ _____ $\frac{17}{3}$ _____

9. $\frac{23}{10}$ _____ $\frac{17}{8}$ _____ $\frac{18}{5}$ _____ $\frac{11}{4}$ _____

Problem Solving Reasoning **Solve. Draw pictures if you need to.**

10. There are **3** pizzas. Each one is cut into **8** slices. Write a fraction to show the total number of eighths.

_____

11. Of the **3** pizzas, you eat **3** slices. Write a mixed number to show the amount of pizza that remains.

_____

Test Prep ★ Mixed Review

12 Which of the following is a prime number?

A 36

B 21

C 18

D 2

13 A total of 2,707,588 people bought tickets to see a movie on its opening weekend. What is the number rounded to the nearest hundred thousand?

F 3,000,000   H 2,070,00

G 2,700,000   J 2,007,000

Adding and Subtracting Mixed Numbers

You can add and subtract with mixed numbers.

Find: $3\frac{3}{5} + 1\frac{1}{5}$.

1. Add fractions.

$$3\frac{3}{5}$$
$$+\ 1\frac{1}{5}$$
$$\overline{\quad \frac{4}{5}}$$

Think: 3 fifths + 1 fifth = 4 fifths

2. Add whole numbers.

$$3\frac{3}{5}$$
$$+\ 1\frac{1}{5}$$
$$\overline{4\frac{4}{5}}$$

Find: $3\frac{3}{5} - 1\frac{1}{5}$.

1. Subtract fractions.

$$3\frac{3}{5}$$
$$-\ 1\frac{1}{5}$$
$$\overline{\quad \frac{2}{5}}$$

Think: 3 fifths − 1 fifth = 2 fifths

2. Subtract whole numbers.

$$3\frac{3}{5}$$
$$-\ 1\frac{1}{5}$$
$$\overline{2\frac{2}{5}}$$

Add.

1.

$4\frac{1}{3}$	$5\frac{3}{6}$	6	$7\frac{3}{4}$	$8\frac{1}{5}$	$\frac{3}{10}$
$+\ 2\frac{1}{3}$	$+\ 2\frac{1}{6}$	$+\ 3\frac{5}{8}$	$+\ 1$	$+\ \frac{2}{5}$	$+\ 2\frac{4}{10}$
$6\frac{2}{3}$	$7\frac{4}{6}$	$10\frac{5}{8}$	$8\frac{3}{4}$	$8\frac{3}{5}$	$2\frac{7}{10}$

Subtract.

2.

$7\frac{5}{8}$	$9\frac{3}{5}$	$4\frac{5}{6}$	$5\frac{1}{3}$	$6\frac{3}{4}$	$8\frac{5}{10}$
$-\ 1\frac{2}{8}$	$-\ 2\frac{1}{5}$	$-\ 3$	$-\ 2\frac{1}{3}$	$-\ \frac{3}{4}$	$-\ 5\frac{4}{10}$
$6\frac{3}{8}$	$7\frac{2}{5}$	$1\frac{5}{6}$	$3\frac{0}{3}$	$6\frac{0}{4}$	$3\frac{1}{10}$

Add or subtract. Watch the signs.

3.

$3\frac{3}{9}$	$7\frac{4}{5}$	$8\frac{2}{6}$	$7\frac{2}{3}$	4	$9\frac{4}{5}$
$+\ 1\frac{5}{9}$	$-\ 5\frac{3}{5}$	$+\ 4\frac{2}{6}$	$-\ 3\frac{1}{3}$	$+\ 4\frac{2}{3}$	$-\ 9\frac{4}{5}$
$4\frac{8}{9}$	$2\frac{1}{5}$	$12\frac{4}{6}$	$4\frac{1}{3}$	$8\frac{2}{3}$	$0\frac{0}{5}$

4.

$3\frac{3}{4}$	$6\frac{1}{4}$	$7\frac{1}{3}$	$8\frac{1}{12}$	$1\frac{3}{4}$	$2\frac{3}{8}$
$-\ 1\frac{2}{4}$	$+\ 3\frac{2}{4}$	$-\ \frac{1}{3}$	$+\ 2\frac{4}{12}$	$-\ \frac{1}{4}$	$+\ 4\frac{4}{8}$
$2\frac{1}{4}$	$9\frac{3}{4}$	$7\frac{0}{3}$	$10\frac{5}{12}$	$1\frac{2}{4}$	$6\frac{7}{8}$

Solve.

5. Damon had $9\frac{1}{4}$ feet of string. He used $7\frac{1}{4}$ feet of the string to tie up a package. How much string was left?

_____

6. Sandy was $5\frac{2}{4}$ feet tall last year. This year he is $5\frac{3}{4}$ feet tall. How much has he grown since last year?

_____

7. Marilyn mailed a package that contained a book. The book weighed $2\frac{4}{8}$ pounds. The entire package weighed $2\frac{7}{8}$ pounds. How much did the mailing materials weigh? _____

8. Julie bought $8\frac{2}{4}$ yards of red fabric and $6\frac{1}{4}$ yards of blue fabric. How many yards of fabric did Julie purchase altogether?

_____

✓ Quick Check

Write each whole number or mixed number as a fraction.

Work Space.

9. $1\frac{1}{4}$ _____

10. 6 _____

11. $2\frac{2}{3}$ _____

12. $2\frac{1}{4}$ _____

13. $2\frac{2}{3}$ _____

14. 2 _____

Add or subtract.

15. $1\frac{1}{3} + 1\frac{1}{3}$ _____

16. $2\frac{1}{5} + 1\frac{2}{5}$ _____

17. $3\frac{3}{6} + 2\frac{2}{6}$ _____

18. $2\frac{4}{5} - 1\frac{1}{5}$ _____

19. $3\frac{2}{3} - 2\frac{1}{3}$ _____

20. $5\frac{5}{8} - 2\frac{3}{8}$ _____

Name _____

Sometimes you may need to decide how to express a remainder to solve a problem.

- You may need to include the remainder in your answer.

  You have **$7** to buy notebooks. Each notebook costs **$2.00**. How many can you buy? How much money is left?
  7 ÷ 2 = 3 R1 → 3 notebooks, **$1.00** left

- You may need to drop the remainder.

  You have **17** oranges to put in bags of **4**. How many complete bags can you make?
  17 ÷ 4 = 4 R1 → 4 complete bags

- You may need to write the answer as the next whole number.

  A van seats **7** people. There are **18** people going on a trip. How many vans do they need?
  18 ÷ 7 = 2 R4 → 3 vans for **18** people

- You may need to write the remainder as a fraction.

  There are **5** apples to share with **4** friends. How much will each friend receive?

$$1\frac{1}{4}$$
$$4\overline{)5}$$
$$\frac{4}{1}$$

The remainder is the numerator. The divisor is the denominator.

$1\frac{1}{4}$ apple for each.

Tips to Remember:

| 1. Understand | 2. Decide | 3. Solve | 4. Look back |

- Try to remember a real-life situation like the one described in the problem. What do you remember that might help you find a solution?
- Ask yourself: Does the answer use the remainder correctly?

Solve.

1. At a picnic, you have **10** sandwiches to divide equally among **8** people. How many sandwiches will each person get?

Think: What would you do with the **2** extra whole sandwiches?

_____

_____

Answer _____

2. A restaurant has a bowl of candy at the checkout. You can buy **4** pieces for a quarter. How much will **1** piece cost?

Think: How do stores round their prices?

_____

_____

Answer _____

Solve.

3. Three juice boxes come in a package. You need **32** juice boxes for a class party. How many packages should you buy?

_____

4. Six boys equally shared **32** ounces of orange juice. How many ounces did each boy get?

_____

5. Martin bought **4** pairs of socks for **$5**. How much did he pay for each pair?

_____

6. A group of **26** students are going on a field trip by car. Each car can fit **4** students. How many cars are needed?

_____

7. A bakery packages left-over bagels for sale the next day at a discounted price. Each package holds **6** bagels. One day, **43** bagels were left over at the end of the day. How many complete packages could be made?

_____

8. There are **18** cars on a ferris wheel. Each car can hold **3** people. For this ride there are **56** people waiting in line. How many people will have to wait until the next ride?

_____

9. Seventy-eight people attended a lecture. There are **10** rows of seats with **7** seats in each row. Will everybody have a seat?

_____

10. A restaurant makes burgers that weigh exactly **6** ounces. How many burgers will be made from **32** ounces of meat? How many ounces will be left over?

_____

Extend Your Thinking

11. Go back to problem **5**. Explain how you solved the problem.

_____

_____

_____

12. Write and solve a word problem for which it would make sense to write the remainder as a fraction.

_____

_____

_____

_____

Adding Unlike Fractions

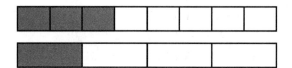

Fractions with different denominators are called **unlike fractions.** You can add unlike fractions.

Find $\frac{3}{8} + \frac{1}{4}$.

1. Write both fractions with like denominators. Find an equivalent fraction.

$$\frac{1 \times 2}{4 \times 2} = \frac{2}{8} \rightarrow \frac{3}{8} + \frac{2}{8}$$

2. Then add the numerators. Write the denominator.

$$\frac{3}{8} + \frac{2}{8} = \frac{5}{8}$$

Think:
3 eighths + 2 eighths

A fraction is in simplest form when **1** is the only number that will divide both the numerator and the denominator evenly.	Simplest Form $\frac{5}{6}$ $\frac{3}{4}$ $\frac{1}{3}$	Not in Simplest Form $\frac{4}{6}$ $\frac{2}{4}$ $\frac{8}{10}$

Add. Write the answer in simplest form.

1. $\frac{1}{2} + \frac{1}{4}$

$\underline{\quad} + \frac{1}{4} = \underline{\quad}$

2. $\frac{1}{3} + \frac{3}{6}$

$\underline{\quad} + \frac{3}{6} = \underline{\quad}$

3. $\frac{5}{12} + \frac{2}{6}$

$\frac{5}{12} + \underline{\quad} = \underline{\quad}$

4. $\frac{1}{3} + \frac{2}{9}$

$\underline{\quad} + \frac{2}{9} = \underline{\quad}$

5. $\frac{2}{4} + \frac{1}{8}$

$\underline{\quad} + \frac{1}{8} = \underline{\quad}$

6. $\frac{3}{5} + \frac{2}{10}$

$\underline{\quad} + \frac{2}{10} = \underline{\quad}$

7. $\frac{2}{8} + \frac{3}{4}$

$\frac{2}{8} + \underline{\quad} = \underline{\quad}$

8. $\frac{5}{12} + \frac{1}{6}$

$\frac{5}{12} + \underline{\quad} = \underline{\quad}$

Add. Write the answer in simplest form.

9. $\frac{3}{8} = \underline{\quad}$
$+ \frac{1}{4} = + \underline{\quad}$

10. $\frac{2}{10} = \underline{\quad}$
$+ \frac{2}{5} = + \underline{\quad}$

11. $\frac{5}{15} = \underline{\quad}$
$+ \frac{1}{5} = + \underline{\quad}$

12. $\frac{3}{8} = \underline{\quad}$
$+ \frac{2}{4} = + \underline{\quad}$

Add. Write the answer in simplest form.

13. $\frac{1}{6} =$ _____
$+\frac{2}{3} = +$ _____

14. $\frac{3}{12} =$ _____
$+\frac{2}{4} = +$ _____

15. $\frac{2}{5} =$ _____
$+\frac{3}{10} = +$ _____

16. $\frac{3}{6} =$ _____
$+\frac{2}{12} = +$ _____

17. $\frac{2}{3} =$ _____
$+\frac{1}{9} = +$ _____

18. $\frac{1}{4} =$ _____
$+\frac{5}{12} = +$ _____

19. $\frac{1}{8} =$ _____
$+\frac{3}{4} = +$ _____

20. $\frac{2}{5} =$ _____
$+\frac{5}{10} = +$ _____

21. $\frac{4}{10} + \frac{3}{5} =$ _____

$\frac{5}{9} + \frac{1}{3} =$ _____

$\frac{4}{10} + \frac{1}{2} =$ _____

22. $\frac{1}{9} + \frac{1}{3} =$ _____

$\frac{8}{12} + \frac{1}{3} =$ _____

$\frac{5}{12} + \frac{1}{2} =$ _____

Problem Solving Reasoning Solve.

23. Sandy walked $\frac{1}{2}$ mile to the pet store and $\frac{4}{10}$ mile to the crafts store.

How far did she walk? _____

Test Prep ★ Mixed Review

24 What number is the common factor of both 18 and 24?

   A 4

   B 6

   C 8

   D 9

25 Which mixed number represents the shaded portion of this model?

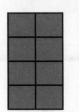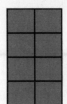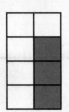

   F $2\frac{3}{8}$ **H** 3

   G $2\frac{5}{8}$ **J** $3\frac{3}{8}$

You also can subtract unlike fractions. Subtracting unlike fractions is similar to adding unlike fractions.

Find $\frac{3}{8} - \frac{1}{4}$.

1. Find an equivalent fraction. Write both fractions with like denominators.

$$\frac{1 \times 2}{4 \times 2} = \frac{2}{8} \rightarrow \frac{3}{8} - \frac{2}{8}$$

2. Then subtract the numerators. Write the denominator.

$$\frac{3}{8} - \frac{2}{8} = \frac{1}{8}$$

Think: 3 eighths − 2 eighths

Subtract. Write the answer in simplest form.

1. $\frac{1}{2} - \frac{1}{4}$

   $\downarrow$

   $\frac{2}{4} - \frac{1}{4} = \frac{1}{4}$

2. $\frac{2}{3} - \frac{3}{6}$

   $\downarrow$

   $\frac{4}{6} - \frac{3}{6} = \frac{1}{6}$

3. $\frac{3}{4} - \frac{3}{8}$

   $\downarrow$

   $\frac{6}{8} - \frac{3}{8} = \frac{3}{8}$

4. $\frac{7}{8} - \frac{2}{4}$

   $\downarrow$

   $\frac{7}{8} - \frac{4}{8} = \frac{3}{8}$

5. $\frac{4}{5} - \frac{5}{10}$

   $\downarrow$

   $\frac{8}{10} - \frac{5}{10} = \frac{3}{10}$

6. $\frac{1}{3} - \frac{3}{12}$

   $\downarrow$

   $\frac{4}{12} - \frac{3}{12} = \frac{1}{12}$

7. $\frac{11}{12} - \frac{1}{6}$

   $\downarrow$

   $\frac{11}{12} - \frac{2}{12} = \frac{9}{12}$

8. $\frac{3}{4} - \frac{3}{12}$

   $\downarrow$

   $\frac{9}{12} - \frac{3}{12} = \frac{4}{12}$

Subtract. Write the answer in simplest form.

9. $\frac{3}{4} = \frac{3}{4}$

   $-\frac{1}{2} = -\frac{2}{4}$

   $\frac{1}{4}$

10. $\frac{1}{2} = \frac{3}{6}$

    $-\frac{1}{6} = -\frac{1}{6}$

    $\frac{2}{6}$

11. $\frac{6}{10} = \frac{6}{10}$

    $-\frac{1}{2} = -\frac{5}{10}$

    $\frac{1}{10}$

12. $\frac{5}{6} = \frac{5}{6}$

    $-\frac{2}{3} = -\frac{2}{6}$

    $\frac{3}{6}$

13. $\frac{3}{4} = \frac{6}{8}$

    $-\frac{1}{8} = -\frac{2}{8}$

    $\frac{4}{8}$

14. $\frac{2}{3} = \frac{6}{9}$

    $-\frac{4}{9} = -\frac{4}{9}$

    $\frac{2}{9}$

15. $\frac{3}{6} = \frac{6}{12}$

    $-\frac{3}{12} = -\frac{3}{12}$

    $\frac{3}{12}$

16. $\frac{8}{10} = \frac{8}{10}$

    $-\frac{3}{5} = -\frac{6}{10}$

    $\frac{3}{10}$

Subtract. Write the answer in simplest form.

17. $\frac{3}{5} =$ *[student handwriting]* $\frac{6}{10}$

  $-\frac{1}{10} = -\frac{1}{10}$

  [answer] $\frac{5}{10}$

18. $\frac{2}{3} =$ *[student handwriting]* $\frac{6}{9}$

  $-\frac{2}{9} = -\frac{2}{9}$

  [answer] $\frac{4}{9}$

19. $\frac{3}{8} =$ *[student handwriting]* $\frac{3}{8}$

  $-\frac{1}{4} = -\frac{2}{8}$

  [answer] $\frac{1}{8}$

20. $\frac{7}{12} =$ *[student handwriting]* $\frac{7}{12}$

  $-\frac{2}{6} = -\frac{4}{12}$

  [answer] $\frac{3}{12}$

21. $\frac{11}{12} - \frac{1}{2} =$ _____ $\frac{6}{9} - \frac{2}{3} =$ _____ $\frac{7}{10} - \frac{1}{5} =$ _____

22. $\frac{1}{2} - \frac{1}{8} =$ _____ $\frac{1}{3} - \frac{1}{9} =$ _____ $\frac{4}{5} - \frac{1}{10} =$ _____

Find the missing addend. Use subtraction.

23. $\frac{1}{2} +$ _____ $= \frac{3}{4}$ $\frac{1}{3} +$ _____ $= \frac{4}{9}$ $\frac{2}{5} +$ _____ $= \frac{7}{10}$

24. $\frac{2}{3} +$ _____ $= \frac{5}{6}$ $\frac{1}{2} +$ _____ $= \frac{9}{10}$ $\frac{1}{6} +$ _____ $= \frac{7}{12}$

Problem Solving Reasoning Solve.

25. Flo swam $\frac{1}{2}$ mile in the morning. She swam $\frac{3}{4}$ mile in the evening. How much farther did she swim in the evening?

_____

 Quick Check

Add or subtract.　　　　　　　　　　　　　　　Work Space.

26. $\frac{2}{3} + \frac{1}{6}$ _____   **27.** $\frac{1}{10} + \frac{3}{5}$ _____

28. $\frac{3}{8} + \frac{1}{2}$ _____   **29.** $\frac{7}{8} - \frac{1}{4}$ _____

30. $\frac{11}{12} - \frac{5}{6}$ _____   **31.** $\frac{8}{10} - \frac{1}{2}$ _____

Name _____

Drawing a picture can help you solve some problems.

It can also help you check an answer to a problem you have solved using computation.

Problem

Taylor rides his bike to and from school every day. The round trip is $\frac{3}{4}$ mile. How many miles does Taylor ride in a 5-day school week?

---

1 Understand   As you reread, ask yourself questions.

- What facts are you given in the problem?

   Taylor rides $\frac{3}{4}$ of a mile each day.

   Taylor rides every day during the school week.

- What do you need to find out?

   _____

---

2 Decide   Choose a method for solving.

Try the strategy Draw a Picture.

- What should your picture show?

   _____

---

3 Solve   Draw a number line divided into fourths. Skip-count five times by three fourths.

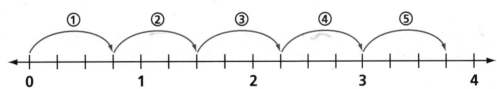

- Write a mixed number to show the point on the number line where you stopped.

   _____

---

4 Look back   Write the answer to the problem below.

   Answer _____

- How might you have solved this problem using addition?

   _____

Solve. Use the Draw a Picture strategy or any other strategy you have learned.

1. Christy cut a $7\frac{1}{2}$ foot piece of ribbon into pieces that were each $1\frac{1}{2}$ feet long. How many pieces were there?

Think: What fraction is the same as $1\frac{1}{2}$?

_____

Answer _____

2. Kim lives $3\frac{1}{4}$ miles from the town library. She decides to walk to the library. After walking $1\frac{3}{4}$ miles, she stops for a break. How far is Kim from the library when she stops?

Think: How could you label the number line to help solve the problem?

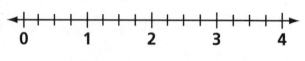

Answer _____

3. Mrs. Lorenz is putting a fence along the back of her yard. The fence will be **72** feet long. There will be a post every **8** feet and a post on each end. How many posts will there be?

_____

4. Grant made a punch by mixing $2\frac{3}{4}$ gallons of orange juice with $1\frac{3}{4}$ gallons of ginger ale. How many gallons of punch did he make?

_____

5. Write the next number in this sequence.

$1\frac{1}{2}$, $1\frac{3}{4}$, 2, $2\frac{1}{4}$, $2\frac{1}{2}$, _____

6. You want to cut a piece of rope into **5** pieces. How many cuts do you need to make?

_____

7. The sum of two numbers is **47**. Their difference is **17**. What are the two numbers?

_____

8. Roberta is thinking of a number. If you add **9** and then multiply the sum by **3**, the result is **45**. What is Roberta's number?

_____

Name _____

Complete each list of multiples. Circle the common multiples.

1. Multiples of 3:   21, 24, _____, _____, _____, _____, 39, _____, _____, _____

Multiples of 4:   _____, _____, _____, _____, 36, _____, _____, _____

Write an equivalent fraction in simplest form.

2. $\frac{10}{16}$ _____   **3.** $\frac{4}{20}$ _____   **4.** $\frac{4}{8}$ _____   **5.** $\frac{6}{10}$ _____

Compare. Write <, >, or =.

6. $\frac{2}{3}$ ◯ $\frac{3}{5}$ **7.** $\frac{3}{4}$ ◯ $\frac{6}{8}$ **8.** $\frac{7}{8}$ ◯ $\frac{3}{4}$ **9.** $\frac{1}{12}$ ◯ $\frac{1}{3}$

Write the fractions in order from least to greatest.

10. $\frac{7}{8}$ $\frac{1}{4}$ $\frac{2}{3}$ $\frac{1}{2}$ _____

11. $\frac{1}{2}$ $\frac{1}{10}$ $\frac{2}{5}$ $\frac{2}{10}$ _____

Write the number as a fraction.

12. 6 _____   **13.** $2\frac{5}{6}$ _____   **14.** $3\frac{2}{3}$ _____   **15.** $3\frac{1}{7}$ _____

Add or subtract. Write your answer in simplest form.

16. $\frac{4}{6}$
        $-\frac{2}{6}$
        ⎯⎯⎯

17. $\frac{2}{5}$
        $+\frac{4}{5}$
        ⎯⎯⎯

18. $1\frac{2}{8}$
        $+4\frac{3}{8}$
        ⎯⎯⎯

19. $6\frac{4}{6}$
        $-2\frac{2}{6}$
        ⎯⎯⎯

20. $\frac{1}{3}$
        $+\frac{1}{6}$
        ⎯⎯⎯

21. $\frac{5}{8}$
        $-\frac{1}{4}$
        ⎯⎯⎯

Solve. Check that your answer is reasonable.

22. Richard brought **6** oranges to the computer club as a snack. If Richard and **3** club members share the oranges equally, what portion will each person get?

_____

23. A pizza had **8** slices. James said, "I ate $\frac{1}{2}$ of $\frac{1}{2}$ of $\frac{1}{2}$ of the pizza." How many slices did James eat?

_____

1 Joanna and Rachel make 20 necklaces to sell at an arts-and-crafts fair. They use 37 beads for each necklace. How many beads do they use in all?

A 7,400   C 640   E NH

B 740   D 57

2 A dripping faucet leaks 4 gallons of water a day. If no one fixes it, how many gallons will it leak in 28 days?

F 96   H 128   K NH

G 112   J 132

3 Painters finished $\frac{1}{2}$ of a house on Wednesday. They finished $\frac{3}{8}$ more of the house on Thursday. How much of the house was finished?

A $\frac{1}{8}$ C $\frac{5}{8}$ E NH

B $\frac{1}{4}$ D $\frac{3}{4}$

4 Which fraction is equivalent to $2\frac{3}{4}$?

F $\frac{6}{4}$ H $\frac{11}{4}$

G $\frac{8}{4}$ J $\frac{12}{4}$

5 Which fraction is in simplest form?

A $\frac{4}{5}$ C $\frac{2}{4}$

B $\frac{6}{9}$ D $\frac{3}{6}$

6 You and 3 friends share 30 books evenly. How many books will you each get?

F 10   H 7   K NH

G 8   J 5

7 What number should go in the ☐ to make the number sentence true?

$$16 \times 4 = (\boxed{} \times 2) \times 4$$

A 4   C 8

B 6   D 16

8 Four students in the choir practice singing at home. Which lists the students in order from the least time to the most time spent practicing?

Name	Time Spent Practicing
Maria	$\frac{1}{3}$ hour
George	$\frac{1}{2}$ hour
Frank	$\frac{3}{4}$ hour
Susan	$\frac{2}{3}$ hour

F Maria, George, Susan, Frank

G Maria, George, Frank, Susan

H Frank, Susan, George, Maria

J George, Maria, Frank, Susan

UNIT 6 • TABLE OF CONTENTS

Geometry

Dear Family,

During the next few weeks, our math class will be learning about geometry.

You can expect to see homework that provides practice with naming polygons and space figures. Here is a sample you may want to keep handy to give help if needed.

Identifying Polygons and Space Figures

A polygon is a closed plane figure made up of line segments that meet only at their end points. A space figure is a figure that takes up space. Here are some examples of polygons and space figures.

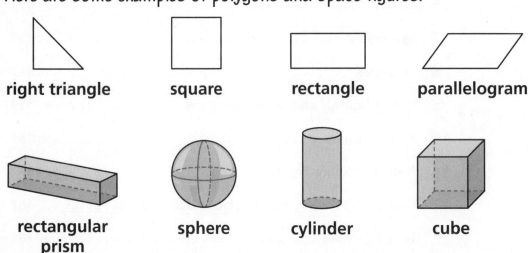

| right triangle | square | rectangle | parallelogram |

| rectangular prism | sphere | cylinder | cube |

Explore your home with your child and try to find examples of each figure shown. You might also look for polygons and space figures while driving or shopping.

During this unit, students will need to continue practicing identifying polygons and space figures, as well as determining congruence and symmetry in figures.

Sincerely,

Name _____

•
B

A **point** is a location in space. A capital letter is used to name a point. The name of this point is **point B**, or just **B**.

You can draw a **line** through any two points. This line is drawn through points **B** and **C**. The arrows show that a line extends in both directions without end.

A line is named by any two points on the line. This is line **BC** or line **CB**. This is how to write line **BC** or line **CB**:

$$\overleftrightarrow{BC} \quad \overleftrightarrow{CB}$$

A **line segment** is part of a line that has two **endpoints**. A line segment is named for its endpoints. This is line segment **BC** or **CB**.

This is how to write line segment **BC** or line segment **CB**:

$$\overline{BC} \quad \overline{CB}$$

Name the line, line segment, or point.

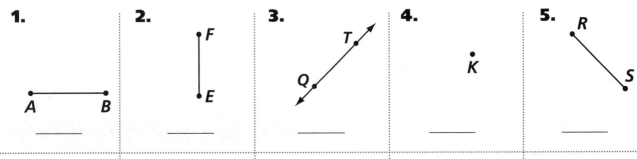

1.   A •———————• B

_____

2.   •F
        |
        •E

_____

3.   T↗
        Q↙

_____

4.   •K

_____

5.   R•
         \
          •S

_____

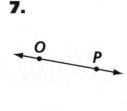 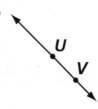 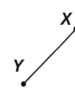

6.   •D

_____

7.   ←O———P→

_____

8.   ↖U
          ↘V

_____

9.   Y •
          \
           • (X)

_____

10. ←——•G——•H——→

_____

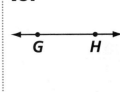

Use a straight edge. Draw the figure.

11.

point **A**

12.

$\overleftrightarrow{BD}$

13.

$\overline{GT}$

14.

$\overleftrightarrow{UV}$

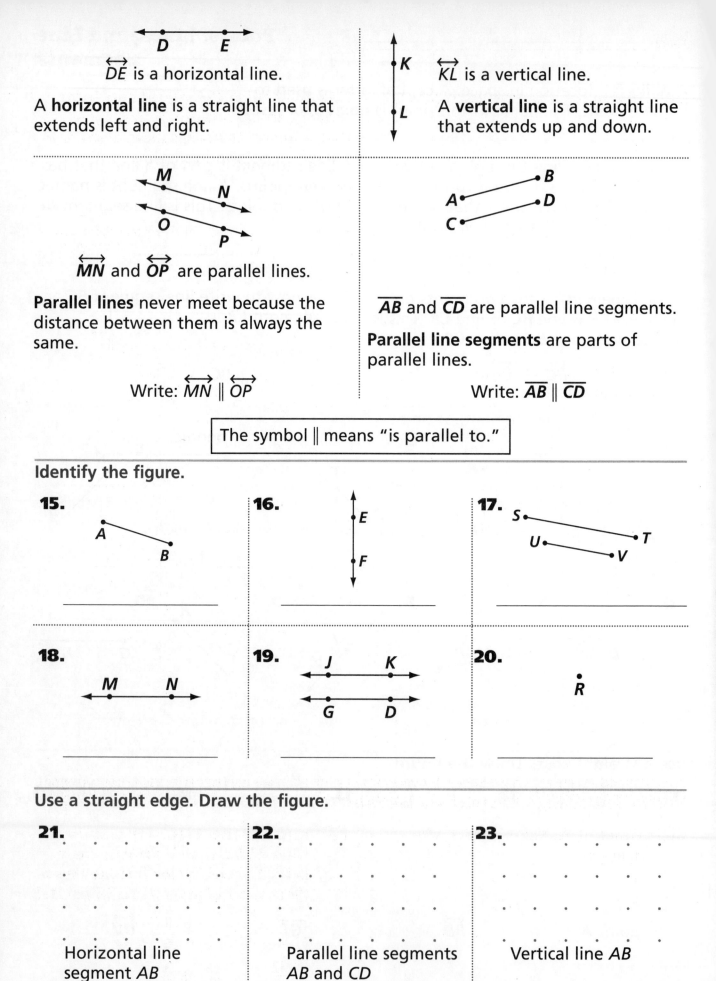

$\overleftrightarrow{DE}$ is a horizontal line.

A **horizontal line** is a straight line that extends left and right.

$\overleftrightarrow{KL}$ is a vertical line.

A **vertical line** is a straight line that extends up and down.

$\overleftrightarrow{MN}$ and $\overleftrightarrow{OP}$ are parallel lines.

Parallel lines never meet because the distance between them is always the same.

Write: $\overleftrightarrow{MN} \parallel \overleftrightarrow{OP}$

$\overline{AB}$ and $\overline{CD}$ are parallel line segments.

Parallel line segments are parts of parallel lines.

Write: $\overline{AB} \parallel \overline{CD}$

The symbol $\parallel$ means "is parallel to."

Identify the figure.

15.

A
B

_____

16.

E
F

_____

17.

S
U   T
V

_____

18.

M   N

_____

19.

J   K
G   D

_____

20.

R

_____

Use a straight edge. Draw the figure.

21.

Horizontal line
segment *AB*

22.

Parallel line segments
AB and *CD*

23.

Vertical line *AB*

Name _____

Line **AB** and line **CD** cross each other.

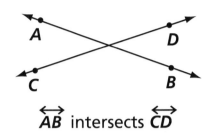

$\overleftrightarrow{AB}$ intersects $\overleftrightarrow{CD}$

Lines that meet or cross are **intersecting lines**.

Line **EF** and line **GH** intersect to form square corners or right angles. Lines that intersect to form square corners are called **perpendicular lines**.

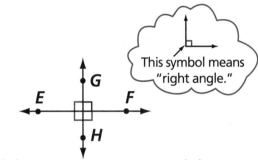

This symbol means "right angle."

$\overleftrightarrow{EF}$ is perpendicular to $\overleftrightarrow{GH}$.

Write: $\overleftrightarrow{EF} \perp \overleftrightarrow{GH}$

The symbol $\perp$ means "is perpendicular to."

Use a straight edge. Draw the figure.

24. $\overleftrightarrow{AB} \perp \overleftrightarrow{DE}$

25. $\overleftrightarrow{CD}$ intersects $\overleftrightarrow{EF}$

26. $\overleftrightarrow{EF} \parallel \overleftrightarrow{GH}$

Test Prep ★ Mixed Review

27 Which of the following is a prime number?

A 7   C 15

B 9   D 27

28 A pizza parlor cuts every pizza into 8 slices. Children at a birthday party finish 4 pizzas. Which fraction shows the number of pizzas the children ate?

F $\dfrac{32}{4}$ H $\dfrac{8}{4}$

G $\dfrac{32}{8}$ J $\dfrac{4}{8}$

Name _____

Rays and Angles

The figure below is a **ray**. A ray has only one endpoint.
When you name a ray, always name its endpoint first.

A   B

This is ray **AB**. Another way to write ray **AB** is:

$$\overrightarrow{AB}$$

| A **ray** is part of a line with only one endpoint. |

Name the ray.

1.

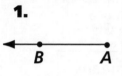

B   A

_____

2.

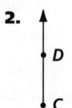

D

C

_____

3.

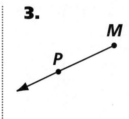

M

P

_____

4.

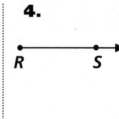

R   S

_____

5.

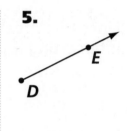

E

D

_____

Name the line, line segment, or ray.

6.

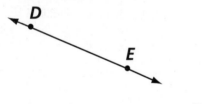

D

E

_____

7.

J

K

_____

8.

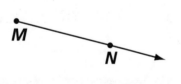

M

N

_____

9.

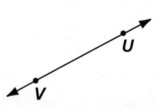

U

V

_____

10.

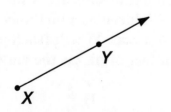

Y

X

_____

11.

V

R

_____

144   Unit 6 Lesson 2

Name _____

This figure is an **angle**. It is made up of two rays with a common **endpoint**. Point **O** is the common endpoint. You say angle **JOL** and write ∠**JOL**. You can also name it ∠**LOJ**.

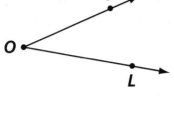

When you write the name of an angle, the common endpoint is always the middle letter. The common endpoint is also called the **vertex**.

A short way to write ∠**JOL** or ∠**LOJ** is ∠**O**.

This is a **right angle**. A right angle is sometimes called a square corner.

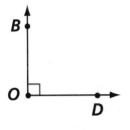

Write two different names for the angle. Circle the right angles.

12.

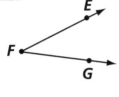

_____

_____

13.

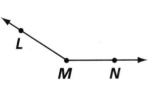

_____

_____

14.

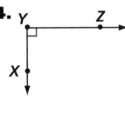

_____

_____

15.

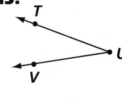

_____

_____

16.

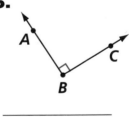

_____

_____

17.

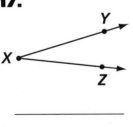

_____

_____

18.

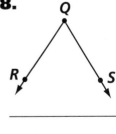

_____

_____

19.

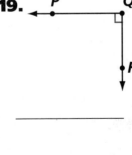

_____

_____

Use a straight edge. Draw and label each angle.

20. ∠*MOP*

21. ∠*RAN*

22. right angle *CAR*

Problem Solving
Reasoning

Solve.

23. How many different angles can you find in this figure? _____ Name the angles.

_____

_____

What vertex do the angles share? _____

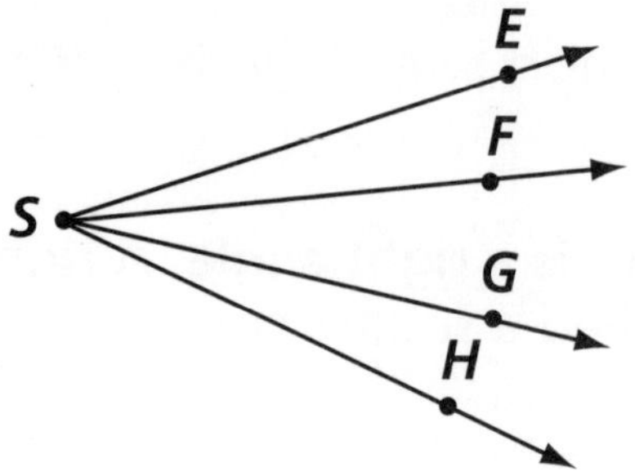

24. Use three letters to name each right angle in square *ABCD*.

_____

_____

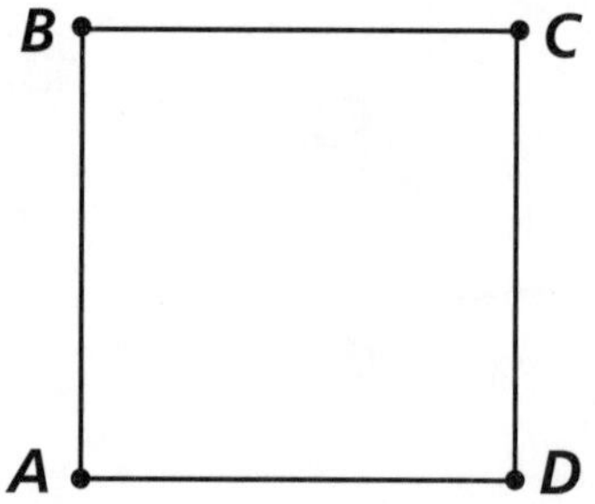

Test Prep ★ Mixed Review

25 Which fraction is in simplest form?

A $\frac{1}{4}$

B $\frac{2}{8}$

C $\frac{2}{6}$

D $\frac{4}{6}$

26 Which mixed number is equivalent to $\frac{7}{3}$?

F $7\frac{1}{3}$

G $2\frac{2}{3}$

H $2\frac{1}{3}$

J $1\frac{2}{3}$

Name _____

Sometimes the best way to solve a
problem is to act it out.

Problem

Can the four figures to the left be arranged
to form a figure congruent to this square
below?

---

1 **Understand**   Be sure you understand what the words in the
problem mean.

- What are congruent figures?

  Congruent figures have the same _____

  and same _____ .

---

2 **Decide**   Choose a method for solving.

Try the strategy Act it Out.

- Trace each of the **4** small figures and cut them out.

---

3 **Solve**   Try to arrange the figures so that they fit **inside**
the large square without overlapping.

- Did you find a way to make all the figures fit

  inside the larger square? _____

- Draw line segments in the square above to
  indicate where you placed each piece.

---

4 **Look back**   Write the answer to the problem below.

Answer _____

- If you take the **4** figures and arrange them to
  form a triangle, would the triangle be congruent
  to the large square? Why or why not?

_____

Solve. Use the Act it Out strategy or any other strategy you have learned.

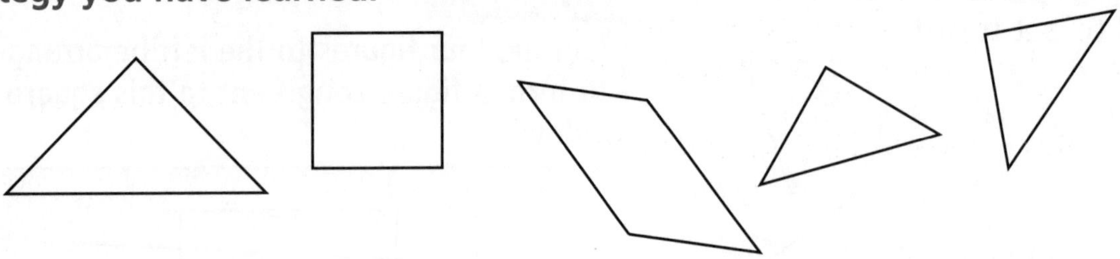

1. Can all the **5** pieces above be arranged to form a figure congruent to the figure below?

Think: Which shapes have sides of the same length as other shapes?

_____

_____

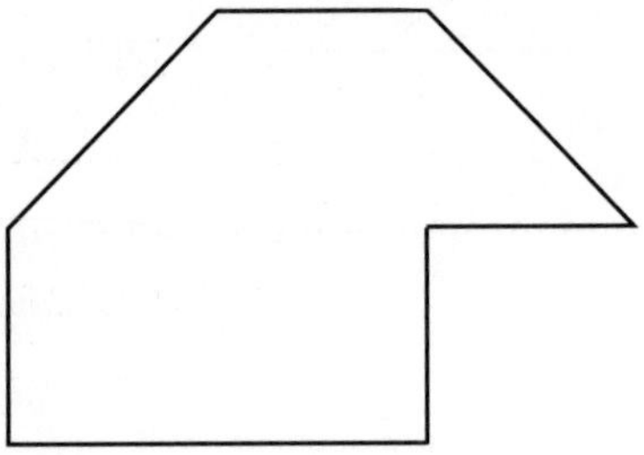

_____

2. Can the **5** pieces above be arranged to form a figure congruent to this figure?

Think: Will the shapes make a figure with **4** square corners the size of the large rectangle?

_____

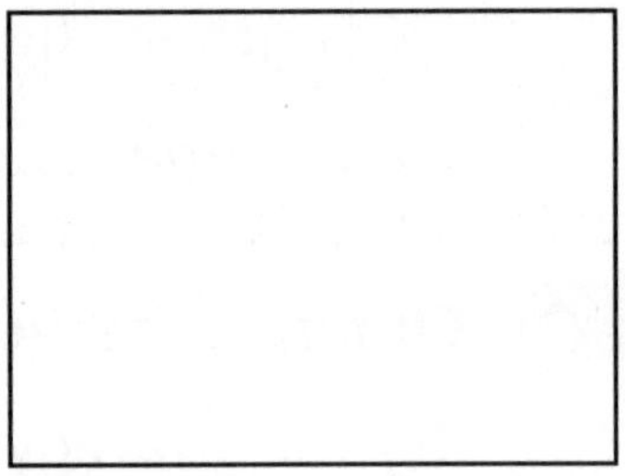

_____

3. Use **12** toothpicks to form **4** congruent squares. Draw the shape.

4. Use **12** toothpicks to form **6** congruent triangles. Draw the shape.

5. Petra and Cecelia are sisters. Petra is $4\frac{1}{2}$ feet tall. Cecelia is $3\frac{3}{4}$ feet tall. How much taller is Petra than Cecelia?

_____

6. Naomi put her dog on a diet. It lost **3** pounds the first month and gained **2** pounds the second month. It then weighed **25** pounds. How much did the dog weigh when it started the diet?

_____

The size or opening of an angle is measured in a unit called a **degree** (°). The figure shown is a **right angle**. A right angle forms a square corner.

| All **right angles** measure **90** degrees or **90°**. |

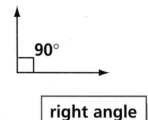

| right angle |

....

This angle measures **45°**. Its measure is less than a right angle. It is called an **acute angle**.

| All angles less than **90°** are **acute angles**. |

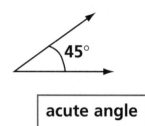

| acute angle |

....

This angle measures **120°**. Its measure is greater than a right angle. It is called an **obtuse angle**.

| All angles greater than **90°** are **obtuse angles**. |

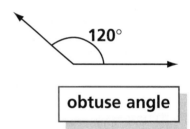

| obtuse angle |

Look at the angle. Write *right, acute,* or *obtuse.*

1.

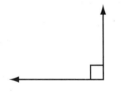

_____

2.

_____

3.

_____

4.

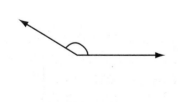

_____

5.

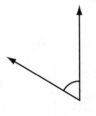

_____

6.

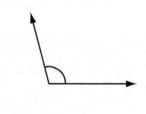

_____

Answer the question next to the figure.

7.

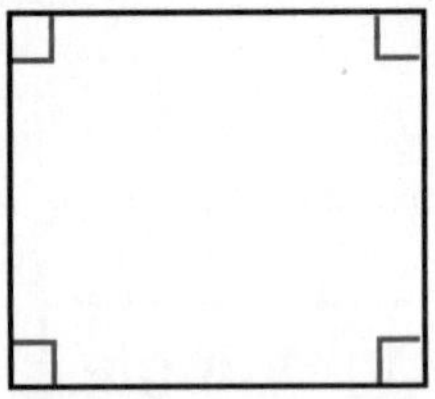

How many
right angles? _____

How many
acute angles? _____

How many
obtuse angles? _____

8.

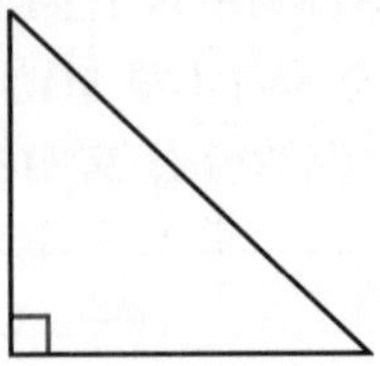

How many
right angles? _____

How many
acute angles? _____

How many
obtuse angles? _____

9.

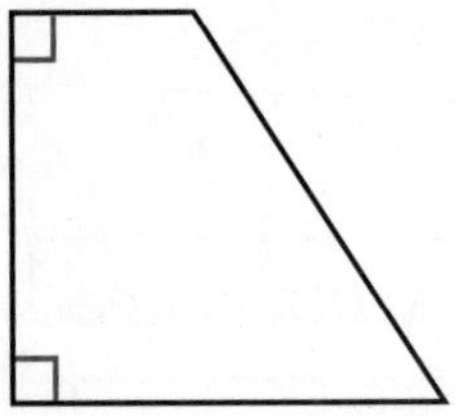

How many
right angles? _____

How many
acute angles? _____

How many
obtuse angles? _____

10.

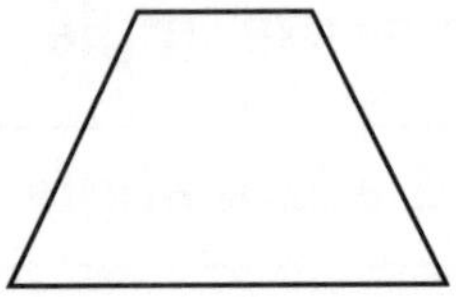

How many
right angles? _____

How many
acute angles? _____

How many
obtuse angles? _____

Use a straight edge. Draw the figure.

11.   acute angle

12.   right angle

13.   obtuse angle

**Problem Solving
Reasoning**   Solve.

14. Name two times when the hour and minute
hands of a clock form a right angle.

_____

Test Prep ★ Mixed Review

15 Which shows all the factors of 32?

A 1, 2, 4, 8, 16, 32

B 30, 2

C 1, 2, 3, 4, 9, 32

D 2, 4, 8, 16

16 What number is the common factor of
both 15 and 27?

F 9

G 6

H 5

J 3

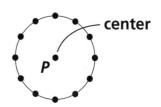

Name _____

Circles

A **circle** is a set of all points that are the same distance from a given point, called the **center**. Point **P** is the center of the circle shown. The points shown on this circle are the same distance from point **P**.

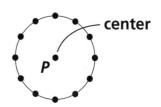
center

Any line segment joining any point on the circle with its center is called a **radius** (plural: **radii**). Point **A** is the center of the circle shown. $\overline{AB}$ or $\overline{BA}$ is a radius.

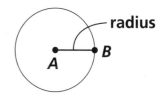
radius

Any line segment that passes across the circle through the center is called a **diameter**. Point **O** is the center of this circle. $\overline{CD}$ or $\overline{DC}$ is a diameter. $\overline{CO}$ and $\overline{OD}$ are radii.

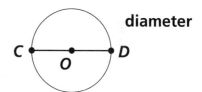
diameter

Use a straight edge and the points given to draw the radius.

1.
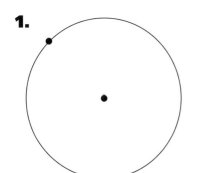

2.
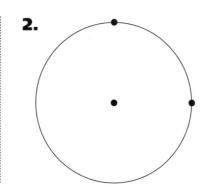

3.
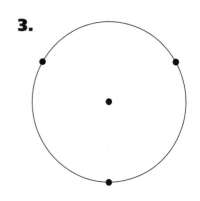

Use a straight edge and the points given to draw the diameter.

4.
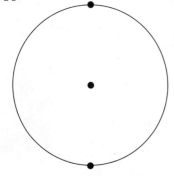

5.
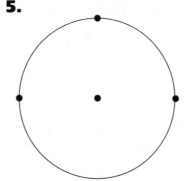

6.
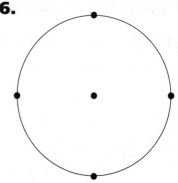

A circle measures **360°**. You can turn an object around the point that is the center of a circle.

Each turn is measured from the start position. The start position is the 0° mark.

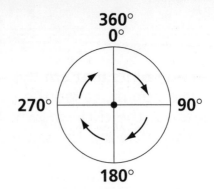

A **quarter turn** is **90°**.   A **half turn** is **180°**.   A **three-quarter turn is 270°.**   A **full turn is 360°.**

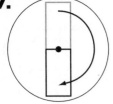   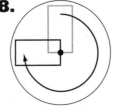   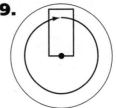   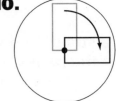

Name the kind of turn and its measure.

7.

8.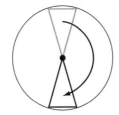

9.

10.

turn _____   turn _____   turn _____   turn _____

degrees _____   degrees _____   degrees _____   degrees _____

Solve.

11. Is the diameter of a circle always twice as long as its radius? Explain.

_____

_____

Test Prep ★ Mixed Review

12 **Which are parallel line segments?**

A   **B**   **C**   **D**

13 **Which fraction represents the shaded part of the model?**

F $\frac{1}{4}$ **H** $\frac{1}{2}$

G $\frac{3}{8}$ **J** $\frac{3}{4}$

Name _____

Figure *ABC* is a triangle. A **triangle** is a figure with three line segments and three angles.

Triangles can be classified by the length of their sides.

An **equilateral triangle** has all three sides the same length.

equilateral

An **isosceles triangle** has at least two sides the same length.

isosceles

A **scalene triangle** has three sides that are all a different length.

scalene

Write whether the triangle is *equilateral, isosceles,* or *scalene.*

1.

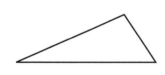

_____

2.

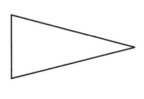

_____

3.

_____

4.

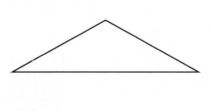

_____

5.

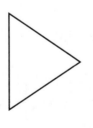

_____

6.

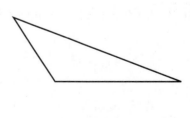

_____

Angle **E** in triangle **DEF** is a right angle. Triangles that have a right angle are called **right triangles**.

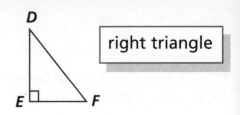

Circle the right triangles.

7.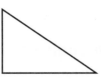

Draw the triangle.

8. equilateral triangle | **9.** isosceles triangle | **10.** scalene triangle

Problem Solving Reasoning Solve.

11. How many different triangles can you find in this figure? _____

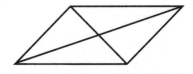

Test Prep ★ Mixed Review

12 Asa practices the piano for $\frac{1}{2}$ an hour each day. Her piano teacher tells her to practice $\frac{1}{3}$ hour more. How much time will she practice in all each day?

A $\frac{5}{8}$ hour   **C** $\frac{3}{4}$ hour

B $\frac{2}{3}$ hour   **D** $\frac{5}{6}$ hour

13 Which group of numbers shows all the factors of 12?

F 1, 2, 8, 11, 12

G 1, 6, 9, 12

H 1, 2, 3, 4, 6, 12

J 1, 4, 5, 7, 12

Name _____

A **polygon** is a closed figure that is made up of line segments.

> Any polygon with **4** sides is a **quadrilateral**.

Some quadrilaterals have other names.

A **square** has four congruent sides and four right angles.

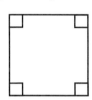

A **rhombus** has four congruent sides and two pairs of parallel sides.

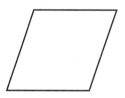

A **trapezoid** has only one pair of parallel sides.

A **rectangle** has two pairs of parallel sides and four right angles.

A **parallelogram** has two pairs of congruent sides and two pairs of parallel sides.

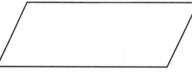

Write the name that best describes the figure.

1.

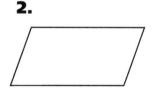

_____

2.

_____

3.

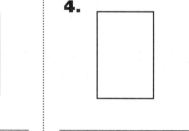

_____

4.

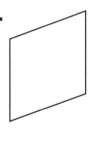

_____

5.

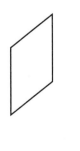

_____

6.

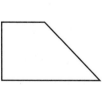

_____

7.

_____

8.

_____

These polygons are called **pentagons**. A **pentagon** has **5** sides and **5** angles.

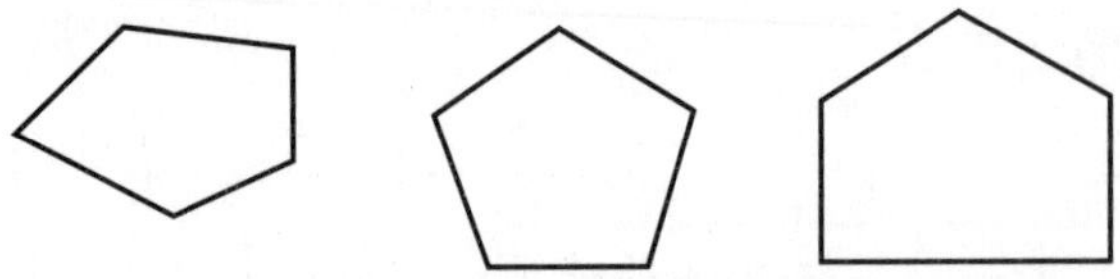

These polygons are called **hexagons**. A **hexagon** has **6** sides and **6** angles.

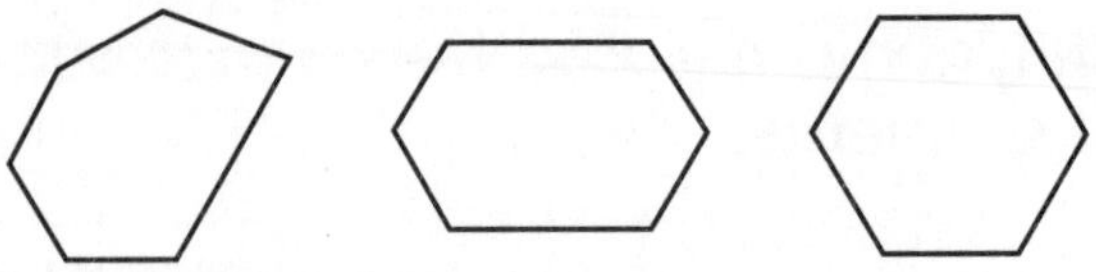

Complete the charts for the figures shown.

Figure	Sides	Right angles	Pairs of parallel sides
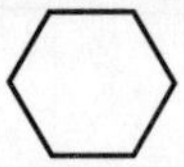 hexagon			
square			

Figure	Sides	Right angles	Pairs of parallel sides
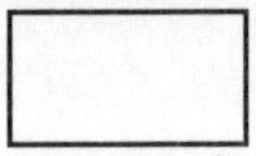 rectangle			
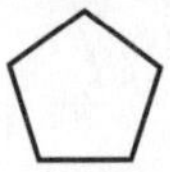 pentagon			

Problem Solving Reasoning   Solve. Write *Yes* or *No*.

9. Is a quadrilateral with four right angles always a square? _____

10. Are all of the angles of a rectangle congruent? _____

☑ **Quick Check**

Write the name of the figure.

Work Space.

11. _____

12. _____

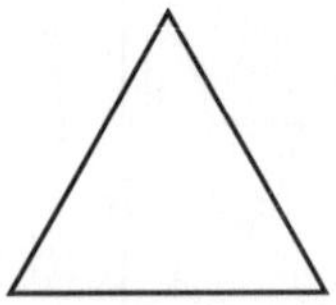

13. _____

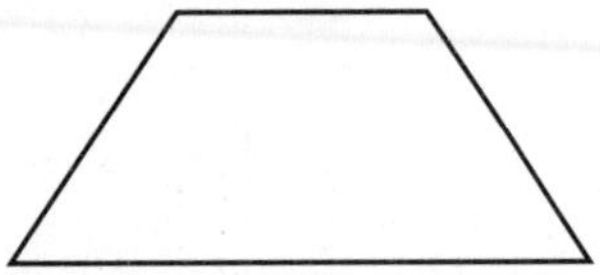

14. _____

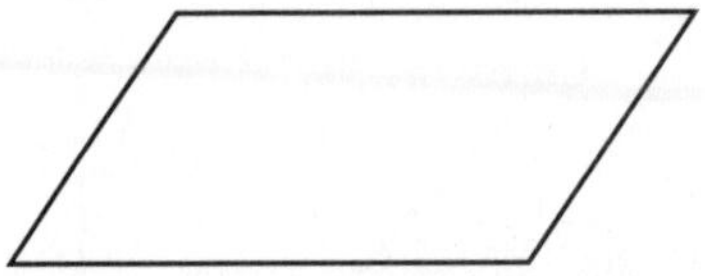

Name _____

Complete the chart.

14.

Space figure	Number of faces	Number of edges	Number of vertices
cube			
triangular pyramid			
rectangular prism			
triangular prism			
rectangular pyramid			

Problem Solving Reasoning Solve.

15. Can one or more faces of a cube be a rectangle?

Explain. _____

_____

Test Prep ★ Mixed Review

16 Which shape is congruent with the square shown?

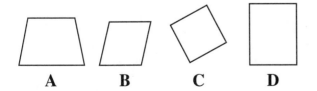

A B C D

17 What is line segment *y*?

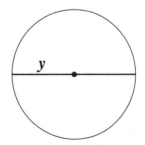

F diameter   **H** parallel lines

G ray   **J** radius

This pattern is called a **net**. You can use nets like this to make space figures. If you cut out this net and fold it on the dotted lines, it will make a cube.

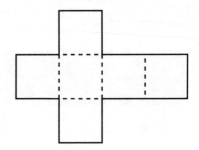

Circle each net that can be folded to make a cube.

1.

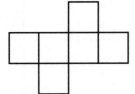

Match the space figure with the correct net.

2.

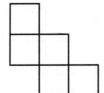

triangular pyramid

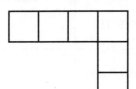 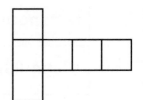

square pyramid

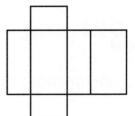

rectangular prism

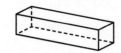

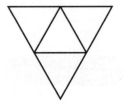

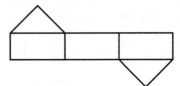

triangular prism

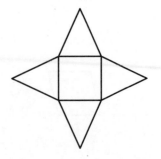

Complete the net for the space figure.

3.

rectangular prism

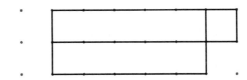

4.

square pyramid

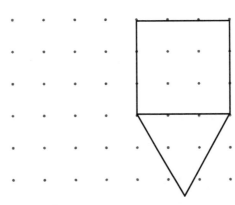

Draw a net for the space figure.

5.

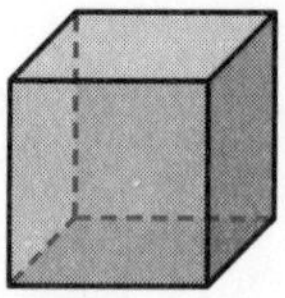

cube

Problem Solving Reasoning **Solve.**

6. How can you tell this net cannot be folded into a cube?

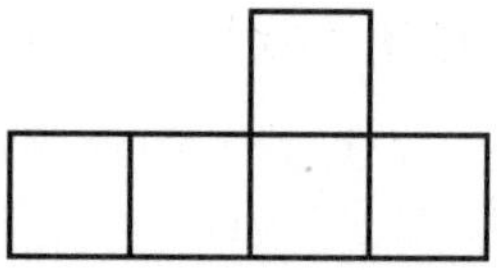

____

____

Quick Check

Answer the question.

Work Space.

7. A cube has how many congruent faces? ______________

How many vertices? ______________

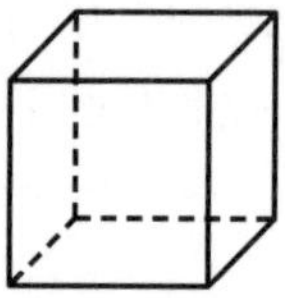

8. A sphere has how many curved surfaces? ______________

How many vertices? ______________

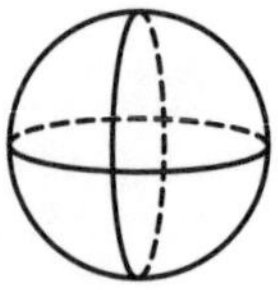

9. Which of these nets can be folded to make a cube? Write the letter.

A 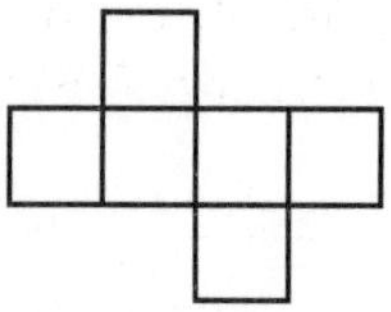

B 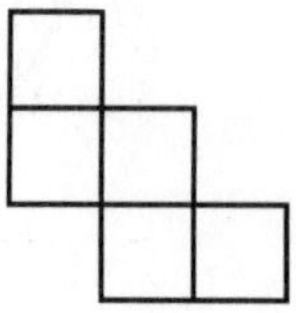

C 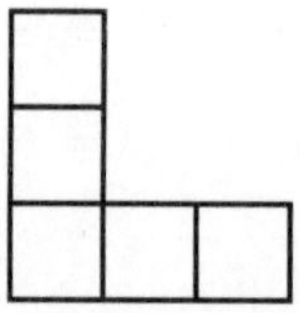

____

Name _____

At a dinner, each person selected a main course. The circle graph shows the choices.

You will use circle graphs to solve the problems in this lesson.

A **circle graph** shows the parts of a whole.

Main Courses Selected

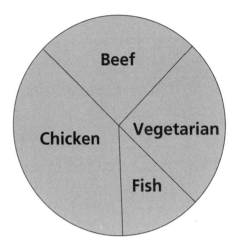

Tips to Remember:

1. Understand	2. Decide	3. Solve	4. Look back

- Reread the problem. Circle important words and numbers.
- Compare the labels on the graph with the words and numbers in the problem. Find the facts you need from the graph.
- Try more than one strategy on the same problem. If one doesn't work, try another.

Solve. Use the circle graph above.

1. Did more people choose chicken or beef?

   Think: What parts of the graph do you need to compare? How could you compare them?

   _____

   _____

   _____

   Answer _____

2. Can you use the graph to find the total number of people at the dinner?

   Think: What information do you need to find the total?

   _____

   _____

   Answer _____

   _____

3. Which two meals were chosen by the same number of people? What fraction of the circle do they each represent?

   _____

   _____

4. Suppose **40** people chose the chicken and **10** people chose fish. Then how many people chose the vegetarian main course? Explain.

   _____

   _____

This circle graph shows how the students in Mrs. Mason's class travel back and forth to school.

How Students Travel to School

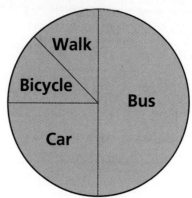

Solve. Use the circle graph above.

5. Do more people walk or take the bus?

_____

6. Do more people go home by car or bicycle?

_____

7. Do more than half of the students in the class go home by car?

_____

8. Suppose there were **24** students in the class. How many students would be going home by bus?

_____

9. If there were **12** students taking the bus, how many students would be going home by car?

_____

10. Suppose **4** students were going home by bicycle. How many students would be walking home?

_____

Extend Your Thinking

11. What fractional part of the whole does each section of the circle graph represent?

_____

12. What fraction represents the combined total of students who walk and students who ride a bicycle?

_____

13. Explain the method you used to solve problem **8**.

_____

_____

_____

14. Explain why this circle graph cannot show data about a class that has a total of **29** students.

_____

_____

_____

Name _____

Identify the figure.

1.

2.

3.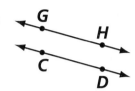

4.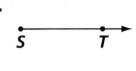

_____   _____   _____   _____

Which figures are congruent?

5. _____ and _____   **6.** _____ and _____

Tell if the angle is right, acute, or obtuse.

7.

8.

9.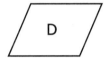

_____   _____   _____

Use the circle to answer the question.

10. Name a radius. _____

11. Name the diameter. _____

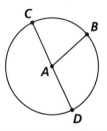

Name the kind of turn and its measure.

12.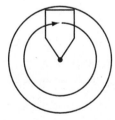

13.

14.

15.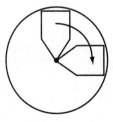

turn _____   turn _____   turn _____   turn _____

degrees _____   degrees _____   degrees _____   degrees _____

Name the figure.

16.

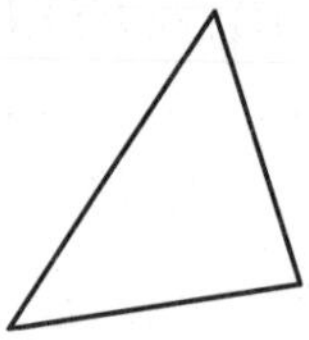

17.

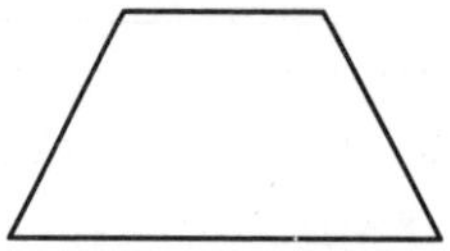

18.

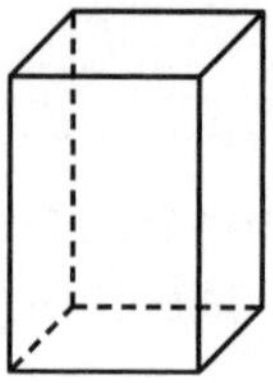

19.

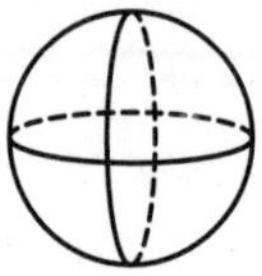

_____   _____   _____   _____

Is the dashed line on the figure a line of symmetry for the figure? Circle _Yes_ or _No_.

20.

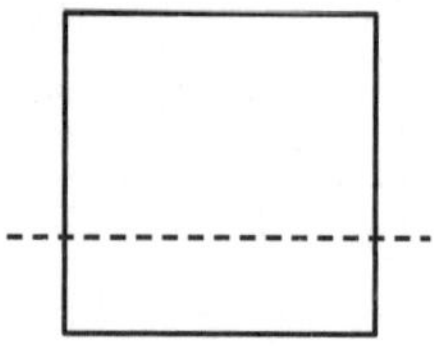

21.

22.

23.

Yes   No   Yes   No   Yes   No   Yes   No

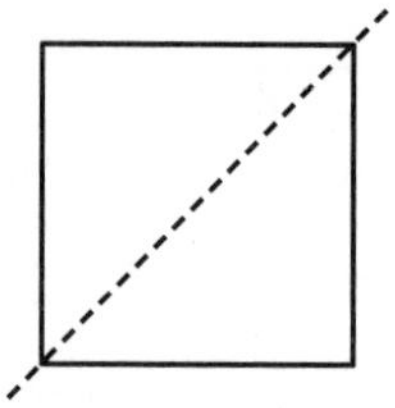

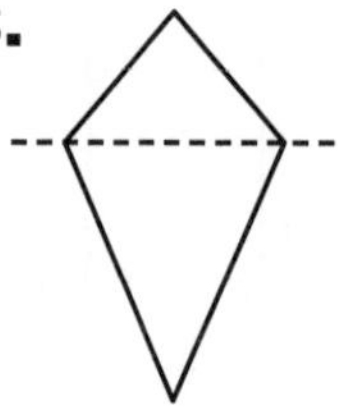

Complete the net for the space figure.

24.

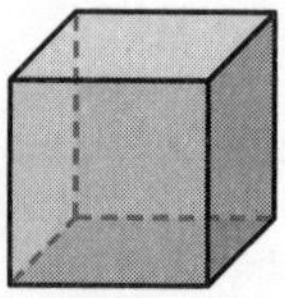

cube

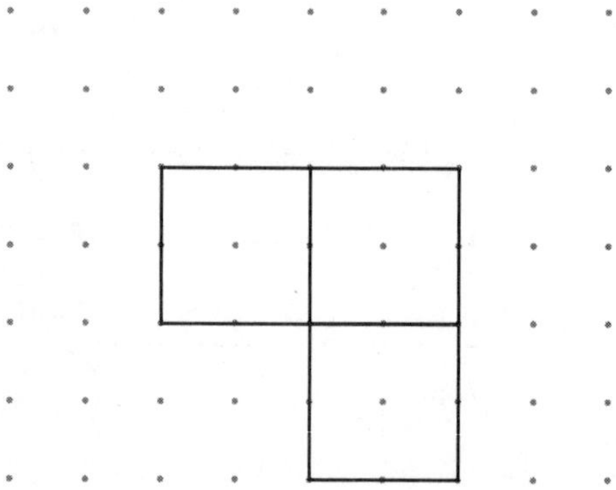

Use the graph to answer the question.

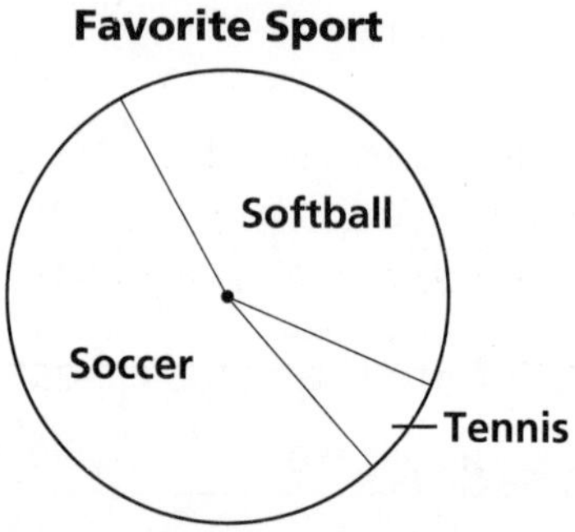

Favorite Sport

Softball

Soccer

Tennis

25. Which sport did about half the students say was their favorite?

_____

Use the Act it Out Strategy to solve the problem.

26. Can **3** of the **4** figures shown be arranged to form a rectangle? Explain.

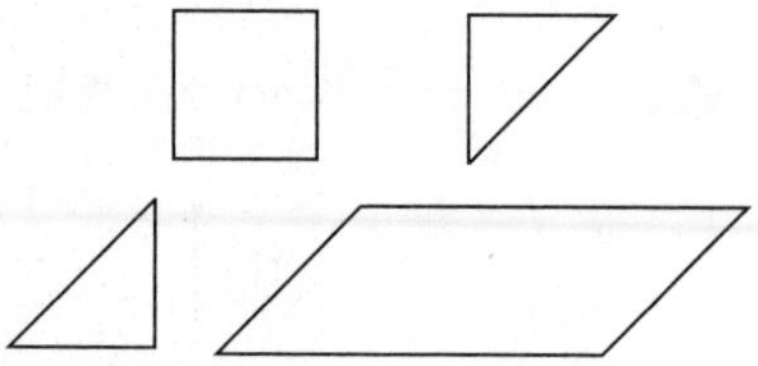

_____

1 A bakery sells 250 muffins in one day. How many muffins does the shop sell in a week?

A 1,750   C 1,450   E NH

B 1,500   D 1,400

2 What fraction of a circle is the right angle shown?

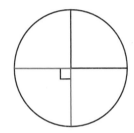

F $\frac{3}{4}$ H $\frac{1}{3}$

G $\frac{1}{2}$ J $\frac{1}{4}$

3 Employees at a music store unpack 12 cartons of CDs. There are 128 CDs in each carton. How many CDs did they unpack in all?

A 1,524   C 1,548   E NH

B 1,536   D 1,560

4 Which figure has the same shape as this traffic sign?

F Triangle   H Hexagon

G Rectangle   J Octagon

5 At a volleyball tournament, 87 students divided into teams with 6 students on each team. How many extra students were there?

A 0   C 2   E NH

B 1   D 3

6 The angles shown below are grouped together because they are similar.

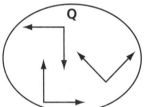

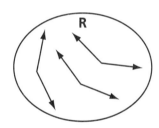

Which angle belongs with group R?

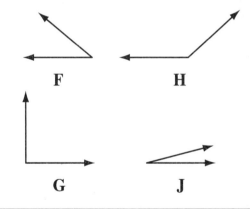

7 Which fraction is in simplest form?

A $\frac{5}{12}$ C $\frac{3}{9}$

B $\frac{4}{10}$ D $\frac{2}{6}$

8 The diameter of Mike's bicycle wheel is 22 inches. What is the radius?

22 inches

F 44 in.   **H** 11 in.

G 22 in.   **J** 2 in.

9 Four students run different distances. The distances are shown below.

Name	Distance Run
Jamail	$\frac{5}{6}$ mile
Kim	$\frac{1}{4}$ mile
Frank	$\frac{2}{3}$ mile
Elena	$\frac{11}{12}$ mile

Which lists the students in order from the *longest* distance run to the *shortest* distance run?

A Frank, Kim, Elena, Jamail

B Kim, Frank, Jamail, Elena

C Elena, Jamail, Kim, Frank

D Elena, Jamail, Frank, Kim

10 What number is equal to
$(6 \times 100{,}000) + (9 \times 10{,}000) + (7 \times 1{,}000) + (6 \times 1)$?

F 6,970,600   **H** 697,060

G 6,097,006   **J** 697,006

11 Which mixed number represents the shaded portion of this model?

A $3\frac{14}{6}$ **C** $3\frac{4}{6}$

B 4   **D** $3\frac{2}{6}$

12 Which of the following is a prime number?

F 15   **H** 22

G 17   **J** 25

13 Averil runs every day. He has run $7\frac{1}{2}$ miles so far this week. If he runs $1\frac{1}{4}$ miles on Friday, how far will he have run all together?

A $7\frac{3}{4}$ **D** $9\frac{3}{4}$

B $8\frac{1}{2}$ **E** NH

C $8\frac{3}{4}$

UNIT 7 • TABLE OF CONTENTS

Measurement

Dear Family,

During the next few weeks, our math class will be learning about and practicing measurement.

You can expect to see homework that provides practice with finding perimeter. Here is a sample you may want to keep handy to give help if needed.

Finding Perimeter

When you find the perimeter of an object, you are finding the distance around it. To find the perimeter of a rectangle, use the formula $P = 2 \times (l + w)$ where P = perimeter, l = the length of the rectangle, and w = the width of the rectangle.

Example Find the perimeter of rectangle **ABCD**.

$P = 2 \times (l + w)$	Write the formula.
$P = 2 \times (10 + 5)$	Substitute for l and w.
$P = 2 \times (15)$	Start inside parentheses.
$P = 30$ in.	Multiply. Label the answer.

Another way to find the perimeter of a figure is to add the measure of its sides.

Example Find the perimeter of square **WXYZ**.

$P = s + s + s + s \quad s$ = the length of one side
$P = 12 + 12 + 12 + 12$
$P = 48$ cm

During this unit, students will need to continue practicing multiplication and addition facts.

Sincerely,

Celsius Temperature

You measure temperature with a **thermometer**. The thermometer shown is a liquid thermometer. The liquid rises when it gets warmer and falls when it gets cooler.

A **degree Celsius (°C)** is a metric unit used to measure temperature. The scale on this thermometer shows degrees Celsius. Each mark represents **2 degrees Celsius**.

The red shading in this thermometer shows that the temperature is **28°C** or **28 degrees Celsius**.

Read the scale on the thermometer.

- Find **0°C**. Water freezes at **0°C**. When it is ⁻**10°C** or minus **10 degrees** Celsius, it is a very cold day.

- Find **100°C**. Water boils at **100°C**.

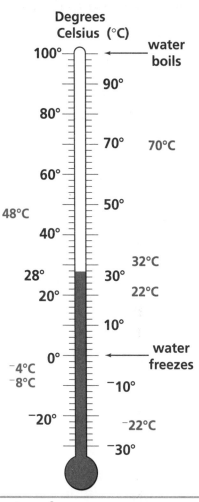

Degrees Celsius (°C)

Use arrows to mark each temperature on the thermometer above.

1. 32°C   ⁻8°C   70°C   ⁻4°C   22°C   48°C   ⁻22°C

Circle the warmer temperature.

2. 10°C	32°C	32°C	36°C	50°C	68°C	⁻10°C	⁻20°C

3. 5°C	⁻5°C	72°C	82°C	0°C	⁻8°C	15°C	12°

Circle the best estimate of temperature.

4. ice   boiling water   a snowy day   a very hot day

12°C   0°C   90°C   100°C   ⁻5°C   25°C   38°C   88°C

A **line graph** organizes and displays data that change during a period of time. This line graph shows how the temperature changed on Saturday.

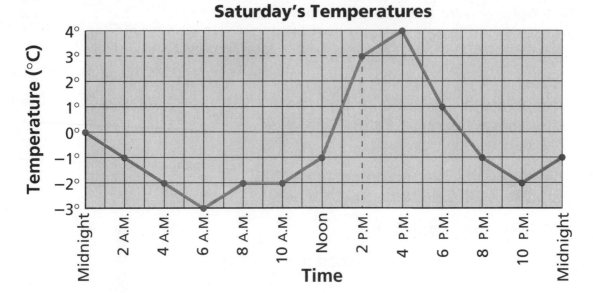

Saturday's Temperatures

To find the temperature at **2 P.M.**, follow these steps.

- Find **2 P.M.** on the horizontal (left-to-right) axis.

- Trace a line up from **2:00 P.M.** until you reach a point on the graph.

- Trace a straight line from that point to the vertical (up-and-down) axis to find the temperature, **3°**. The temperature at **2 P.M.** was **3°C.**

Use the graph to answer the questions.

5. What was the warmest temperature on Saturday? _____

   At what time did that temperature occur? _____

6. What was the coldest temperature? _____

   At what time did that temperature occur? _____

7. When was the temperature –1°C? _____ , _____ , _____

8. For how many hours was the temperature less than –2°C? _____

Test Prep ★ Mixed Review

9 What is line segment *Q*?

   A Ray   **C** Diameter

   B Radius   **D** Chord

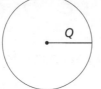

10 There are 360° in a circle. What is the degree measure of the angle shown?

   F 60°   **H** 180°

   G 90°   **J** 270°

Name _____

In this lesson, you will learn to make a table to help you solve a problem.

Problem
Beginning at **6:30** A.M., buses leave to go to the airport. A bus leaves every **45** minutes. The trip takes $1\frac{1}{2}$ hours. If Marcia takes the second bus of the day, what time will she get to the airport?

Understand   As you reread, ask yourself questions.

- What facts do you know?
  The first bus leaves at **6:30** A.M.

  Buses leave every _____ minutes.

  The trip takes _____ hours.
- What do you need to find out?

  _____

- What will you need to find out first?

  _____

Decide   Choose a method for solving.

Try the strategy Make a Table.

Bus	Leaves	Arrives
1		
2		

---

3 **Solve**   Find the times you need. Write them in the table.

- What time can you fill in first?

  _____

- Find the time the second bus leaves.

  6:30 A.M. $\xrightarrow{\textbf{+30} \text{ min}}$ _____ A.M. $\xrightarrow{\textbf{+15} \text{ min}}$ _____ A.M.

- Find the time the second bus arrives at the airport.

  7:15 A.M. $\xrightarrow{\textbf{+1} \text{ hr}}$ _____ A.M. $\xrightarrow{\textbf{+30} \text{ min}}$ _____ A.M.

---

4 **Look back**   Write the answer to the problem. _____

- Why is it not necessary to complete the entire table?

  _____

Solve. Use the Make a Table strategy or any other strategy you have learned.

1. At an amusement park, a musical show starts every **35** minutes and lasts for **20** minutes. If the first show is at **9:30** A.M., what time does the third show end?

Think: What could you label the columns and rows of a table?

_____

Answer _____

2. T-shirts are on sale, buy **2**–get one free. If one T-shirt costs **$6**, how much will Mrs. Simon pay for **7** shirts?

Think: How would you set up a table to help you solve the problem?

_____

Answer _____

3. Move **4** toothpicks to make **3** congruent squares.

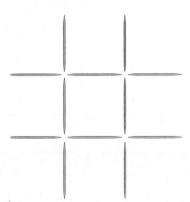

4. Are these two figures congruent?

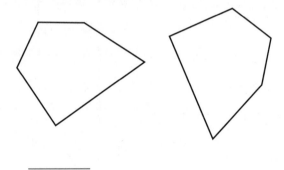

_____

5. A movie lasts **90** minutes. The movie is shown at **1:30** P.M., **3:25** P.M., **5:20** P.M., **7:15** P.M., and **9:05** P.M. Sarah can get from the theater to her house in **15** minutes. What is the latest show Sarah can go to and still be home by **8:30** P.M.?

_____

6. Sean bowled three games. His scores were **79**, **76**, and **83**. What score will he need to get in the next game to have an average of exactly **80**?

_____

7. The sum of two numbers is **60**. Their difference is **12**. What are the two numbers?

_____

8. Write the next number in this sequence.

$5\frac{1}{3}$, $6\frac{2}{3}$, 8, $9\frac{1}{3}$, $10\frac{2}{3}$, _____

Name _____

Customary Units of Length: Inch, Half Inch, Quarter Inch

In the **customary system** of measurement, the **inch (in.)** is a standard unit of length. This ruler is marked with inches and half inches.

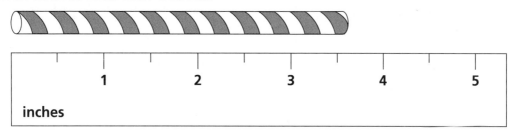

- You can use a ruler to measure to the **nearest inch**. The straw is between **3** and **4** inches long. Because it is nearer to **4** inches than to **3** inches, the length of the straw is **4 inches to the nearest inch**. If the object you are measuring is **halfway** between two whole inches, use the greater number.

- You can also measure to the **nearest half inch**. The straw is between $3\frac{1}{2}$ and **4** inches long. But it is nearer to $3\frac{1}{2}$ inches, so the length of the straw is $3\frac{1}{2}$ **inches to the nearest half inch**.

Measure the pen to the nearest inch or half inch.

1. Pen **A** is about _____ inches long.

Pen **B** is about _____ inches long.

Pen **C** is about _____ inches long.

Pen **D** is about _____ inches long.

A

C

B

D

2. Pen **A** is _____ to the nearest half inch.

Pen **B** is _____ to the nearest half inch.

3. Pen **C** is _____ to the nearest half inch.

Pen **D** is _____ to the nearest half inch.

The units on this ruler are whole inches, half inches, and quarter inches. The straw is $3\frac{3}{4}$ inches long, **to the nearest quarter-inch.**

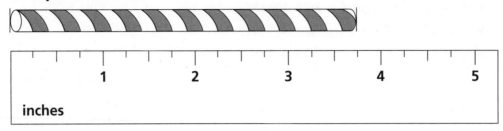

Complete.

4. What is the length of this pencil to the nearest inch? _____

to the nearest half inch? _____

to the nearest quarter inch? _____

Measure the line to the nearest quarter inch.

5. |————————————————————| _____

6. |————————————————| _____

| Problem Solving |
| Reasoning |

Solve.

7. Is it more accurate to measure to the nearest quarter inch, half inch, or inch? Explain.

_____

_____

Test Prep ★ Mixed Review

8 What number is a common factor of both 14 and 28?

A 7   **C** 4

B 6   **D** 3

9 The distance from Brian's house to the park is 3,000 meters. What is the distance in kilometers?

F 3   **H** 300

G 30   **J** 30,000

Name _____

In the Customary System, temperature is measured in **degrees Fahrenheit (°F)**. Each mark on this thermometer is **1°F**. Temperatures below 0° are written with a negative sign (⁻).

Read the scale.

Find **32°F**. Water freezes at **32°** Fahrenheit.

Water boils at **212°F**.

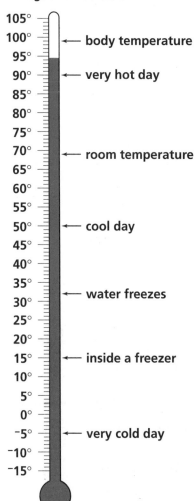

Fahrenheit Temperature and Negative Numbers

- 105°
- 100° ← body temperature
- 95°
- 90° ← very hot day
- 85°
- 80°
- 75°
- 70° ← room temperature
- 65°
- 60°
- 55°
- 50° ← cool day
- 45°
- 40°
- 35°
- 30° ← water freezes
- 25°
- 20°
- 15° ← inside a freezer
- 10°
- 5°
- 0°
- ⁻5° ← very cold day
- ⁻10°
- ⁻15°

Read the thermometer to find the temperature.

1. the inside of a freezer _____

2. body temperature _____

3. room temperature _____

4. a very cold day _____

5. a very hot day _____

6. a cool day _____

Draw an arrow pointing to the temperature on the thermometer.

7.   85°F   20°F   58°F   23°F

8. ⁻10°F   17°F   ⁻3°F   ⁻14°F

Circle the colder temperature.

9. 83°F or 73°F   16°F or 26°F   10°F or 0°F

10. ⁻4°F or 0°F   ⁻8°F or 8°F   ⁻6°F or ⁻12°F

Circle the best estimate.

11. ice cubes	**12.** hot soup	**13.** a day at the beach
32°F 80°F 50°F	230°F 125°F 70°F	49°F 99°F 149°F
14. a glass of cold water	**15.** water in a swimming pool	**16.** snowballs
72°F 40°F 95°F	114°F 84°F 34°F	20°F 52°F 81°F

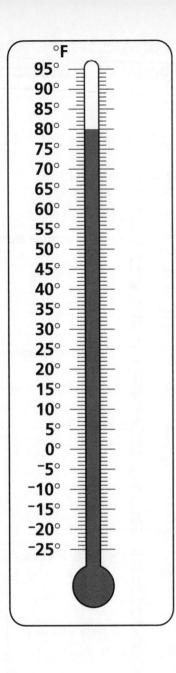

You can think of a thermometer as a vertical **number line.**

Find **0°** on the thermometer. Look at the numbers below or less than zero. You write these numbers with a negative sign.

$^-$**15°F** $^-$**12°F** $^-$**10°F** $^-$**5°F** $^-$**3°F**

Look at the numbers above or greater than zero. These numbers are positive numbers, but the positive sign is usually not written.

3°F **5°F** **10°F** **12°F** **15°F**

Use the thermometer to answer each question.

17. What temperature is **10 degrees** above **0°F**? _____

18. What temperature is **10 degrees** below **0°F**? _____

19. How many degrees is it from **0°F** to **20°F**? _____

20. How many degrees is it from **0°F** to $^-$**20°F**? _____

21. What temperature is **5 degrees** warmer than $^-$**10°F**? _____

22. What temperature is **5 degrees** colder than $^-$**10°F**? _____

23. What temperature is **5 degrees** warmer than **25°F**? _____

Find the number of degrees from one temperature to the other.

24. **55°F and 65°F** _____   **25°F and 65°F** _____   **10°F and 18°F** _____

25. **0°F and 32°F** _____ $^-$**10°F and 0°F** _____ $^-$**10°F and 10°F** _____

26. $^-$**20°F and 20°F** _____ $^-$**12°F and 10°F** _____ $^-$**5°F and 25°F** _____

27. $^-$**5°F and** $^-$**10°F** _____ $^-$**25°F and** $^-$**5°F** _____ $^-$**13°F and** $^-$**6°F** _____

Name _____

Write the temperature. Use the thermometer if you need to.

28. Was **10°F.** Increased **20 degrees.** _____

29. Was **75°F.** Increased **12 degrees.** _____

30. Was **62°F.** Decreased **8 degrees.** _____

31. Was **32°F.** Decreased **7 degrees.** _____

32. Was **0°F.** Decreased **6 degrees.** _____

33. Was **0°F.** Increased **16 degrees.** _____

34. Was **10°F.** Decreased **10 degrees.** _____

35. Was **5°F.** Decreased **15 degrees.** _____

36. Was **⁻10°F.** Increased **15 degrees.** _____

37. Was **⁻5°F.** Decreased **5 degrees.** _____

38. Was **⁻16°F.** Increased **12 degrees.** _____

39. Was **⁻6°F.** Decreased **8 degrees.** _____

| **Problem Solving** |
| **Reasoning** |

Solve.

40. At midnight the temperature was **⁻4°F.** Three hours later the temperature was **10 degrees** colder. What was the temperature? _____

41. At dawn the temperature was **⁻7°F.** By noon the temperature had risen **15 degrees.** What was the noon temperature? _____

°F
95°
90°
85°
80°
75°
70°
65°
60°
55°
50°
45°
40°
35°
30°
25°
20°
15°
10°
5°
0°
⁻5°
⁻10°
⁻15°
⁻20°
⁻25°

Test Prep ★ Mixed Review

42 Which is the most likely temperature outside when Angel is swimming?

  A 93° C
  B 38° C
  C 10° C
  D 0° C

43 The width of Glenda's room is 24 feet. What is the width in yards?

  F 3
  G 6
  H 8
  J 12

Name _____

Sometimes you can use a diagram to solve a problem.

In this lesson, you will use a number line to keep track of changes and to compare numbers.

Tips to Remember:

| 1. Understand | 2. Decide | 3. Solve | 4. Look back |

- Picture the situation described in the problem. Tell what is happening in your own words.
- When you can, make predictions about the answer. Then compare your answer and your prediction.
- Compare the numbers on the number line with the words and numbers in the problem.

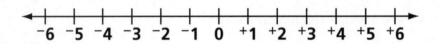

$$^-6 \quad ^-5 \quad ^-4 \quad ^-3 \quad ^-2 \quad ^-1 \quad 0 \quad ^+1 \quad ^+2 \quad ^+3 \quad ^+4 \quad ^+5 \quad ^+6$$

Solve. Use the number line above.

1. Jim is at his house (point **0** on the number line). He walks **3** blocks west (move left **3** on the number line). Then he walks **4** blocks east and **6** blocks west. What point on the number line shows where Jim is then?

Think: At what point is Jim after he walks **4** blocks east? How did you use the number line to help you?

_____

_____

Answer _____

2. Every morning, Luis records the temperature. Monday's temperature was **2°** F. Tuesday's temperature was **1°**F higher than Monday's. Wednesday's temperature was **4°**F lower than Tuesday's. What was Wednesday's temperature?

Think: Where on the number line should you begin?

_____

Answer _____

Name _____

The **length (*l*)** of this rectangle is **4** cm.
The **width (*w*)** is **3** cm.
To find the perimeter, add the lengths of the four sides:

$$P = 4 \text{ cm} + 4 \text{ cm} + 3 \text{ cm} + 3 \text{ cm or } 14 \text{ cm}$$

$$P = 2 \times 4 + 2 \times 3 \text{ or } 14 \text{ cm}$$

For any rectangle with length *l* and width *w*,
$$P = (2 \times l) + (2 \times w)$$

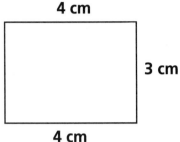
4 cm

3 cm   3 cm

4 cm

Use a formula to find the perimeter.

13. a rectangle **4** m long
and **2** m wide _____

14. a rectangle **15** cm long
and **10** cm wide _____

15. a square **6** mm on each side _____

16. a square **23** m on each side _____

 Quick Check

Compare. Write >, <, or =.

17. 1 lb ☐ 19 oz

18. 4,400 lb ☐ 2 T

19. 1 gal ☐ 5 qt

20. 2 pt ☐ 1 qt

Work Space.

Solve.

21. When would it be
warm enough to
swim outside? Circle
the better estimate
of temperature.

A. 40°F   B. 90°F

22. The temperature was
⁻3°F at dawn. By
noon, it was 10°F.
How much did the
temperature rise?

_____

23. Find the perimeter
of the rectangle shown.

_____

4 feet

8 feet

Name _____

Area

Area is the number of square units in a region.
The area of this region is **6** square units.

....

A **square centimeter** can be used to measure
area. A square centimeter is a square with
1 cm sides.

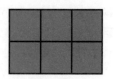

A rectangle has two dimensions: length (*l*) and
width (*w*). The rectangle at the right has a length
of **2** centimeters, a width of **1** centimeter,
and an area (*A*) of **2** square centimeters.

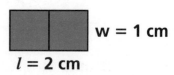

A = **2** square centimeters

Find the area in square units.

1.

_____   _____   _____   _____

Find the area in square centimeters.

2.

A = _____

3.

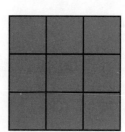

A = _____

4.

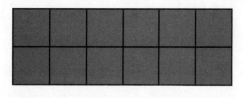

A = _____

5.

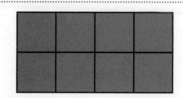

A = _____

198   Unit 7 Lesson 12

Name _____

You can find the **perimeter** of this figure by adding the length of each side.

3 in. + 4 in. + 3 in. + 8 in. + 6 in. + 12 in. = 36 in.

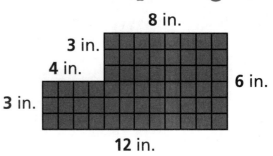

You can also find the **area** of the figure by first dividing it into two rectangles.

Find the area of both rectangles.

Use $A = l \times w$.

Rectangle 1: 4 in. × 3 in. = 12 square in.

Rectangle 2: 8 in. × 6 in. = 48 square in.

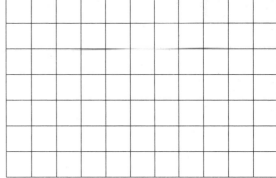

Rectangle 1   **Rectangle 2**

Then add the areas of the two rectangles to find the total area of the figure:

48 square in. + 12 square in. = 60 square in.

Find the perimeter for each figure.
Draw the figure as two rectangles to find the area.

1.

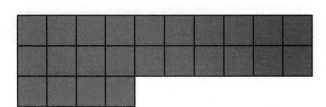

Perimeter = _____ units

Area = _____ square units

2.

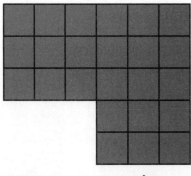

Perimeter = _____ units

Area = _____ square units

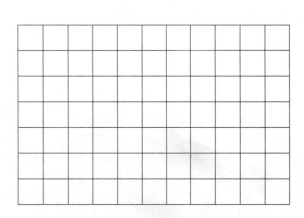

Find the area of this figure.

3.

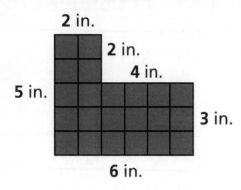

2 in.

2 in.

4 in.

5 in.

3 in.

6 in.

A = _____

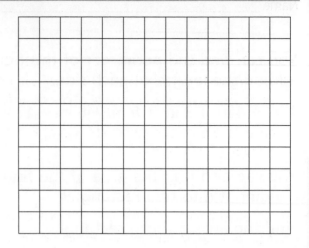

Solve.

4. What is the perimeter of this figure?

_____

5. What is the area of this figure?

_____

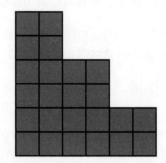

 Quick Check

6. Find the area of the rectangle shown. Give the measurement in square units.

7 cm

3 cm

_____

Work Space.

7. Find the perimeter of the figure shown. Then find the area. Write the measurement for area in square units.

2 ft

2 ft

2 ft

3 ft

1 ft _____

4 ft

Name _____

Surface area is the sum of the areas of all the faces of a space figure. A cube has **6** faces. The surface area of a cube is the sum of the areas of its **6** faces.

To find the surface area of a cube, first find the area of one face of the cube.

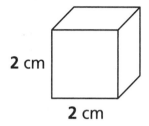

2 cm × 2 cm = **4** square cm

2 cm

2 cm

Since all **6** faces of a cube are **congruent**, or the same size and shape, you can add the area of one face six times to find the surface area.

4 + 4 + 4 + 4 + 4 + 4 = 24 square cm

Or, you can multiply the area of one face by **6**.

6 × 4 square cm = 24 square cm

Find the surface area for each cube.

1.

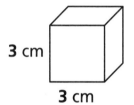

3 cm

3 cm

surface area _____

2.

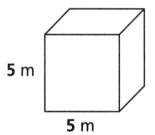

5 m

5 m

surface area _____

3.

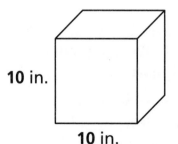

10 in.

10 in.

surface area _____

A rectangular prism also has **6** faces. But the faces are not all congruent. To find the surface area of a rectangular prism, first make a drawing of what the rectangular prism would look like if it was unfolded.

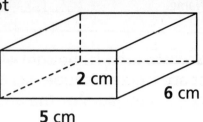

2 cm

6 cm

5 cm

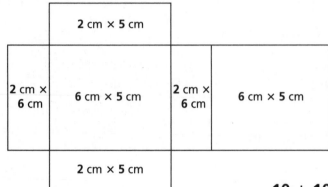

| 2 cm × 5 cm |
| 2 cm × 6 cm | 6 cm × 5 cm | 2 cm × 6 cm | 6 cm × 5 cm |
| 2 cm × 5 cm |

Find the area of each face.

Then add the areas.

10 + 10 + 12 + 12 + 30 + 30 = 104 square cm

Find the surface area of this rectangular prism.

4.

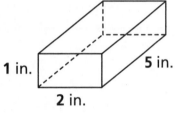

1 in.   5 in.

2 in.

A = _____

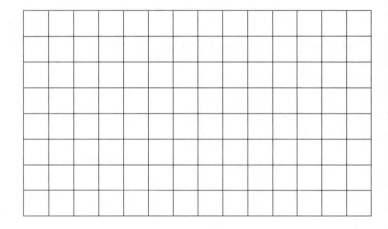

Problem Solving Reasoning Solve.

5. Look at the rectangular prism above. How many

pairs of faces are congruent? _____

Test Prep ★ Mixed Review

6 You return a library book that is exactly 4 weeks overdue. The fine is $.12 a day. How much do you owe?

A $33.36

B $3.36

C $.84

D $.48

7 Frank's vegetable garden is 15 feet wide and 10 feet long. What is the area of his garden?

F 25 square feet

G 50 square feet

H 150 square feet

J 200 square feet

Volume is the amount of space inside a space figure.

You can find the volume of this rectangular prism by counting the unit cubes it would take to fill it.

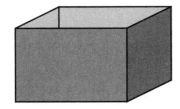

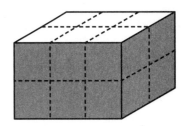

The volume of this rectangular prism is **12 cubic units**.

A standard unit that is used for measuring volume is a cube with each edge **1** centimeter long. This unit is called a **cubic centimeter**.

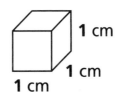

1 cubic centimeter

A rectangular prism has three dimensions, length (**l**), width (**w**), and height (**h**). You can find its volume (**V**) by multiplying these dimensions.

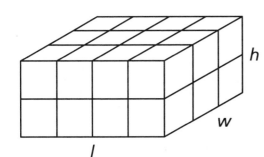

$V = l \times w \times h$
$V = 4$ cm $\times 3$ cm $\times 2$ cm
$V = 24$ **cubic cm**

Name the volume in cubic units.

1.

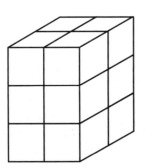

$V = $ _____

2.

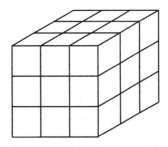

$V = $ _____

Write a number sentence to describe the volume. Then name the volume.

3.

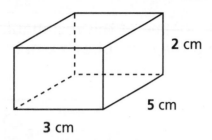

2 cm

5 cm

3 cm

number sentence: _____

volume: _____

4.

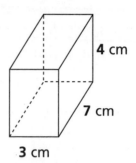

4 cm

7 cm

3 cm

number sentence: _____

volume: _____

Problem Solving Reasoning

Solve.

5. Betty filled a box with **5** layers of centimeter cubes. Each layer had **6** rows with **4** cubes in each row. How many cubes were in the box?

_____

6. A box of candies had **3** layers. Each layer had **8** rows with **6** candies in each row. How many candies were in the box?

_____

 Quick Check

Solve.

7. Find the surface area of the cube shown. Write the measurement in square units.

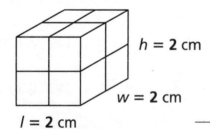

$h = 2$ cm

$w = 2$ cm

$l = 2$ cm

_____

8. Find the volume of the rectangular prism shown. Write the measurement in cubic units.

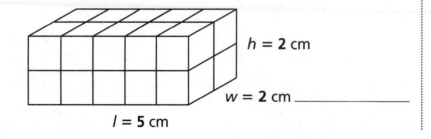

$h = 2$ cm

$w = 2$ cm

$l = 5$ cm

Work Space.

Name _____

Use a ruler to measure the length of this segment to the nearest inch and to the nearest half inch.

1. •————————————————•

_____   _____

Use a ruler to measure the length of this segment to the nearest centimeter and to the nearest millimeter.

2. •————————————————•

_____   _____

Circle the better estimate.

3. mass of a textbook

1 kg   1 mg

4. capacity of a spoon

5 L   5 mL

5. weight of a coin

1 oz   1 lb

6. capacity of a drinking glass

1 qt   1 pt

Name the equivalent measure.

7. 2 kg = _____ g

8. 5 cm = _____ mm

9. 4,000 mL = _____ L

10. 1,000 m = _____ km

11. 6,000 mg = _____ g

12. 2 L = _____ mL

13. 8 yd = _____ ft

14. 3 gal = _____ qt

15. 6 lb = _____ oz

16. 24 pt = _____ gal

17. 2 T = _____ lb

18. 2,640 ft = _____ mi

Write the letter that indicates the temperature.

19. 4°C _____

20. ⁻1°C _____

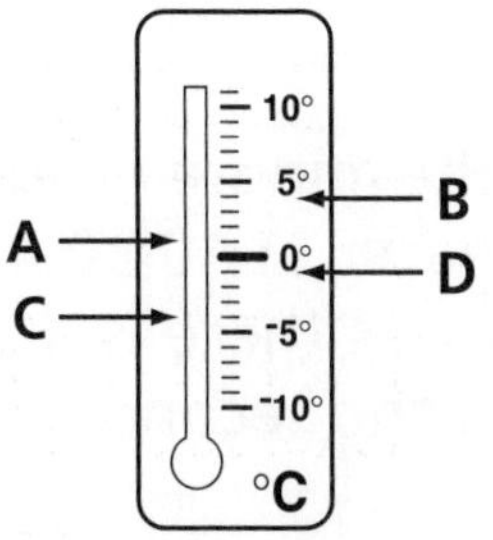

Write the letter that indicates the temperature.

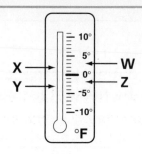

21. 2°F _____

22. ⁻2°F _____

Find the perimeter and area of the figure.

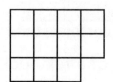

23. Perimeter = _____ units

24. Area = _____ square units

25. Perimeter = _____ cm

4 cm

2 cm

26. Area = _____ square cm

27. Perimeter = _____ units

28. Area = _____ square units

Find the surface area and volume of each rectangular prism.

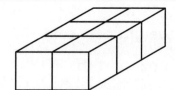

29. Surface area = _____ square units

30. Volume = _____ cubic units

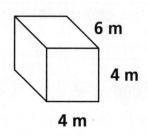

6 m

4 m

31. Surface area = _____ square m

32. Volume = _____ cubic m

4 m

Solve.

33. Which two letters on this number line are **6** units apart?

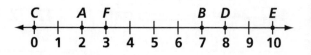

_____

34. A **90**–minute long movie begins showing in a theater at **10:30** A.M. every morning. Between movies there is a **30**-minute break. What time will the second movie of the day end?

_____

1 A contest has 5 winners. Each winner gets $7,600 in prize money. What is the total amount of prize money?

A $34,600   C $36,600   E NH

B $35,000   D $38,000

2 Which phrase describes the intersection of Green Street and Maple Street?

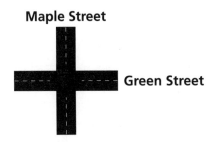

Maple Street

Green Street

F Perpendicular lines

G Vertical lines

H Parallel lines

J Horizontal lines

3 Waiters at a restaurant put two rectangular tables together. One table is $4\frac{1}{3}$ feet long. The second table is $5\frac{1}{2}$ feet long. They place these tables end to end to make one long table. How long a table will they make?

A $9\frac{5}{6}$ feet   C $9\frac{2}{3}$ feet   E NH

B $9\frac{3}{4}$ feet   D $8\frac{5}{6}$ feet

4 Suppose you folded each of these letters in half. Which could you fold to show line symmetry?

F   G   H   J

5 A field has 33 rows of tomato plants. Each row has 25 plants. How many plants are in the field?

A 825   C 800   E NH

B 815   D 750

6 The Celsius thermometers show the temperature at noon and at midnight. How many degrees colder was the temperature at midnight?

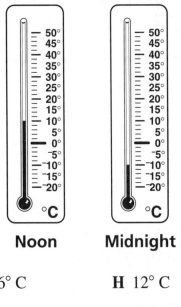

Noon   Midnight

F 26° C   H 12° C

G 20° C   J 10° C

7 Which angle shown is less than a right angle?

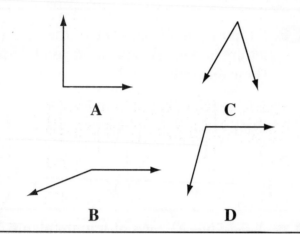

A

C

B

D

8 Four students record the time it takes them to finish eating their lunch.

Name	Time Spent Eating Lunch
Jackson	$\frac{1}{4}$ hour
An	$\frac{1}{8}$ hour
Maria	$\frac{1}{2}$ hour
Bernard	$\frac{3}{8}$ hour

Which lists the students in order from the *least* time to the *most* time spent eating lunch?

F An, Jackson, Bernard, Maria

G Maria, Jackson, Bernard, An

H Maria, Bernard, Jackson, An

J An, Jackson, Maria, Bernard

9 Choose the shape that answers this riddle.

I have exactly 3 sides that are the same length. What shape am I?

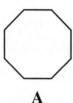

A

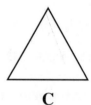

C

B

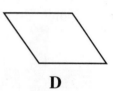

D

10 Which mixed number is equivalent to $\frac{17}{4}$?

F $4\frac{1}{4}$ **H** $5\frac{3}{4}$

G $4\frac{1}{2}$ **J** $17\frac{1}{4}$

11 What number is a common factor of both 18 and 42?

A 9   **C** 7

B 8   **D** 6

12 Lorraine rode her bicycle $\frac{3}{4}$ of a mile. Joanne rode her bicycle $\frac{5}{8}$ of a mile. How much farther did Lorraine ride her bicycle?

F $\frac{1}{2}$ mile   **H** $\frac{1}{4}$ mile   **K** NH

G $\frac{3}{8}$ mile   **J** $\frac{1}{8}$ mile

UNIT 8 • TABLE OF CONTENTS

Decimals

Dear Family,

During the next few weeks, our math class will be learning about decimals.

You can expect to see homework that provides practice with comparing and ordering decimals. Here is a sample you may want to keep handy to give help if needed.

Comparing and Ordering Decimals

To put decimals such as **2.04**, **1.9**, **3.1**, and **2.77** in order from least to greatest, you can use place value.

First, align the decimal points in each number.

2.04
1.9
3.1
2.77

Compare the digits in each column starting at the greatest place value. The digit in the ones place has the greatest value in each of these decimals. Since **3** has the greatest value, **3.1** is the greatest number. Since **1** has the least value, **1.9** is the least number. The other two numbers are between **1.9** and **3.1**.

↓
2.04
1.9
3.1
2.77

Both of the numbers have **2** in the ones place. So, you need to compare their digits in the next column, the tenths place. Compare these digits. Since **7** is greater than **0**, **2.77** is greater than **2.04**.

↓
2.04
1.9
3.1
2.77

Once all the numbers have been compared, you can put them in order from least to greatest.

least → greatest
1.9   2.04   2.77   3.1

During this unit, students will need to continue practicing addition and subtraction facts.

Sincerely,

Each of these squares is divided into **10** equal parts.

The mixed number $1\frac{4}{10}$ represents the shaded regions.

You can write the mixed number $1\frac{4}{10}$ like this: **1.4**

decimal point

Read **1.4** as "one **and** four tenths." Say "and" for the decimal point.

Numbers such as **1.4, 3.5** (three and five tenths), and **0.8** (eight tenths) are called **decimals**.

Circle the decimal that represents the shaded regions.

1.    3.2   2.3   2.5

2.    6.1   2.6   1.6

3. 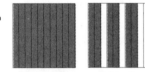   2.7   1.7   7.2

4. 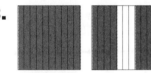   9.0   0.9   1.9

Write a mixed number and a decimal for the shaded regions.

5.   ___ ___   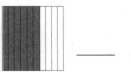   ___ ___

6.    ___ ___      ___ ___

You can show decimals on a number line. Notice that the distance between **0** and **1** on the number line below is **10** times as great as the distance between each tenth.

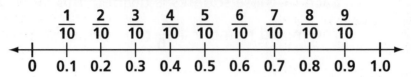

Write the missing decimals and fractions on the number line.

7.

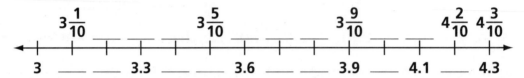

Write the fraction or mixed number as a decimal.

8. $\dfrac{3}{10} =$ _____ $\dfrac{6}{10} =$ _____ $\dfrac{10}{10} =$ _____ $\dfrac{15}{10} =$ _____

9. $4\dfrac{2}{10} =$ _____ $2\dfrac{8}{10} =$ _____ $38\dfrac{7}{10} =$ _____ $55\dfrac{4}{10} =$ _____

Write the decimal as a fraction or mixed number.

10. $0.9 =$ _____ $0.2 =$ _____ $4.8 =$ _____ $39.0 =$ _____

11. $0.7 =$ _____ $1.3 =$ _____ $7.4 =$ _____ $8.2 =$ _____

Problem Solving
Reasoning   **Solve.**

12. Chet has a block of wood that measures **0.1** meter on each side. How many blocks would he need to make a row of blocks **1** meter long?

_____

Test Prep ★ Mixed Review

13 Angela is 60 inches tall. What is her height in feet?

   A 4   **C** 6

   B 5   **D** 7

14 A rectangle has an area of 36 square meters. Which of the following could be the measurement of its perimeter?

   F 72 meters   **H** 12 meters

   G 24 meters   **J** 8 meters

Name _____

Each of these squares is divided into **100** equal parts. These parts are called hundredths.

You can show hundredths in mixed numbers, decimals, or words.

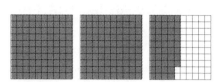

$2\dfrac{48}{100}$ ← **mixed number**

2.48 ← **decimal**

two **and** forty-eight hundredths ← **words**

Circle the decimal that represents the shaded parts.

1.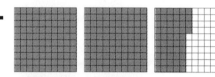

2.01   2.10   1.02

2.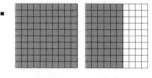

1.60   1.10   1.06

3.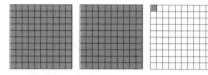

2.05   2.54   2.45

4.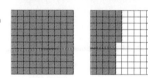

1.45   1.40   1.54

Write a mixed number and a decimal for the shaded parts.

5.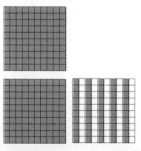

_____ _____   _____ _____

6.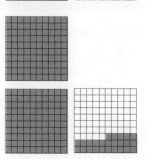

_____ _____   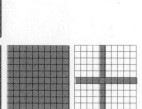 _____ _____

A number line can show how fractions, mixed numbers, and decimals are related. Write the missing fractions, mixed numbers, and decimals on the number line below.

7.

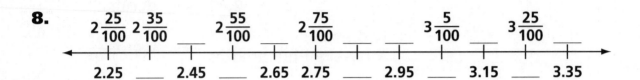

$\frac{5}{100}$ ___ $\frac{25}{100}$ ___ ___ ___ ___ ___ ___

0 ___ 0.15 ___ ___ 0.50 ___ ___ 0.90 1

8.

$2\frac{25}{100}$ $2\frac{35}{100}$ ___ $2\frac{55}{100}$ ___ $2\frac{75}{100}$ ___ ___ $3\frac{5}{100}$ ___ $3\frac{25}{100}$ ___

2.25 ___ 2.45 ___ 2.65 2.75 ___ 2.95 ___ 3.15 ___ 3.35

Write the number as a decimal and as a mixed number.

9. three and two tenths   seven and seven hundredths

_____   _____

Write the decimal in words.

10. 4.6 _____

11. 0.7 _____

12. 5.09 _____

| Problem Solving |
| Reasoning |

Solve.

13. Jorge said **0.1** mile is **10** times as far as **0.01** mile. Is he correct? Use a number line to show why.

_____

14. Helen said **0.4** is less than **0.40**. Peter said the numbers were equal. Who is correct? Use shaded squares to show why.

_____

Test Prep ★ Mixed Review

15 Which fraction is in simplest form?

A $\frac{7}{8}$ **C** $\frac{6}{10}$

B $\frac{4}{12}$ **D** $\frac{4}{6}$

16 Which group of fractions is in order from *greatest* to *least*?

F $\frac{3}{4}, \frac{2}{3}, \frac{1}{2}, \frac{1}{4}$ **H** $\frac{2}{3}, \frac{3}{4}, \frac{1}{2}, \frac{1}{4}$

G $\frac{1}{4}, \frac{1}{2}, \frac{2}{3}, \frac{3}{4}$ **J** $\frac{1}{4}, \frac{1}{2}, \frac{3}{4}, \frac{2}{3}$

Name _____

Comparing and Ordering Decimals

One way to compare decimals is to use models.

These models show **2.1** and **2.8**.   These models show **2.05** and **2.04**.

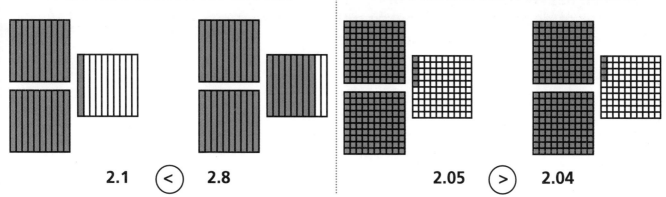

2.1 (<) 2.8   2.05 (>) 2.04

Another way to compare decimals is to use a number line.

Compare 2.73 and 2.68.

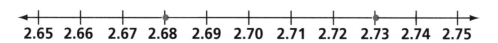

2.65 2.66 2.67 2.68 2.69 2.70 2.71 2.72 2.73 2.74 2.75

- Locate each decimal on the number line.

- Compare. The decimal farther to the left is less.   2.73 (>) 2.68
  The decimal farther to the right is greater.

- Write >, <, or =.

Compare. Write >, <, or =.

1. 1 ◯ 0.1   0.3 ◯ 0.7   0.8 ◯ 0.80

2. 2.35 ◯ 2.26   3.46 ◯ 3.46   5.37 ◯ 5.4

Compare these decimals. Then write them in order from least to greatest.

| 8.03 | 3.80 | 3.08 | 4.56 | 4.05 | 5.00 |

3. _____ _____ _____ _____ _____ _____
       least   greatest

| 9.10 | 12.1 | 10.9 | 1.10 | 9.12 | 1.29 |

4. _____ _____ _____ _____ _____ _____
       least   greatest

You can also use place value to compare decimals.

1. Align the decimal points. You may have to add zeros so each decimal has the same number of decimal places.

3.10
3.15

2. Compare the digits in each place. Start with the greatest place value. Work to the right until you find the digits that are different.

↓
3.10
3.15
↑

3. Write >, <, or =.

Think: 0 < 5

3.1 (<) 3.15

Other Examples

↓
2.34
2.14   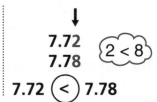 3 > 1

2.34 (>) 2.14

↓
4.24
2.89   4 > 2

4.24 (>) 2.89

↓
7.72
7.78   2 < 8

7.72 (<) 7.78

Is the statement True or False? Write *T* or *F*.

5. 4.78 < 5.79 _____   49.08 = 49.80 _____   11.3 < 10.8 _____

6. 52.71 > 25.71 _____   260.7 = 260.07 _____   201 > 20.19 _____

7. 68.46 > 684.60 _____   831.45 < 543.47 _____   72.98 = 72.980 _____

✓ Quick Check

Write a fraction and decimal for the shaded part.

Work Space.

8. _____ _____

9. _____ _____

10. _____ _____

11. 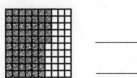 _____ _____

Compare. Write >, <, or =.

12. 0.2 ◯ 0.20   **13.** 0.23 ◯ 0.21   **14.** 0.45 ◯ 0.4

15. 6.45 ◯ 2.89   **16.** 7.05 ◯ 7.03   **17.** 9.46 ◯ 9.48

Name _____

Problem Solving Strategy:
Find a Pattern

To find the missing number in a sequence, you need to look for a pattern and find the rule.

Problem

What would be the next number in this sequence?
0.26, 0.36, 0.46, 0.56, 0.66, 0.76, _?_

---

1 Understand   As you reread, ask yourself questions.

- What information do you have?
  The first six numbers in a sequence:
    0.26, 0.36, 0.46, 0.56, 0.66, 0.76

- What do you need to find out?

_____

---

2 Decide   Choose a method for solving.

Try the strategy Find a Pattern.

- Look at how each number is related to the next number.

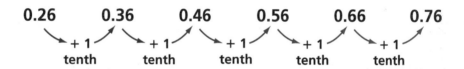

0.26   0.36   0.46   0.56   0.66   0.76
       + 1   + 1   + 1   + 1   + 1
       tenth   tenth   tenth   tenth   tenth

---

3 Solve   What is the pattern?

- How does each number change?

_____

Use the pattern to find the missing number.

0.76 _____ = _____

---

4 Look back   Check your answer. Write the answer below.

Answer _____

- Why was it important to try the pattern with all the numbers?

_____

_____

Solve. Use the **Find a Pattern** strategy or any other strategy you have learned.

1. What is the missing number in this sequence?

<u>?</u>, 0.15, 0.25, 0.35, 0.45

Think: Why would working backward help with this problem?

_____

Answer _____

2. What is the missing number in this sequence?

4.3, <u>?</u>, 4.2, 4.15, 4.1, 4.05, 4.00

Think: What is the relationship between each number and the next?

_____

Answer _____

3. Use **9** toothpicks to form **5** triangles. Draw a picture.

4. The distance around a bicycling course is $1\frac{3}{4}$ mi. Danusa rode around the course **3** times. How many miles did she ride?

_____

5. Luann needs **20** minutes to get dressed, eat breakfast, and get ready for school. It takes her **15** minutes to walk to school. If school starts at **8:30** A.M. and Luann likes to arrive **10** minutes early, what time should she get up?

_____

6. The distance Alex jogs follows a pattern. On Sunday, he jogs **1.5** mi, on Monday **1.75** mi, on Tuesday **2** mi, and on Wednesday **2.25** mi. If he continues this pattern, how many miles will Alex jog on Saturday?

_____

7. Use the clues to find Katherine's favorite number.

- It is less than **20**.
- When you divide it by **3**, the remainder is **1**.
- When you divide it by **4**, the remainder is **3**.
- When you divide it by **5**, the remainder is **2**.

_____

8. At a certain grocery store, the amount you save increases according to a pattern. On the first visit, you save **$.25**. On the second visit you save **$.50**, On the third visit, you save **$.75**, and so on. How much will you save on your fifth visit?

_____

Decimals and Fractions

A number line can help you write a fraction as a decimal.
Study the number line below.

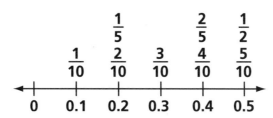

Equivalent fractions can be used to write fractions as decimals.

Write $\frac{1}{5}$ as a decimal.

Rewrite $\frac{1}{5}$ as a fraction with a denominator of **10**.

$\frac{1 \times 2}{5 \times 2} = \frac{2}{10}$; and $\frac{2}{10} = 0.2$

Write $\frac{3}{4}$ as a decimal.

Rewrite $\frac{3}{4}$ as a fraction with a denominator of **100**.

$\frac{3 \times 25}{4 \times 25} = \frac{75}{100}$; and $\frac{75}{100} = 0.75$

Write the missing fractions and decimals on each number line.

1.

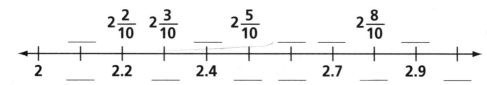

2.

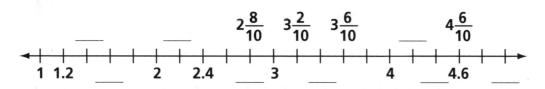

Write a decimal for the fraction or mixed number.

3. $\frac{3}{10} =$ _____ $\frac{1}{2} =$ _____ $2\frac{1}{5} =$ _____ $3\frac{9}{10} =$ _____

4. $\frac{2}{4} =$ _____ $5\frac{2}{5} =$ _____ $3\frac{7}{10} =$ _____ $7\frac{3}{5} =$ _____

Write a fraction or mixed number for the decimal.

5. $0.8 = \frac{8}{10}$ $0.9 = \frac{9}{10}$ $4.2 =$ _____ $1.3 =$ _____

6. $0.5 =$ _____ $1.6 =$ _____ $0.7 =$ _____ $0.4 =$ _____

Is the statement True or False? Write *T* or *F*.

7. Decimals and fractions both show parts of a whole. _____

8. You can write **0.7** as a fraction in more than one way. _____

9. There is only one way to write a decimal such as **7.5** as a mixed number. _____

10. On the number line there are only 2 decimal numbers between **0.2** and **0.5**. _____

Circle the equivalent decimal for the fraction. (Hint: Write the decimals as fractions, then simplify if possible.)

11. $\frac{6}{25}$ 0.06   0.24

12. $\frac{3}{20}$ 0.15   0.60

13. $1\frac{9}{25}$ 1.70   1.36

14. $\frac{3}{12}$ 0.25   0.24

15. $\frac{3}{15}$ 0.15   0.20

16. $\frac{16}{20}$ 1.80   0.8

Problem Solving Reasoning Solve.

17. Chris knows that $\frac{1}{4}$ equals **0.25**, $\frac{2}{4}$ equals **0.50**, and $\frac{3}{4}$ equals **0.75**. What pattern can he use to write a decimal that equals $\frac{5}{4}$? What decimal does he write?

_____

_____

Test Prep ★ Mixed Review

18 The length of a desk is 2 meters. What is the length of the desk in centimeters?

A 0.2   C 24

B 20   D 200

19 An athlete ran a 200-meter race 0.03 seconds faster than she ran this distance the day before. What is 0.03 in words?

F Thirty   H Three tenths

G Three   J Three hundredths

Name _____

You can use a number line to help round decimals to the nearest whole number.

Round **4.8** to the nearest whole number.

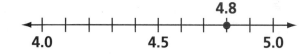

Since **4.8** is closer to **5** than to **4**, **4.8** rounds to **5**.

Round **9.4** to the nearest whole number.

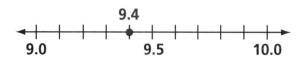

Since **9.4** is closer to **9** than to **10**, **9.4** rounds to **9**.

> When a decimal number is halfway between two whole numbers, round up to the next whole number. For example, **7.5** rounds to **8**.

You can also use place value to help round decimals.

Round **5.78** to the nearest tenth.	Round **12.79** to the nearest whole number.
• First look at the digit in the hundredths place.	• First look at the digit in the tenths place.
5.78	**12.79**
• If it is equal to or greater than **5**, round up. **8 > 5**, so **5.78** rounds to **5.8**.	• If it is equal to or greater than **5**, round up. **7 > 5**, so **12.79** rounds to **13**.

**Round the decimal to the nearest whole number.
Use a number line if you need to.**

1. 3.7 _____   0.9 _____   4.7 _____   13.8 _____   17.0 _____

2. 10.1 _____   0.1 _____   0.5 _____   4.5 _____   1.90 _____

Round the decimal to the nearest tenth.

3. 0.39 _____   0.22 _____   1.09 _____   34.92 _____   0.67 _____

4. 6.48 _____   12.00 _____   0.15 _____   5.55 _____   9.09 _____

You can use rounding to estimate sums and differences.
Estimate by rounding to the nearest whole number.

5. 5.78 rounds to __   5.38 rounds to __ $12.07
     + 6.89 rounds to + __   − 1.07 rounds to − __   + $5.01

6.   9.38   0.44   88.00   34.75 $3.54 $14.36
      + 4.55   − 0.20   − 4.02   + 9.4   + $6.14   − $6.92

| Problem Solving Reasoning | Solve. |

7. Greg bought lunch at the school cafeteria. He spent **$3.75** for a sandwich and **$.75** for a drink. Dessert cost **$1.25**. To the nearest dollar, how much did he spend?

_____

8. Three friends are going to the movies. Tickets cost **$6.75** each. They expect to pay about **$21** for the **3** tickets. Is this reasonable? Explain.

_____

_____

 Quick Check

Find the point on the number line that represents the fraction or decimal. Write the letter next to the fraction or decimal.

Work Space.

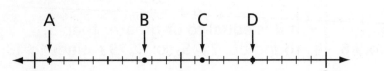

9. 1.5 ____   **10.** $\frac{3}{4}$ ____   **11.** $\frac{1}{10}$ ____   **12.** 1.15 ____

Round the decimal to the nearest whole number.

13. 2.7 ____   **14.** 7.2 ____   **15.** 6.5 ____

Round the decimal to the nearest tenth.

16. 3.67 ____   **17.** 10.85 ____   **18.** 1.77 ____

Name _____

You can use what you know about adding whole numbers to add decimals.

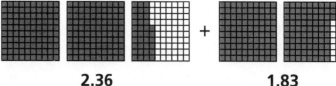

2.36   +   1.83

Find 2.36 + 1.83.

1. Line up the decimal points. Add as you would whole numbers.	2. Write the decimal point in the answer.	3. Use estimation to check your answer.

1. Line up the decimal points. Add as you would whole numbers.

$$\begin{array}{r} 2.36 \\ + 1.83 \\ \hline 4.19 \end{array}$$

2. Write the decimal point in the answer.

$$\begin{array}{r} \overset{1}{2.36} \\ + 1.83 \\ \hline 4.19 \end{array}$$
↑

3. Use estimation to check your answer.

$$\begin{array}{r} \overset{1}{2.36} \\ + 1.83 \\ \hline 4.19 \end{array} \quad \begin{array}{c} \text{rounds down} \\ \longrightarrow \\ \text{rounds up} \\ \longrightarrow \end{array} \quad \begin{array}{r} 2 \\ + 2 \\ \hline 4 \end{array}$$

Since **4.19** is close to **4**, the answer is reasonable.

Whenever you add decimals:

• Place a decimal point in the answer.

• Use estimation to check if your answer is reasonable.

Use estimation to place the decimal point in the answer.

1. 5.46 + 3.56 = 9 0 2   0.03 + 1.2 = 1 2 3   4.39 + 3.0 + 1 = 8 3 9

2. 0.34 + 0.3 = 0 6 4   288 + 3.4 = 2 9 1 4   1.38 + 20.4 + 13 = 3 4 7 8

Find the sum. Estimate to help make sure your answer is reasonable.

3.
$$\begin{array}{r} 2.35 \\ + 4.55 \end{array} \quad \begin{array}{r} 8.42 \\ + 0.20 \end{array} \quad \begin{array}{r} 8.00 \\ + 4.02 \end{array} \quad \begin{array}{r} 54.05 \\ + 9.4 \end{array} \quad \begin{array}{r} 5.54 \\ + 5.84 \end{array}$$

4.
$$\begin{array}{r} 15.05 \\ + 8.61 \end{array} \quad \begin{array}{r} 4.11 \\ + 0.99 \end{array} \quad \begin{array}{r} 6.81 \\ + 0.04 \end{array} \quad \begin{array}{r} 4.89 \\ + 7.12 \end{array} \quad \begin{array}{r} 8.32 \\ + 9.41 \end{array}$$

Find the sum. Estimate to help make sure your answer is reasonable.

5.

13.01	6.72	7.99	15.9	4.33
1.66	3.61	2.09	5.77	2.41
+ 4.9	+ 8.52	+ 5.77	+ 8.32	+ 0.31

Find the sum. Be sure to line up the decimal points.

6. 35.9 + 25.44 _____   0.38 + 23.95 _____

7. 14.79 + 3.56 _____   7.39 + 6.2 _____

8. 1.24 + 4.5 + 1.02 _____   8.25 + 7.55 + 0.29 _____

Problem Solving
Reasoning

Solve.

9. Jeff rode **13.75** kilometers on his bike one month and **12.4** kilometers the next month. What was the total number of kilometers he rode in both months?

_____

10. Ellen has **3.5** yards of ribbon for a project. She buys **4.75** yards more. She estimates she now has about **9** yards of ribbon in all. Is her estimate greater or less than the actual amount she has? Explain.

_____

_____

_____

Test Prep ★ Mixed Review

11. A square has a perimeter of 24 feet. Which of the following could be the measurement of its area in square feet?

A 36   C 24

B 28   D 18

12. Manuel rode his bicycle $3\frac{1}{4}$ kilometers. What decimal is equivalent to $3\frac{1}{4}$?

F 3.41   H 3.20

G 3.25   J 3.14

Subtracting Decimals

You can use what you know about subtracting whole numbers to help subtract decimals.

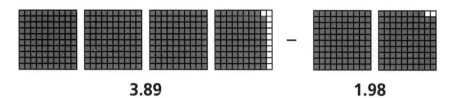

3.89   1.98

Find 3.89 − 1.98.

1. Line up the decimal points. Subtract as you would whole numbers.

$$\begin{array}{r} 3.89 \\ -\ 1.98 \\ \hline 1\,91 \end{array}$$

2. Write the decimal point in the answer.

$$\begin{array}{r} \overset{2}{\cancel{3}}.\overset{18}{\cancel{8}}9 \\ -\ 1.98 \\ \hline 1.91 \end{array}$$
↑

3. Use estimation to check your answer.

$$\begin{array}{r} \overset{2}{\cancel{3}}.\overset{18}{\cancel{8}}9 \\ -\ 1.98 \\ \hline 1.91 \end{array}$$

rounds up → 4
rounds up → − 2
⎯⎯
2

Since **1.91** is close to **2**, the answer is reasonable.

Whenever you subtract decimals:

- Place a decimal point in the answer.

- Use estimation to check if your answer is reasonable.

Use estimation to place the decimal point correctly in the answer.

1. 6.43 − 0.26 = 6 1 7   8.77 − 0.9 = 7 8 7   45.0 − 1.9 = 4 3 1

2. 67.34 − 3.2 = 6 4 1 4   9.62 − 8.4 = 1 2 2   9.7 − 2.5 = 7 2

Find the difference. Estimate to be sure your answer is reasonable.

3.
$$\begin{array}{r} 9.75 \\ -\ 3.55 \\ \hline \end{array}$$
$$\begin{array}{r} 6.32 \\ -\ 0.60 \\ \hline \end{array}$$
$$\begin{array}{r} 9.90 \\ -\ 7.04 \\ \hline \end{array}$$
$$\begin{array}{r} 84.04 \\ -\ 7.16 \\ \hline \end{array}$$
$$\begin{array}{r} 10.24 \\ -\ 8.04 \\ \hline \end{array}$$

4.
$$\begin{array}{r} 9.66 \\ -\ 8.51 \\ \hline \end{array}$$
$$\begin{array}{r} 3.91 \\ -\ 0.39 \\ \hline \end{array}$$
$$\begin{array}{r} 2.21 \\ -\ 0.24 \\ \hline \end{array}$$
$$\begin{array}{r} 5.49 \\ -\ 3.77 \\ \hline \end{array}$$
$$\begin{array}{r} 4.38 \\ -\ 3.21 \\ \hline \end{array}$$

Find the difference. Estimate to be sure your answer is reasonable.

5.

	7.6	9.41	12.00	8.77	3.21
	− 4.2	− 3.54	− 2.99	− 0.02	− 0.91

Find the difference. Be sure to line up the decimal points.

6. 21.9 − 20.44 _____   82.9 − 81.95 _____

7. 14.12 − 7.50 _____   8.32 − 7.8 _____

8. 1.24 − 1.03 _____   33.22 − 10.29 _____

9. 6.4 − 4.7 _____   14.1 − 6.05 _____

Problem Solving Reasoning Solve.

10. Josh saved **$5.89** one week. The next week he saved **$4.75**. How much more did he save the first week?

_____

11. Maria ran **1** mi in **8.7** minutes. Her friend Teresa ran the same distance in **7.9** minutes. Is the difference in minutes more or less than **1** minute?

_____

 Quick Check

Solve.

Work Space.

12.

	1.53
	+ 2.33

13.

	2.78
	+ 2.13

14.

	3.45
	+ 3.67

15.

	3.69
	− 1.43

16.

	4.52
	− 2.37

17.

	5.47
	− 1.79

Name _____

Some problems give more facts than you need. You need to decide which facts are necessary.

Some problems do not give enough facts. In this lesson, you will decide what fact or facts you need to solve a problem.

Tips to Remember:

| 1. Understand | 2. Decide | 3. Solve | 4. Look back |

- Read each problem more than once. Circle the important words and numbers. Cross out the words and numbers that you don't need.
- Think about each fact in the problem. Ask yourself: Is this an extra fact? Or do I need it to find a solution?
- Predict the answer. Then solve the problem. Compare your answer with your prediction.

Cross out the extra information. Then solve the problem. If information is missing, name the fact or facts needed on the answer lines.

1. In Florida, the highest monthly average temperature is **91.7** °F. The lowest monthly average is **39.9** °F. The highest temperature ever recorded in Florida is **109** °F. What is the difference between the highest and lowest monthly temperatures?

Think: How does the question help you decide what facts are needed?

_____

_____

Answer _____

_____

2. The population of the state of New Jersey is **7,945,298**. It has an average of **1065.4** people per square mile. Massachusetts has an average of **770.7** people per square mile. What is the difference in the populations of the two states?

Think: What two numbers do you need to compare?

_____

_____

Answer _____

_____

Cross out the extra information. Then solve the problem. If information is missing, name the fact or fact that you need.

3. California has more public schools than any other state. California has **1,481** more public schools than Texas, which has **4,185**. Illinois has **4,032** and New York has **4,032**. How many more public schools does California have than New York?

_____

_____

4. New Mexico is the fifth largest state. The land area of New Mexico is **121,364** square miles. Its water area is **234** square miles. What is the total area of New Mexico?

_____

_____

5. Here are the populations of the major cities in Nebraska.

Bellevue	30,982
Grand Island	39,386
Kearney	24,396
Lincoln	191,972
Omaha	335,795

What is the population of Nebraska?

_____

_____

6. Alaska and Hawaii were the last two states to become part of the United States. Alaska became the forty-ninth state on January **3, 1959**. Hawaii became the fiftieth state in August of the same year. For how many days did the United States have exactly **49** states?

_____

_____

Extend Your Thinking

7. Explain the method you used to solve problem **3**.

_____

_____

_____

_____

8. Make up a word problem using facts from this lesson. Solve the problem.

_____

_____

_____

_____

Write the decimal in words.

1. 2.08 _____

2. 0.4 _____

Write the fraction or mixed number as a decimal.

3. $\frac{3}{4}$ _____

4. $7\frac{1}{10}$ _____

5. $\frac{1}{2}$ _____

6. $8\frac{3}{100}$ _____

Write the decimal as a fraction or mixed number.

7. 0.3 _____

8. 13.01 _____

9. 6.7 _____

Compare. Write >, <, or =.

10. 0.03 ◯ 0.21

11. 1 ◯ 0.72

12. 9.2 ◯ 9.1

13. 5.3 ◯ 5.35

Write these decimals in order from greatest to least.

1.14, 0.8, 2.3, 0.9

2.15, 2.05, 2.75, 2.09

14. _____ _____ _____ _____

15. _____ _____ _____ _____

Round the decimal to the nearest tenth.

16. 3.61 _____

17. 7.66 _____

18. 13.55 _____

19. 8.12 _____

Round the decimal to the nearest whole number.

20. 4.76 _____

21. 17.07 _____

22. 7.51 _____

23. 8.43 _____

Find the sum or difference.

24. 8.3
    + 14.02

25. 5.05
    + 9.1

26. 4.72
    − 2.31

27. 6.4
    − 3.66

Solve. Which number comes next in the sequence?

28. 0.8, 0.85, 0.9, 0.95, 1.0, 1.05 _____

Cross out the extra information. Then solve the problem.

29. In a class of **24** students, **11** girls and **9** boys like to play soccer. How many students in the class like to play soccer? _____

1 Which are parallel line segments?

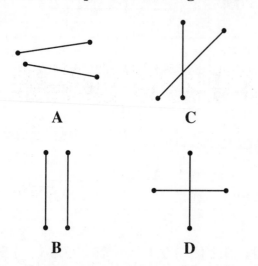

A   C

B   D

2 Four students timed how long they waited for the bus one morning.

Student	Time Spent Waiting
Steven	**7.55** minutes
Emily	**6.97** minutes
Sarah	**7.7** minutes
Ralph	**7.35** minutes

Which lists them in order from the *greatest* to the *least* time waiting?

F Emily, Ralph, Steven, Sarah

G Sarah, Steven, Emily, Ralph

H Sarah, Steven, Ralph, Emily

J Steven, Sarah, Ralph, Emily

3 Arthur's family drove 72.9 miles on Saturday. What is this distance rounded to the nearest mile?

A 70 miles   **C** 73 miles   **E** NH

B 72 miles   **D** 74 miles

4 Which angle shown is greater than a right angle?

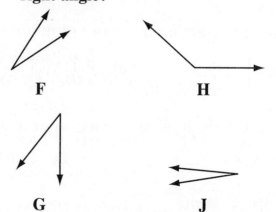

F   H

G   J

5 Amanda added $\frac{1}{3}$ c milk and $\frac{1}{2}$ c water to a recipe. How much liquid did she add in all?

A $\frac{3}{6}$ c   **C** $\frac{3}{4}$ c   **E** NH

B $\frac{2}{3}$ c   **D** $\frac{5}{6}$ c

6 The Fahrenheit thermometers show the temperature in the morning and in the afternoon. How many degrees warmer was the temperature in the afternoon?

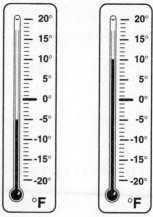

Morning   Afternoon

F 3°F   **H** 15°F

G 5°F   **J** 20°F

UNIT 9 • TABLE OF CONTENTS

Division with 2-Digit Divisors

We will be using this vocabulary:

dividend the number that is divided
divisor the number that is divided by
quotient the answer to a division problem

Dear Family,

During the next few weeks, our math class will be learning and practicing division of whole numbers by **2**-digit numbers.

You can expect to see homework that provides practice with dividing whole numbers by **2**-digit numbers. Here is a sample you may want to keep handy to give help if needed.

Four-Digit Dividends

Divide: $61\overline{)1{,}285}$

1. $\begin{array}{r} ? \\ 61\overline{)1{,}285} \end{array}$ Not enough thousands to divide.

2. $\begin{array}{r} ? \\ 61\overline{)1{,}285} \end{array}$ Not enough hundreds to divide.

3. $\begin{array}{r} ? \\ 61\overline{)1{,}285} \\ -1\,22 \\ \hline 6 \end{array}$ Divide tens. Think: $\begin{array}{r} 2 \\ 60\overline{)120} \end{array}$

4. $\begin{array}{r} 2\,? \\ 61\overline{)1{,}2\,8\,5} \\ -1\,2\,2 \\ \hline 6\,5 \\ -\,6\,1 \\ \hline 4 \end{array}$ Divide ones. Think: $\begin{array}{r} 1 \\ 60\overline{)60} \end{array}$

5. Write the answer using a remainder. $\begin{array}{r} 21 \text{ R4} \\ 61\overline{)1{,}285} \end{array}$

During this unit, students will need to continue practicing division and multiplication facts.

Sincerely,

Dividing with 2-Digit Divisors

You can use estimation to help you know where to place the first digit in a quotient.

Divide 83 by 38.

1. Estimate. Round the divisor and the dividend. Try **2**. Write it in the ones place in the quotient.	2. Try the estimate. Multiply. Subtract. Write the remainder in the quotient.
$38\overline{)83}^{?}$ rounds to $40\overline{)80}^{?}$ Think: $4\overline{)8}^{2}$ Then $40\overline{)80}^{2}$	$38\overline{)83}^{\ 2\ R7}$ $-76 \leftarrow 2 \times 38$ 7

Estimate to place the digit in each quotient. Then divide.

Estimate.

1. $31\overline{)94}$ rounds to: $30\overline{)90}^{?}$

Try **3**.

2. $39\overline{)89}$ rounds to: $40\overline{)90}^{?}$

Try **2**.

3. $41\overline{)84}$ rounds to: $\overline{)}^{?}$

Try _____.

4. $54\overline{)78}$ rounds to: $\overline{)}^{?}$

Try _____.

5. $39\overline{)94}$ rounds to: $\overline{)}^{?}$

Try _____.

6. $28\overline{)81}$ rounds to: $\overline{)}^{?}$

Try _____.

7. $19\overline{)74}$ rounds to: $\overline{)}^{?}$

Try _____.

8. $22\overline{)93}$ rounds to: $\overline{)}^{?}$

Try _____.

Divide.

9. $33\overline{)54}$ $19\overline{)45}$ $21\overline{)93}$ $55\overline{)84}$

10. $36\overline{)82}$ $54\overline{)65}$ $69\overline{)77}$ $24\overline{)32}$

11. $39\overline{)83}$ $28\overline{)87}$ $18\overline{)82}$ $43\overline{)93}$

12. $37\overline{)89}$ $19\overline{)83}$ $41\overline{)93}$ $52\overline{)79}$

| Problem Solving |
| Reasoning |

Solve.

13. If **24** apples can fit in a tray and there are **89** apples altogether, how many trays can be filled? How many apples will be left over?

14. If **32** potatoes can fit in a sack and there are **74** potatoes altogether, how many sacks can be filled? How many potatoes will be left over?

Test Prep ★ Mixed Review

15 Sam's sneakers have a mass of 2 kilograms. What is the mass of his sneakers in grams?

A 20

B 200

C 2,000

D 20,000

16 The course for the bicycle race is 27.75 kilometers long. What is this distance rounded to the nearest tenth?

F 27.5 kilometers

G 27.7 kilometers

H 27.8 kilometers

J 28 kilometers

Sometimes when you divide, your first estimate
will be too large.

Divide: $34\overline{)62}^{?}$

1. Estimate.

$$30\overline{)60}^{2}$$

Try **2**.

2. Divide.

$$\begin{array}{r} 2 \\ 34\overline{)62} \\ -68 \\ \uparrow \end{array}$$

Too large. Try **1**.

3. Adjust.

$$\begin{array}{r} 1 \ \ R28 \\ 34\overline{)62} \\ -34 \\ \hline 28 \end{array}$$

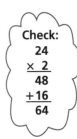

Check:
$$\begin{array}{r} 34 \\ \times\ 1 \\ \hline 34 \\ +48 \\ \hline 62 \end{array}$$

Divide: $24\overline{)64}^{?}$

1. Estimate.

$$20\overline{)60}^{3}$$

Try **3**.

2. Divide.

$$\begin{array}{r} 3 \\ 24\overline{)64} \\ -72 \\ \uparrow \end{array}$$

Too large. Try **2**.

3. Adjust.

$$\begin{array}{r} 2 \ \ R16 \\ 24\overline{)64} \\ -48 \\ \hline 16 \end{array}$$

Check:
$$\begin{array}{r} 24 \\ \times\ 2 \\ \hline 48 \\ +16 \\ \hline 64 \end{array}$$

---

1. Estimate.

Think:

$$30\overline{)90}^{3} \qquad \begin{array}{r} 3 \\ 32\overline{)94} \\ -96 \\ \uparrow \end{array}$$

Try **3**.   Too large.

Try _____.

$$32\overline{)94}$$

2. Estimate.

Think:

$$40\overline{)80}^{2} \qquad \begin{array}{r} 2 \\ 41\overline{)81} \\ -82 \end{array}$$

Try **2**.

Try _____.

$$41\overline{)81}$$

---

3. $23\overline{)66}$

Estimate.   Divide.

4. $12\overline{)73}$

Estimate.   Divide.

---

5. $44\overline{)87}$

Estimate.   Divide.

6. $24\overline{)69}$

Estimate.   Divide.

Sometimes your first estimate will be too small.

Divide: $16\overline{)84}$?

Estimate.   Check.   Divide.
Try **5**.

Think:
$$20\overline{)80} \quad 4$$

$$\begin{array}{r} 4 \\ 16\overline{)84} \\ -64 \\ \hline 20 \uparrow \end{array}$$

$$\begin{array}{r} 5\ \text{R4} \\ 16\overline{)84} \\ -80 \\ \hline 4 \end{array}$$

Try **4**.   The remainder is greater than the divisor. Try again.

Find: $15\overline{)62}$?

Estimate.   Check.   Divide.
Try **4**.

Think:
$$20\overline{)60} \quad 3$$

$$\begin{array}{r} 3 \\ 15\overline{)62} \\ -45 \\ \hline 17 \uparrow \end{array}$$

$$\begin{array}{r} 4\ \text{R2} \\ 15\overline{)62} \\ -60 \\ \hline 2 \end{array}$$

Try **3**.   The remainder is greater than the divisor. Try again.

> **Remember:** The remainder must always be less than the divisor.

Estimate to place the digit in each quotient. Then divide.

7. Estimate.   Try _____.

$$30\overline{)50} \qquad \begin{array}{r} 1 \\ 26\overline{)53} \\ -26 \\ \hline 27 \uparrow \end{array} \qquad 26\overline{)53}$$

Try **1**.   Too large.

8. Estimate.   Try _____.

$$20\overline{)70} \qquad \begin{array}{r} 3 \\ 18\overline{)73} \\ -54 \\ \hline 19 \end{array} \qquad 18\overline{)73}$$

Try **3**.

9. $28\overline{)84}$

Estimate.   Divide.

10. $16\overline{)33}$

Estimate.   Divide.

11. $36\overline{)74}$

Estimate.   Divide.

12. $16\overline{)84}$

Estimate.   Divide.

Name _____

Estimate to place the digit in each quotient. Then divide.

13. 31)‾96̅   41)‾86̅   12)‾74̅

14. 18)‾93̅   34)‾89̅   17)‾87̅

15. 40)‾78̅   45)‾93̅   27)‾82̅

Problem Solving
Reasoning   Solve.

16. A librarian had **84** books to pack in boxes. Each box held **16** books. How many boxes were filled? How many books were left over?

_____

17. Henry uses **12** oranges to make one pint of juice. How many pints can he make from **75** oranges? How many oranges will not be used?

_____

Test Prep ★ Mixed Review

18 Choose the shape that answers this riddle.

I have more than **2** sides that are parallel. What shape am I?

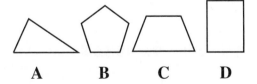

  A   B   C   D

19 Which of these models shows fifty-five hundredths shaded?

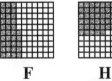

  F   H

  G   J

You can use the same steps to divide with **3**-digit
dividends as you would with **2**-digit dividends.

Divide: $19\overline{)187}^{?}$

Estimate. Round to the nearest **10**. Then
divide.

$20\overline{)190}^{?}$ $19\overline{)187}^{9\ R16}$
Try **9**. $\underline{-171} \leftarrow 9 \times 19$
                              16

| $9 \times 20 = 180$ |

Divide: $64\overline{)203}^{?}$

Estimate. Round to the nearest **10**. Then
divide.

$60\overline{)200}^{?}$ $64\overline{)203}^{3\ R11}$
Try **3**. $\underline{-192} \leftarrow 3 \times 64$
                              11

| $3 \times 60 = 180$ |

| **Remember:** Check your answer. |

Estimate to place the digit in each quotient. Then divide.

1. $54\overline{)221}$

2. $43\overline{)194}$

3. $54\overline{)110}$

4. $44\overline{)134}$

5. $62\overline{)321}$

6. $31\overline{)198}$

7. $37\overline{)219}$

8. $23\overline{)118}$

9. $18\overline{)161}$

Name _____

To divide **105** by **54**, you can estimate first. Since you know that **100 ÷ 50 = 2**, then you know that the first digit of the quotient of **105 ÷ 54** will be in the ones place.

Divide: 54$\overline{)105}$?

1. Estimate.

50$\overline{)100}$ 2

54$\overline{)105}$ 2
$-\ 108$
         ↑
Try **2**.   Too large.

2. Adjust. Try 1.
   Then divide.

54$\overline{)105}$ 1 R51
$-\ 54$
    51

3. Check.

54
$\times\ 1$
54
$+\ 51$
105

Divide: 17$\overline{)104}$?

| The remainder must always be less than the divisor. |

1. Estimate.

20$\overline{)100}$ 5

17$\overline{)104}$ 5
$-\ 85$
    19
     ↑
Try **5**.   Too large.

2. Adjust. Try 6.
   Then divide.

17$\overline{)104}$ 6 R2
$-\ 102$
     2

3. Check.

17
$\times\ 6$
102
$+\ 2$
104

Estimate to place the first digit in the quotient. Then divide.

10. 22$\overline{)163}$

11. 32$\overline{)151}$

12. 82$\overline{)732}$

13. 43$\overline{)341}$

14. 45$\overline{)431}$

15. 57$\overline{)461}$

Estimate to place the first digit in the quotient. Then divide.

16. $28\overline{)205}$ $18\overline{)156}$ $32\overline{)284}$ $56\overline{)472}$

17. $16\overline{)107}$ $66\overline{)635}$ $83\overline{)762}$ $44\overline{)336}$

18. $48\overline{)460}$ $31\overline{)202}$ $43\overline{)294}$ $17\overline{)137}$

| Problem Solving |
| Reasoning |

Solve.

19. Billy had **156** stamps in his collection. He pasted **16** stamps on each page of his album. How many pages were filled? How many stamps were left over?

 Quick Check

Estimate to place the digit in each quotient. Then divide.

Work Space.

20. $37\overline{)82}$ **21.** $23\overline{)75}$ **22.** $45\overline{)93}$

23. $23\overline{)42}$ **24.** $33\overline{)96}$ **25.** $44\overline{)86}$

26. $17\overline{)121}$ **27.** $43\overline{)227}$ **28.** $62\overline{)394}$

2-Digit Quotients

When you divide by a **2**-digit number, you may need to place the first digit in the quotient in the tens or ones place.

Divide 533 by 23.

1. Divide the hundreds.

Not enough hundreds. Regroup to tens.

$$23\overline{)533}$$

2. Regroup hundreds as tens. Estimate. Divide.

Try **2.**
$$\begin{array}{r} 2 \\ 23\overline{)533} \\ -46 \\ \hline 7 \end{array}$$

3. Regroup tens as ones. Bring down the ones digit. Divide.

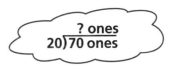

Try **3.**
$$\begin{array}{r} 23\ \text{R4} \\ 23\overline{)533} \\ -46 \\ \hline 73 \\ -69 \\ \hline 4 \end{array}$$

Divide. $\overset{?}{24\overline{)879}}$

1. Estimate. Try **4.** Divide.

$$\begin{array}{r} 4 \\ 24\overline{)879} \\ 96 \end{array} \leftarrow \text{Too large.}$$

2. Adjust. Try **3.** Bring down the next digit.

$$\begin{array}{r} 3 \\ 24\overline{)879} \\ -72 \\ \hline 159 \end{array}$$

3. Multiply. Subtract. Write the remainder in the quotient.

$$\begin{array}{r} 36\ \text{R15} \\ 24\overline{)879} \\ -72 \\ \hline 159 \\ -144 \\ \hline 15 \end{array}$$

4. Check.

$$\begin{array}{r} 24 \\ \times\ 36 \\ \hline 144 \\ +720 \\ \hline 864 \end{array}$$

Divide and check.

1. $36\overline{)823}$ $\quad$ $21\overline{)657}$ $\quad$ $42\overline{)913}$ $\quad$ $18\overline{)624}$

2. $43\overline{)814}$ $\quad$ $14\overline{)683}$ $\quad$ $12\overline{)732}$ $\quad$ $33\overline{)864}$

Divide and check.

3. $27\overline{)865}$ $26\overline{)891}$ $17\overline{)734}$ $16\overline{)641}$

4. $15\overline{)344}$ $26\overline{)834}$ $18\overline{)942}$ $17\overline{)689}$

5. $24\overline{)729}$ $14\overline{)637}$ $19\overline{)854}$ $49\overline{)938}$

6. $12\overline{)562}$ $35\overline{)421}$ $28\overline{)663}$ $50\overline{)748}$

| Problem Solving |
| Reasoning |

Solve.

7. A theater holds **892** people. There are **27** rows of seats. All the rows except **1** have the same number of seats. How many seats are in each row?

8. Betty has **521** flowers. She uses **15** flowers to make a bouquet. How many bouquets can she make? How many flowers will she have left over?

Test Prep ★ Mixed Review

9 A square has a perimeter of 48 meters. Which could be the measurement of its area?

  A 12

  B 24

  C 80

  D 144

10 What number should go in the ☐ to make the number sentence true?

$$\frac{1}{2} = 0.50$$

$$\frac{3}{4} = \boxed{}$$

  F 0.25   **H** 0.5

  G 0.34   **J** 0.75

When you divide, you may need to write a zero in the quotient.

Divide 595 by 56.

1. Not enough hundreds. Regroup hundreds as tens. Divide.

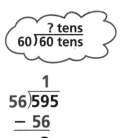

$$\begin{array}{r} 1 \\ 56\overline{)595} \\ -56 \\ \hline 3 \end{array}$$

2. Regroup tens as ones. Bring down the next digit. Divide.

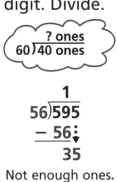

$$\begin{array}{r} 1 \\ 56\overline{)595} \\ -56 \\ \hline 35 \end{array}$$

Not enough ones.

3. Write a **0** in the quotient. Write the remainder.

$$\begin{array}{r} 10\ \mathbf{R35} \\ 56\overline{)595} \\ -56 \\ \hline 35 \\ -\ 0 \\ \hline 35 \end{array}$$

4. Check:

$$\begin{array}{r} 56 \\ \times\ 10 \\ \hline 560 \end{array}$$

$$\begin{array}{r} 560 \\ +\ 35 \\ \hline 595 \end{array}$$

Divide and check.

1. $24\overline{)741}$ $32\overline{)658}$ $13\overline{)922}$ $17\overline{)462}$

2. $26\overline{)785}$ $39\overline{)806}$ $24\overline{)752}$ $27\overline{)830}$

3. $23\overline{)920}$ $17\overline{)863}$ $16\overline{)851}$ $36\overline{)720}$

4. $44\overline{)469}$ $32\overline{)355}$ $18\overline{)850}$ $35\overline{)710}$

Divide and check.

5. $17\overline{)584}$ $28\overline{)391}$ $36\overline{)857}$ $13\overline{)661}$

6. $21\overline{)473}$ $32\overline{)931}$ $18\overline{)972}$ $29\overline{)654}$

7. $15\overline{)762}$ $12\overline{)467}$ $23\overline{)926}$ $33\overline{)993}$

Problem Solving
Reasoning

Solve.

8. Tony has **124** video tapes. Each shelf in his video cabinet holds **12** tapes. How many shelves will he fill? How many tapes will be left over?

9. Maria has a collection of **285** CDs. She wants to show her collection on shelves that hold **14** CDs each. How many shelves does she need? Explain.

Test Prep ★ Mixed Review

10 What number is a common factor of both 12 and 24?

    A 12

    B 10

    C 9

    D 8

11 Which fraction is equivalent to $\frac{8}{12}$?

    F $\frac{1}{4}$

    G $\frac{1}{2}$

    H $\frac{2}{3}$

    J $\frac{3}{4}$

Problem Solving Application: Solving Multi-Step Problems

Sometimes you need to use several steps in order to solve a problem.

Try to break the problem into parts. Write simpler problems that will help you find each fact you need. Solve each simpler problem. Then use the answers to solve the original problem.

Tips to Remember:

1. Understand	2. Decide	3. Solve	4. Look back

- Try to remember a real-life situation like the one described in the problem. What do you remember that might help you find a solution?
- Think about the action in the problem. Is there more than one action? Which operation best represents each action—addition, subtraction, multiplication, or division?
- When you can, make a prediction about the answer. Then compare your answer and your prediction.

Solve.

1. A wall-to-wall carpet costs **$15** per square yard. Mrs. Sullivan paid **$630** to carpet a room **6** yards long. What was the width of the room?

Think: What do you need to find first? How can you find it?

_____

_____

Answer _____

2. A shoe box **11** inches long and **4** inches high has a volume of **330** cubic inches. What is the width of the shoe box?

Think: How do you find the volume of a rectangular prism?

_____

_____

Answer _____

3. A square garden has a perimeter of 48 ft. What is the area?

_____

4. Jim doubled the length of his square garden to 24 ft. What is the area now?

_____

Solve.

5. A certain custom frame costs $.75 per inch. How much will it cost Carla to frame an oil painting 26 inches by 18 inches?

_____

6. You can buy a school lunch for $1.75 or you can buy 5 lunch tickets for $7.50. How much can you save on each lunch by using a ticket?

_____

7. A full-year family membership to the Museum of Science costs $79. A one-day visit costs $9 for adults and $7 for children. If the LeBlanc family has 2 adults and 2 children, how many times would they need to visit the museum in a year for the family membership to be a good value?

_____

8. Package A weighs 2.43 pounds. Package B weighs $4\frac{3}{4}$ pounds. Package C weighs 1.6 pounds. Package D weighs 1.2 pounds. Is the total weight of the four packages more than 10 pounds?

_____

9. Mrs. Li and 15 other people equally share the cost of dinner in a restaurant. The total bill, including tip is $192. If Mrs. Li puts in a $20 bill, how much change should she take out?

_____

10. Chelsea wants to buy 3 books. One costs $3.99, one costs $2.75, and one costs $4.98. She has 8 dollars, 15 quarters, 9 dimes, and 7 nickels. Does Chelsea have enough money to buy the books?

_____

Extend Your Thinking

11. Go back to problem 5. Carla wants to use the same kind of frame for a square painting. It turns out that the price will be the same as for the rectangular painting. How long is each side of the square painting?

_____

12. Describe the method you used to solve problem 10. Tell whether you used exact calculations or estimates.

_____

_____

_____

_____

Name _____

You can use what you know about dividing **3**-digit numbers to divide **4**-digit numbers.

Divide: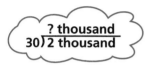

1. Divide the thousands.

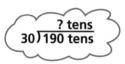

$$29\overline{)1,948}$$

Not enough thousands.

2. Regroup thousands as hundreds.

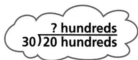

$$29\overline{)1,948}$$

Not enough hundreds.

3. Regroup hundreds as tens. Divide.

$$\begin{array}{r} 6 \\ 29\overline{)1,948} \\ -1\,74 \\ \hline 20 \end{array}$$

4. Regroup tens as ones. Bring down the next digit. Divide the ones.

$$\begin{array}{r} 67\text{ R5} \\ 29\overline{)1,948} \\ -1\,74 \\ \hline 208 \\ -203 \\ \hline 5 \end{array}$$

? ones
30)200 ones

| Remember to multiply and add to check your answer. |

Divide and check.

1. $38\overline{)2,371}$ $45\overline{)3,056}$ $23\overline{)2,164}$

2. $19\overline{)1,073}$ $52\overline{)3,134}$ $61\overline{)4,892}$

3. $72\overline{)4,103}$ $57\overline{)4,980}$ $67\overline{)5,042}$

4. $52\overline{)4,187}$ $83\overline{)6,014}$ $17\overline{)1,092}$

Divide and check.

5. 16)8,384   82)9,430   14)8,614

6. 71)9,236   46)9,755   55)6,380

Problem Solving Reasoning **Solve.**

7. Jose's family traveled **4,200** miles during their **12**-day vacation. If they traveled the same number of miles each day, how many miles each day did they travel?

8. Judy's Nursery planted **1,216** flower bulbs. They planted **4** dozen bulbs in each row. How many rows did they plant? How many bulbs were left over?

 Quick Check

Divide and check.

9. 23)356   **10.** 54)657   **11.** 41)953

12. 36)724   **13.** 17)693   **14.** 24)965

15. 21)1,019   **16.** 37)2,523   **17.** 58)3,617

Work Space.

Zeros in 3-Digit Quotients

A quotient can sometimes contain one or more zeros.

Divide: $37\overline{)7{,}646}$ with ? above

1. Not enough thousands to divide. Regroup thousands as hundreds. Divide.

? hundreds
40)80 hundreds

$$
\begin{array}{r}
2 \\
37\overline{)7{,}646} \\
-74 \\
\hline
2
\end{array}
$$

2. Regroup hundreds as tens. Bring down the next digit.

? tens
40)20 tens

$$
\begin{array}{r}
20 \\
37\overline{)7{,}646} \\
-74 \\
\hline
24
\end{array}
$$

Not enough tens. Write a zero in the quotient.

3. Regroup tens as ones. Divide. Write the remainder in the quotient.

? ones
40)250 ones

$$
\begin{array}{r}
206\ \text{R24} \\
37\overline{)7{,}646} \\
-74 \\
\hline
246 \\
-222 \\
\hline
24
\end{array}
$$

Check your answer. Multiply and add.

Divide and check.

1. $31\overline{)8{,}756}$ $26\overline{)5{,}983}$ $19\overline{)5{,}834}$

2. $16\overline{)8{,}457}$ $56\overline{)4{,}487}$ $72\overline{)7{,}421}$

3. $71\overline{)2{,}852}$ $47\overline{)5{,}082}$ $32\overline{)6{,}489}$

Divide and check.

4. $35\overline{)1,482}$ $68\overline{)1,164}$ $56\overline{)3,928}$

5. $28\overline{)3,248}$ $17\overline{)4,309}$ $27\overline{)5,623}$

6. $52\overline{)5,324}$ $35\overline{)2,352}$ $43\overline{)8,781}$

Problem Solving Reasoning Solve.

7. Niles has a puzzle with **2,496** pieces. If he puts **24** pieces together a day, how many days will it take to finish the puzzle?

_____

8. The total attendance for **12** performances of a play was **1,860** people. The same number of people attended each performance. How many people attended each performance?

_____

Test Prep ★ Mixed Review

9 What is the area in square feet of the figure shown?

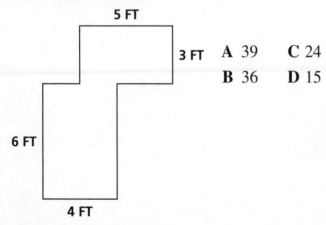

A 39   C 24
B 36   D 15

10 Which of these shows thirty-four hundredths shaded?

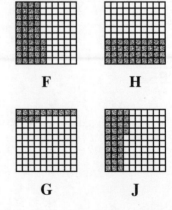

F   H

G   J

Name _____

One way to estimate a quotient is to round the dividend and divisor. Another way to estimate a quotient is to use compatible numbers.

Compatible numbers are numbers that are easy to divide mentally.

Examples of Compatible Numbers		
2 and 4	3 and 9	7 and 35
4 and 16	8 and 24	9 and 36

With **1**-digit divisors, find a compatible number for the dividend.

Estimate: 7)‾431‾

1. Find a number for the dividend compatible with **7**.

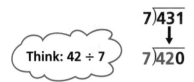

2. Estimate.

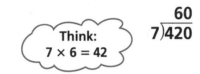

With **2**-digit divisors, find compatible numbers for both the dividend and the divisor.

Estimate: 62)‾192‾

1. Find the compatible numbers.

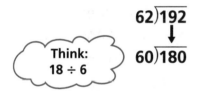

2. Estimate.

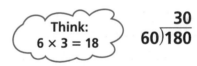

Estimate each quotient using compatible numbers. Then circle the correct answer.

1. 7)‾492‾ $\frac{70}{7)490}$ 7 R2   700 R2   70 R2

2. 21)‾336‾ $\frac{20}{20)400}$ 1 R20   108 R16   16

3. 57)‾582‾   57)‾570‾   101 R12   10 R12   1 R12

4. 76)‾795‾   )‾___‾   1 R48   104 R48   10 R35

5. 52)‾4,546‾   )‾___‾   8 R22   807 R22   87 R22

Unit 9 Lesson 9   **253**

Estimate each quotient using compatible numbers.
Then circle the correct answer.

6. $24\overline{)539}$ $25\overline{)}$ **200 R2**   **22 R11**   **70 R11**

7. $41\overline{)7,962}$ $40\overline{)}$ **194 R8**   **94 R8**   **294 R8**

8. $78\overline{)5,617}$ $80\overline{)}$ **177 R5**   **17 R5**   **72 R1**

9. $39\overline{)3,440}$ $40\overline{)}$ **903 R1**   **10 R5**   **88 R8**

**Problem Solving
Reasoning** | Solve.

10. A tool company shipped **3,672** small tools in **18** boxes. Each box contained the same number of tools. About how many tools were in each box?

_____

11. A toy company shipped **3,914** marbles in **38** boxes. Each box contained the same number of marbles. About how many marbles were in each box?

_____

 Quick Check

Divide and check.

12. $17\overline{)3,521}$ **13.** $26\overline{)7,956}$ **14.** $14\overline{)8,537}$

Work Space.

Estimate the quotient using compatible numbers.

15. 240 ÷ 63 _____   **16.** 3,627 ÷ 92 _____

17. 4,243 ÷ 74 _____

Problem Solving Strategy:
Solve a Simpler Problem

Sometimes using simpler numbers can make it easier to decide what steps you need to take to solve a problem.

Problem

Mr. Kim is driving his car a total distance of **3,339** miles. He used **58** gallons of gasoline to drive the first **1,218** miles. How many gallons of gasoline will he need to complete the trip?

Understand As you reread, ask yourself questions.

- What do you need to find out? _____

② Decide Choose a method for solving.

Try the strategy Use a Simpler Problem.

- Find simpler numbers to use. One way to make a simpler number is to replace all the digits, except the first digit, with zeros.

Original number	3,339	58	1,218
Simpler number	3,000	50	_____

Solve Solve the simpler problem and the original problem.

- Break the simpler problem into parts and solve.
  a. Find the miles per gallon (mpg).

     1,000 ÷ _____ = _____ mpg

  b. Find the number of miles left.

     3,000 − _____ = _____ mi

  c. Find the number of gallons needed.

     _____ ÷ _____ = **100** gal

- Now use the same steps for the original problem.

  a. Find the miles per gallon (mpg). _____ mpg

  b. Find the number of miles left. _____ miles

  c. Find the number of gallons needed. _____ gallons

④ Look back Write the answer to the problem. _____

Solve. Use the Use a Simpler Problem strategy or any other strategy you have learned.

1. Mr. Kay bought **3** shirts for **$15.99** each. Mrs. Kay bought **2** shirts for **$29.50** each. How much more money did Mrs. Kay spend than Mr. Kay?

   Think: How can you round dollars and cents?

   _____

   Answer _____

2. Mr. Johnson cut a **25**-foot rope into **12** equal-sized pieces. How many cuts did he make?

   Think: What numbers could you choose that would be simpler?

   _____

   Answer _____

3. Write the missing number in this sequence.

   2.34, 2.44, 2.43, 2.53, _____, 2.62

4. Find the missing digits.

   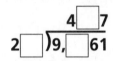

5. To celebrate a shopping mall's **fifteenth** anniversary, a cake **15** feet long and **15** feet wide will be served. How many square pieces with **3**-inch sides can be cut from the cake?

   _____

6. Six people at a party all shake hands with each other. How many handshakes is that? (Hint: Try solving the problem for fewer people. Look for a pattern.)

   _____

7. The Kleiner family is making a trip to Connecticut. The total distance is **364** miles. So far they have driven **208** miles in **4** hours. If they continue at the same speed, how many hours will it take them to complete the trip?

   _____

8. A special fundraiser concert is being held in the school gym. Tickets cost **$12** each. Ticket sales so far total **$3,768**. Chairs for all ticket holders plus **50** extra chairs will be set up. Each row will have **14** chairs. How many rows will there be?

   _____

9. The choir is standing on steps in a specific pattern. The bottom step has **18** people. The next step has **15** people, then **12** people and so on. How many people are in the choir?

   _____

10. A local play is offering a special discount rate on tickets: **2** tickets for **$12**. A class of **18** students can use the special discount rate or a special student rate of **3** tickets for **$15**. Which is cheaper?

   _____

Divide.

1. $12\overline{)84}$ 2. $41\overline{)68}$ 3. $29\overline{)93}$ 4. $32\overline{)197}$

5. $27\overline{)763}$ 6. $17\overline{)680}$ 7. $26\overline{)785}$ 8. $17\overline{)688}$

9. $64\overline{)3,306}$ 10. $35\overline{)7,245}$ 11. $84\overline{)7,057}$ 12. $12\overline{)8,530}$

Use compatible numbers to estimate each quotient.

13. $41\overline{)451}$

Estimate _____

14. $67\overline{)556}$

Estimate _____

15. $25\overline{)2,197}$

Estimate _____

16. $51\overline{)3,526}$

Estimate _____

Solve.

17. During a grand opening, a store gave every fourth customer a discount coupon. Every tenth customer was given a discount coupon and a free gift. During the grand opening, **240** people visited the store. How many coupons and gifts were given away?

_____

_____

18. A 20-foot length of ribbon is to be cut in half. Each length will then be cut into **5** equal lengths. How many equal lengths of ribbon will there be altogether?

_____

_____

Name _____

1 At track practice, 4 students ran different distances.

Student	Distance Run
Amanda	2.65 meters
Wilson	2.75 meters
Robert	2.6 meters
Alexia	2.8 meters

Which lists the students in order from the *shortest* distance run to the *longest* distance run?

A Amanda, Robert, Wilson, Alexia

B Robert, Amanda, Wilson, Alexia

C Robert, Amanda, Alexia, Wilson

D Alexia, Wilson, Amanda, Robert

2 The Celsius thermometers show the temperature at noon on Monday and the temperature at noon on Tuesday. How many degrees colder was the temperature on Tuesday?

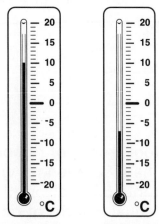

Monday	Tuesday

F 17° C   **H** 10° C

G 12° C   **J** 7° C

3 The Lawsons are driving 1,235 miles to visit relatives in Colorado. If they drive 65 miles an hour, how many hours will the trip take?

A 15 hours   **C** 19 hours   **E** NH

B 17 hours   **D** 21 hours

4 Which shape is congruent with the triangle shown?

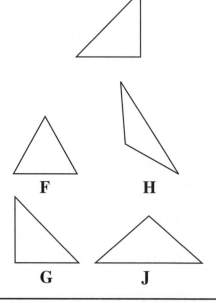

5 What decimal should go in the ☐ to make the number sentence true?

$$\frac{3}{10} = 0.30 \qquad \frac{1}{2} = \boxed{}$$

A 0.75   **C** 0.25

B 0.50   **D** 0.1

6 An employee is arranging 170 CDs on a display rack. Each shelf of the rack holds 15 CDs. How many shelves will he use to display all the CDs?

F 10 shelves   **H** 12 shelves   **K** NH

G 11 shelves   **J** 13 shelves

UNIT 10 • TABLE OF CONTENTS

Data, Statistics, and Probability

Dear Family,

During the next few weeks, our math class will be learning about data, statistics, and probability.

You can expect to see homework that provides practice with describing sets of data. Here is a sample you may want to keep handy to give help if needed.

Finding Median, Mode, and Range

To find the median of the set of data {3, 9, 4, 2, 9, 16, 5}:

First arrange the numbers from least to greatest or from greatest to least.

2 3 4 5 9 9 16

The median is the middle number. The median is **5**.

2 3 4 5 9 9 16
          ↑

If a set of data has two middle data numbers, the median is the number halfway between the two middle numbers.

To find the mode of the set of data {3, 9, 4, 2, 9, 16, 5}:

Look for the number or numbers that occurs most often. The mode is **9**.

3 9 4 2 9 16 5

To find the range of the set of data {3, 9, 4, 2, 9, 16, 5}:

Subtract the greatest number from the least. The range is **14**.

3 9 4 2 9 16 5
$16 - 2 = 14$

During this unit, students will need to continue practicing working with data, as well as addition and subtraction facts.

Sincerely,

Name _____

When you conduct a **survey**, you collect **data** or facts.

• Record the data in a table.

• Make a tally mark each time a choice is made.

• After all the people have been surveyed, find the total number of the tallies in all the choices.

Survey question: "What is your favorite color for a car?"

Title →
Column Headings →
Categories {

Favorite Color for a Car		
Color	Tally	Total
Blue |卌 |||	8
Green	卌 卌 ||	12
Red	卌 |||	8

Number of people surveyed

$8 + 12 + 8 = 28$

Conduct a survey. Use the table to record your data.

1. Choose an idea for your survey. Write a question to ask that has **3** possible responses.

2. Make a table with a title, headings, and three choices.

3. Survey **20** people. Tally the results.

4. Count the tally marks for each choice.

5. Which choice received the most tallies? The least?

_____

_____

Title:		
	Tally	Total

A **line plot** is a way to show the frequency of data. This line plot shows the number of books members of the book club have read this month.

Number of Books Read	
Jan	3
Paul	5
Steve	7
Karen	6
Mia	3
Kim	2
Tara	5
Andy	7
Kris	2
Tim	5
Roland	5
Juan	2

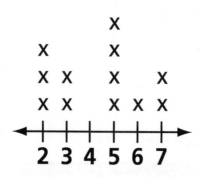

```
            X
      X     X
    X X   X   X
    X X   X X X
    +-+-+-+-+-+-+-+
    2 3 4 5 6 7
```

Number of Books Read

The four X's above **5** mean that four members of the book club have read **5** books. One X above **6** means that one member has read **6** books.

Use the line plot to answer each question.

6. How many members of the book club read exactly **2** books this month? _3_

7. A total of _0_ club members read **8** books this month.

8. In all, there are _12_ club members.

9. How many club members read at least **5** books? _4_

10. What was the least number of books read this month? _2_

Test Prep ★ Mixed Review

11 Which shows all the factors of 28?

A 3, 4, 6, 19

B 1, 2, 6, 8, 28

C 1, 2, 4, 7, 14, 28

D 2, 4, 7, 14

12 The course for a cross-country skiing race is 20.13 kilometers long. What is this distance rounded to the nearest tenth?

F 21 kilometers

G 20.2 kilometers

H 20.1 kilometers

J 20 kilometers

Name _____   **Mean, Mode, Range, Median**

This line plot shows the results of the survey shown in the table.

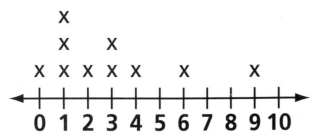

Number of Apples

Number of Apples	
Chris	1
Pat	3
Ann	2
Mark	4
Andy	9
Doug	1
Angela	1
Susan	0
Erin	3
Shelly	6

You can use the data in the line plot to find the **mode**. The mode is the number in the data that occurs most often. If no number occurs more than once, there is no mode.

There are more X's above **1** than above any other number. The mode is **1**.

You can also find the range. The **range** is the difference between the greatest value and the least value in the set of numbers.

To find the range, subtract the least number from the greatest.

$9 - 0 = 9$ The range is **9**.

An **outlier** is one or more numbers in the data that is much greater or much less than the other numbers. In this set of data, **9** is an outlier.

The **mean**, or average, is the sum of the numbers divided by the number of addends.

$0 + 1 + 1 + 1 + 2 + 3 + 3 + 4 + 6 + 9 = 30$ $30 \div 10 = 3$

In this set of data, **3** is the mean.

The middle number in the data is called the **median**.

Write the numbers in order from least to greatest.

0, 1, 1, 1, 2, 3, 3, 4, 6, 9

This set of data has **10** numbers, so it has two middle numbers. The middle numbers are **2** and **3**. The median is the mean of the two middle numbers:

$2 + 3 = 5$ $5 \div 2 = 2\frac{1}{2}$

In this set of data, $2\frac{1}{2}$ or **2.5** is the median.

Use the line plot to answer the question.

1. How many responses are shown in this survey? _16_

2. What is the mode? _6_

3. What is the range? _3_

4. What is the median? _0_

5. What is the mean? _15_

6. Is there an outlier? _no_
   If so, what is it? _no_

Amount of Money Spent Last Week

Number of Dollars

Find the mean, range, median, mode, and outlier of the set of data.

7. 1, 1, 1, 3, 3, 4, 6, 6, 11

   mean: _37_   range: _____   median: _____
                 mode: _____   outlier: _____

8. 3, 3, 4, 4, 4, 4, 5, 6, 7, 7, 8

   mean: _55_   range: _____   median: _____
                 mode: _____   outlier: _____

9. 22, 22, 23, 25, 25, 26, 26, 26, 39

   mean: _____   range: _____   median: _____
                    mode: _____   outlier: _____

10. 1, 18, 18, 19, 20, 20, 20, 21, 21, 22

    mean: _____   range: _____   median: _____
                     mode: _____   outlier: _____

Arrange the data in order from least to greatest.
Then find the range, median, mode, and outlier.

11. 4, 8, 5, 2, 2, 5, 5, 9, 15, 5 _____

    range: _____ median: _____ mode: _____ outlier: _____

12. 3, 1, 4, 3, 6, 4, 7, 5, 8, 6, 3, 7 _____

    range: _____ median: _____ mode: _____ outlier: _____

13. 7, 14, 2, 1, 7, 19, 28, 7, 4, _____

    range: _____ median: _____ mode: _____ outlier: _____

Name _____

In sets without numbers, the mode depends on the group you select.

This set of buttons is grouped by color.

The mode color of this set is **red**. Red is the group with the most buttons.

Use the set of buttons above to answer each question.

Draw the buttons grouped in another way.

14. How did you group them?

_____

15. What is the mode?

_____

Problem Solving
Reasoning
Solve. Use this set of buttons to answer problems 16-18.

16. What is the mode number of holes in this set?

_____

17. What is the mode shape of this set?

_____

18. What is the mode color of this set?

_____

Test Prep ★ Mixed Review

19 An Olympic athlete runs 200 meters in 19.75 seconds. What is 19.75 in words?

A Nineteen and seventy hundredths

B Nineteen and seven tenths

C Nineteen and seventy-five hundredths

D Nineteen and seventy-five tenths

20 Miranda hopped on one foot for $4\frac{1}{2}$ meters. What decimal is equivalent to $4\frac{1}{2}$?

F 4.05

G 4.12

H 4.21

J 4.50

Name _____

Sometimes you will need to use the information in a table in order to solve a problem.

Molly and Katy worked together on a project. They collected information about three brands of oatmeal-raisin cookies. All the cookies were about the same size. They made this table to show the number of cookies in each bag and the cost of each bag.

	Price per bag	Number of cookies
Granny's Best	$5.50	50
Just Like Home	$3.60	20
Uncle Erno's	$3.50	25

Tips to Remember:

1. Understand	2. Decide	3. Solve	4. Look back

- Think about what the problem is asking you to do. What information does the problem give you? What do you need to find out?
- Try to break the problem into parts.
- Do you need to use both addition and subtraction to show what is happening? Which should you use first?

Solve. Use the table above.

1. Which brand of cookies was most expensive?

Think: How would you find the cost of **1** cookie?

_____

_____

Answer _____

2. You want to buy **200** of Granny's Best cookies. How much will they cost?

Think: How would you find the number of bags you need?

_____

Answer _____

3. Write the unit price of the cookies in order from least to greatest.

_____

4. How much would **100** cookies from Uncle Erno's cost?

_____

Name _____

Molly and Katy took **5** cookies from each bag and counted the number of raisins in each cookie. This table shows their results.

Number of raisins					
	1	**2**	**3**	**4**	**5**
Granny's Best	6	5	4	8	7
Just Like Home	9	8	9	10	9
Uncle Erno's	10	10	18	11	12

Solve. Use the table above.

5. Which brand had the greatest range in the number of raisins?

_____

6. For which brand does the data not have a mode?

_____

7. For which brand does the data have an outlier? What is it?

_____

8. What is the median number of raisins for Just Like Home?

_____

9. What is the median number of raisins for Uncle Erno's?

_____

10. What is the mean number of raisins for Granny's Best?

_____

Extend Your Thinking

11. Go back to problem **10.** Suppose the number of raisins in the first cookie were different. What number of raisins would have to be in the first cookie for the mean to be **7** raisins? Explain how you solved this problem.

_____

_____

_____

_____

12. The line plot below shows data for **10** cookies of one brand. Which brand do you think the data is for? Explain your thinking.

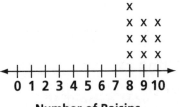

Number of Raisins

_____

_____

You can use a **line graph** to show how data change during a period of time. This graph shows how the temperature outside changed during twelve hours.

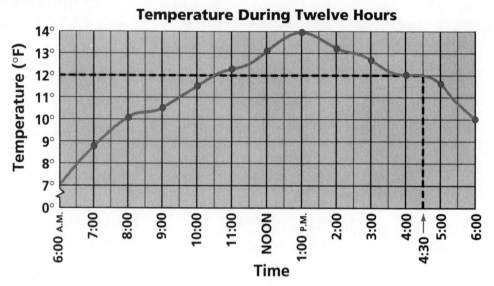

Temperature During Twelve Hours

The vertical scale should always start at 0. You can save space by using a jagged line to show a gap.

To find the temperature at **4:30** P.M. follow these steps:

• Find **4:30** P.M. on the Time scale.

• Trace a straight line up from **4:30** P.M. until you reach a point on the line segment.

• Trace another line from that point to the Temperature scale to find the temperature, **12°F.**

You can show the temperature at **4:30** P.M. by writing this coordinate: (**4:30** P.M., **12°F**).

Use the graph to answer the question.

1. What was the greatest temperature? _____

2. At what time did the greatest temperature occur? _____

3. When was the temperature **10°F**? _____ and _____

4. What time was the temperature **13°F**? _____ and _____

5. Describe how the temperature changed between **6:00** A.M. and **1:00** P.M. _____ By how much? _____

6. Would you expect the temperature at **7:00** P.M. to be greater or less than **10°F**? Explain. _____

_____

Name _____

Monthly Balloon Sales at Helium Joe's	
June	$100
July	$300
August (Aug.)	$100
September (Sept.)	$100
October (Oct.)	$600
November (Nov.)	$500

Follow these steps to make a line graph of the sales data in the table.

1. Write the months on one scale. Use abbreviations. Label it *Months*.

2. Write the number of dollars using multiples of **100** on the other scale. Label it *Dollars*.

3. Plot the amount of money for each month on the graph. Here's how June was plotted.
   • Find June on the Month scale.
   • Find **100** on the Dollars scale.
   • Place a point where both lines meet.

4. Connect the points with line segments.

Monthly Balloon Sales

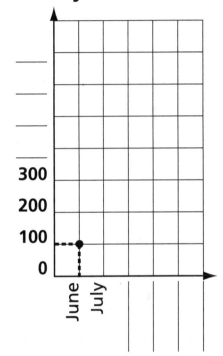

Complete.

7. Which month had the greatest sales? _____

8. In which three months were the sales $100? _____
_____

9. Between June and November, which month had the greatest decrease in sales?
_____

10. What is the difference in sales between the least point and the greatest point on the graph?
_____

11. What might have caused the sales during August to be so low?
_____

12. Use this data to make a line graph.

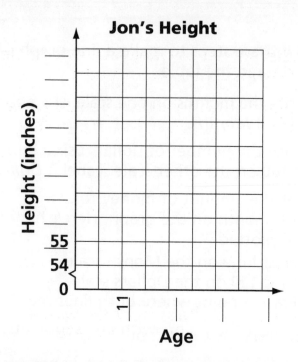

| Jon's Height from Ages 11 to 14 ||
Age	Height (inches)
11	55
12	59
13	62
14	63

 Quick Check

13. The tally chart shows results of a survey. How many more people liked orange juice than liked

cherry juice? _____

Favorite Juices		
Apple	**Orange**	**Cherry**
𝍿𝍿 𝍿𝍿 II	𝍿𝍿 𝍿𝍿 IIII	𝍿𝍿 II

Work Space.

14. The ages of people at a family dinner were **12, 15, 20, 21, 48, 51, 78, 81.** Find the range of ages.

_____

15. Manuel records how long he spends walking to school every morning: Monday, **10** min.; Tuesday, **15** min.; Wednesday, **9** min.; Thursday **15** min.; Friday **18** min. Show this data on the line graph below.

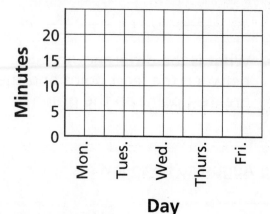

Name _____

A **prediction** uses as many facts as possible to describe what is likely to happen.

OUTCOMES:
Red, gray, white

An **experiment** is an activity you do to gather data. An **outcome** is a result of an experiment.

You can conduct an experiment and record the outcomes to make a prediction.

The tally chart and the line plot show the outcomes of an experiment:

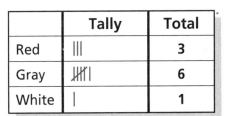

	Tally	Total
Red	|||	3
Gray	Ж|||	6
White			1

- Without looking, a cube was removed from the bag.

- The cube's color was recorded with a tally mark, and it was put back in the bag.

- Ten draws were made from the bag. The chart shows **10** tally marks.

What color will be picked on the eleventh draw?

To predict the outcome of the next draw, study the data. Since **6** out of **10** cubes chosen were gray, you can predict that the next cube chosen most likely will be gray.

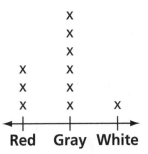

```
                    x
                    x
                    x
           x        x
           x        x
           x        x        x
         ←─┼────────┼────────┼──→
          Red     Gray    White
```

Follow these steps to conduct an experiment.

1. Make ten **1**-inch paper squares. On **5** squares write M. On **2** squares write A. On **2** squares write T, and on **1** square write H.

2. What are the possible outcomes in this experiment? _____

```
←─┼────┼────┼────┼──→
  M    A    T    H
```

3. Put the squares in a bag. Without looking, take a square from the bag, record the outcome on the line plot, and put the square back into the bag.

4. Repeat step **3** eleven more times.

5. Which letter is most likely to be picked on the next draw?

   Explain. _____

   _____

Solve.

6. Ricky put several cubes in a bag and conducted an experiment. He used a tally of his results to make this bar graph.

When it was time to hand his chart and graph in for a grade, he could not find his tally chart. Use the data in the graph to recreate Ricky's tally chart.

Experiment Results

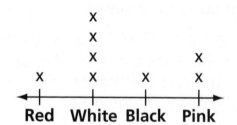

Number Drawn

	Tally	Total

7. Of the cubes in the bag, do you think the least number were red? If not, explain.

_____

_____

_____

8. This line plot shows the results of an experiment. Circle the bag of cubes that may have been used. Then explain your choice.

_____

_____

_____

_____

_____

_____

```
                    x
                    x
                    x              x
        x           x        x     x
    ←———+———————+————————+—————+———→
       Red    White   Black  Pink
```

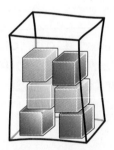  

Test Prep ★ Mixed Review

9 A warehouse is packing an order for 3,264 books. If each box holds 24 books, how many boxes will the warehouse need?

A 130

C 134

B 132

D 136

10 The area of a square is 64 square meters. What is the length of one side?

F 16 meters

G 12 meters

H 8 meters

J 4 meters

The possible results of an experiment can be described in words or in numbers.

Will you choose a green cube?

- There are **0** chances out of **6**, or $\frac{0}{6}$, to choose a green cube from the bag.

- It is **impossible** to choose a green cube from this bag.

Will you choose a gray or red cube?

- There are **6** chances out of **6**, or $\frac{6}{6}$, to choose a red or a gray cube from the bag.

- It is **certain** that either a red or gray cube will be chosen from this bag.

Will you choose a gray cube?

- There are **2** chances out of **6**, or $\frac{2}{6}$, to choose a gray cube from the bag.

Will you choose a red cube?

- There are **4** chances out of **6**, or $\frac{4}{6}$, to choose a red cube from the bag.

Are you more likely to choose a red or a gray cube?

- There are more red than gray cubes. Red is a greater part of the whole.

- Since $\frac{4}{6} > \frac{2}{6}$, you are **more likely** to choose a red cube than a gray cube.

4 red cubes
2 gray cubes

$$0 \qquad \frac{2}{6} \quad \frac{1}{2} \quad \frac{4}{6} \qquad 1$$

Use the spinner to answer the question.

1. How many equal sections does the spinner have? _____

2. How many sections have squares? _____

Triangles? _____ Circles? _____

Suppose the spinner is spun once.

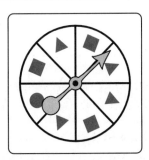

3. What is the chance that the spinner will point to a square?

_____ out of _____ or _____

4. What is the chance that the spinner will point to a triangle?

_____ out of _____ or _____

The spinner shown is the same as on p. 273. Suppose it is spun once.

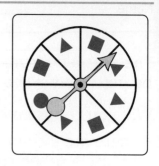

5. What is the chance that the spinner will point to a circle?

_____ out of _____ or _____

6. What is the chance that the spinner will point to a pentagon? A pentagon is a five-sided figure.

_____ out of _____ or _____

Problem Solving Reasoning Solve. Choose the spinner that describes the statement.

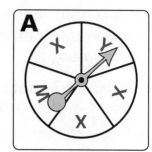

A

7. For which spinner is W an impossible outcome? Explain.

_____

8. For which spinner is there a $\frac{1}{5}$ probability of pointing to Y?

Explain. _____

_____

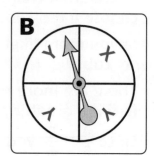

B

9. In which spinner is there a $\frac{1}{4}$ probability of pointing to X? Explain. _____

_____

10. Which spinner is more likely to point to X than to Y? Explain. _____

_____

Test Prep ★ Mixed Review

11 Which group of numbers shows all the factors of 18?

A 1, 2, 9, 18   C 3, 9, 18

B 1, 2, 3, 6, 9, 18   D 18, 36, 54

12 A class trip costs a total of $682 for 22 students. How much does it cost for each student?

F $29   H $33

G $31   J $35

You are deciding what to wear. You have **1** pair of jeans, but you have a choice of a red or blue T-shirt and sneakers or hiking boots. How many different outfits could you wear?

You can use a **tree diagram** to show all the possible outcomes.

1. Write down *jeans*. It will be the trunk of the tree.

2. Draw two branches from the trunk. Label one *red shirt* and the other *blue shirt*.

3. Draw two branches from each shirt. Label one *sneakers* and the other *hiking boots*.

4. Count the number of branches made in step **3**. This is the number of possible outcomes.

Tree Diagram

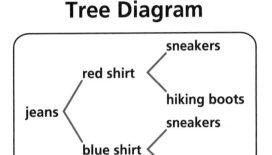

4 possible outcomes

You could wear four different outfits:

Jeans, red shirt, sneakers   Jeans, red shirt, hiking boots

Jeans, blue shirt, sneakers   Jeans, blue shirt, hiking boots

---

The tree diagram shows choices for wrapping a present. Use it to answer each question.

1. How many different ribbon colors are there to choose from? __2__

2. How many different kinds of wrapping papers are there to choose from? __3__

3. How many different possible outcomes are there so far? _____

4. Extend the tree diagram to show two different colors of bows.

5. How many different possible outcomes are there now? _____

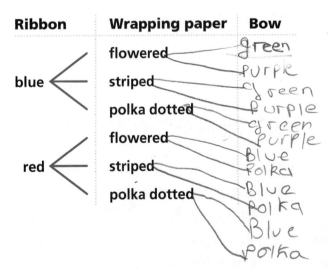

Make a tree diagram to solve the problem.

6. A restaurant has round and square tables. It has 3 kinds of tablecloths: red, blue or white. The vases on the table have a rose or a daisy. Show all of the possible combinations.

table	tablecloth	flower

✔ Quick Check

Answer each question.

Work Space.

7. There are **12** cubes in a bag. Four are red, **2** are yellow, and **6** are green. Which color will you probably pick most often? _____

8. What are the chances of the spinner stopping on red? Write your answer both in words and as a fraction. _____

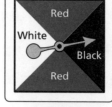

9. You flip a coin three times. How many ways could the coin flips turn out? _____ Complete the tree diagram shown.

H   T

Name _____

In the last lesson, you used a tree diagram to show possible outcomes. Another way to show possible outcomes is to make an organized list.

Problem

Mia bought a pair of blue jeans and a pair of black jeans. She also bought a red shirt, a white shirt, and a yellow shirt. How many different outfits can she make?

---

1 Understand As you reread, ask yourself questions.

- What information do you have?

  Mia bought _____ jeans and _____ jeans.

  Mia bought a _____ shirt, a _____ shirt, and

  a _____ shirt.

- What do you need to find out?

  _____

---

2 Decide Choose a method for solving.

Try the strategy Make a List.

- First list all the outfits with the blue jeans.

  blue jeans—red shirt

  blue jeans—white shirt

  blue jeans—yellow shirt

- Then list all the outfits with the black jeans.

  black jeans—red shirt

  _____ jeans—_____ shirt

  _____ jeans—_____ shirt

---

3 Solve Count the number of outfits in the list.

Mia can make _____ outfits with the blue jeans.

Mia can make _____ outfits with the black jeans.

Mia can make _____ outfits altogether.

---

4 Look back Check your answer. Write the answer below.

Answer _____

- Why was it helpful to list the items in the same order as they are given in the problem?

  _____

Solve. Use the Make a List strategy or any other strategy you have learned.

1. Mrs. Norton is making sandwiches. She has white bread and whole wheat bread. She has turkey and ham and she has Swiss cheese and American cheese. Each sandwich will have one kind of bread, one kind of meat, and one kind of cheese. How many different kinds of sandwiches can she make?

   Think: How many different sandwiches can she make with white bread?

   _____

   Answer _____

2. At the department store, you can have your purchase gift-wrapped. The store has blue, gold, and silver paper. It has white, blue, and green ribbon. You want to get a package wrapped. You can choose one color paper and one color ribbon. How many different combinations are available?

   Think: How many different ways are available using blue paper?

   _____

   Answer _____

3. You have **12** square tiles. Each tile measures **1** foot on each side. How many noncongruent rectangles can you make? Each rectangle must use all **12** tiles.

   _____

4. Three boys – Andrew, Jamie, and Sean – are lining up for a picture. If they stand in a row, how many different ways can they line up?

   _____

5. List all **2**-digit numbers for which the sum of the digits is **5**.

   _____

6. List all **3**-digit numbers for which the sum of the digits is **3**.

   _____

7. How many strips of paper **4** inches long and **1** inch wide can be cut from a piece of paper **8** inches long and **6** inches wide?

   _____

8. How many strips of wood **4** inches long and **1** inch wide can be cut from a piece of board **8** inches long and **36** inches wide?

   _____

9. Mrs. Washington purchased a refrigerator that is **6** feet high, **3** feet deep and **4** feet wide. How much floorspace does she need to fit the refrigerator?

   _____

10. There are **60** people in a line for a local concert. Every third person will be given a ticket so they can sit on the stage. How many people will be sitting on the stage?

   _____

**Arrange the data in order from least to greatest.
Then find the range, median, and mode.**

1. **49, 34, 43, 63, 50, 26, 2, 50** _____

   range: _____ median: _____ mode: _____

2. **17, 15, 22, 25, 14, 22, 19** _____

   range: _____ median: _____ mode: _____

Use the table to make a line graph on the grid.

3. Use a scale of **0, 5, 10, 15, 20, 25, 30** to complete
the vertical axis.

4. Complete the horizontal axis by writing a
number for each week.

5. Graph the height of the tomato plant for each
week. Connect the points with line segments.

6. When was the tomato plant **15** inches tall?

   _____

7. Describe how the height of the tomato plant
changed between Week **2** and Week **3**.

   _____

Tomato Plant Growth	
Week	**Height (in.)**
1	0
2	5
3	10
4	15
5	25
6	30

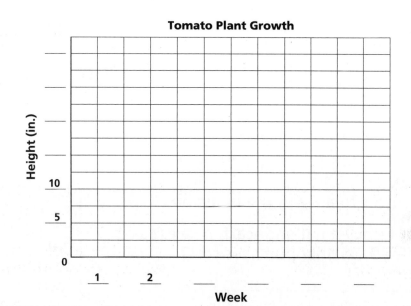

Tomato Plant Growth

Use the spinner to answer each question.

8. What is the chance that the spinner will point to a red section? A gray section? A white section? Express each outcome as a word and as a fraction.

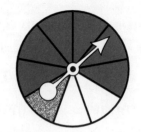

_____

9. Which outcome is more likely to occur: the spinner pointing to a gray section or to a white section?

_____

Make a tree diagram to show all the possible lunch combinations. The sandwich is chicken. The salad is vegetable, potato, or fruit. The drinks are spring water or fruit juice.

10.

Sandwich	Choice of Salad	Choice of Drink

Chicken

Tuna

Fruit Punch

Ice tea

Shrimp salad

Fruit punch

Ice tea

Chicken

Fruit punch

Ice tea

11. How many different lunch combinations are there?

 6

Solve.

12. List all 4-digit whole numbers whose digits have a sum of **2**.

_____

_____

Use the table of prices to answer the question.

13. Maria wants to buy a hat and scarf. If sales tax is **$1.17**, how much will her purchase cost?

_____

Clothing Sale	
hat	$ 9.00
sweater	$25.99
scarf	$12.50

Name_____

1 Amelia has 113 raffle tickets. She wants to divide them equally among 9 people. How many tickets will she have left over?

A 2   C 6   E NH

B 4   D 8

2 The line graph shows the number of visitors to a new museum. How many more people visited the museum in August than in June?

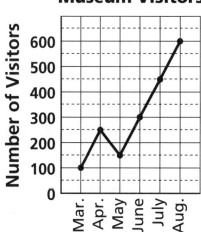

Museum Visitors

F 300   H 450

G 400   J 500

3 A room is 24.56 meters long. What is 24.56 in words?

A twenty-four and six hundredths

B twenty-four and fifty hundredths

C twenty-four and fifty-six hundredths

D twenty-four and sixty-five hundredths

4 Students recorded the hours that they spent doing their homework each week. They displayed the results on a line plot.

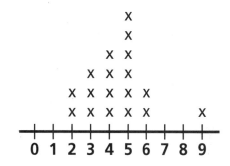

What is the range of hours that students spent on homework?

F 4   H 7

G 5   J 9

5 The chart shows rainfall for one storm in 4 different California cities.

City	Amount of Rain Fallen
Monterey	1.8 inches
Salinas	1.71 inches
Santa Cruz	1.9 inches
San Jose	1.29 inches

Which lists the cities in order from the *greatest* amount of rain to the *least* amount of rain fallen?

A San Jose, Salinas, Santa Cruz, Monterey

B Santa Cruz, Salinas, Monterey, San Jose

C San Jose, Salinas, Monterey, Santa Cruz

D Santa Cruz, Monterey, Salinas, San Jose

6 Melissa's books have a mass of 6 kilograms. What is the mass of her books in grams?

F 60

G 600

H 6,000

J 60,000

7 What decimal should go in the ☐ to make the number sentence true?

$$\frac{7}{10} = 0.70$$

$$\frac{1}{2} = 0.50$$

$$\frac{1}{4} = \boxed{}$$

A 0.80

B 0.4

C 0.25

D 0.14

8 Which of these decimal models shows seventy-eight hundredths shaded?

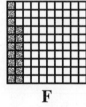
F

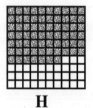
H

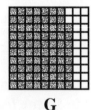
G

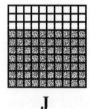
J

9 Which fraction is equivalent to $\frac{4}{16}$?

A $\frac{2}{3}$

B $\frac{4}{8}$

C $\frac{1}{2}$

D $\frac{1}{4}$

10 Which fraction is in simplest form?

F $\frac{4}{6}$

G $\frac{8}{10}$

H $\frac{7}{8}$

J $\frac{14}{16}$

11 The distance between two towns is 76.78 kilometers. What is this distance rounded to the nearest tenth?

A 77 kilometers

B 76.8 kilometers

C 76.7 kilometers

D 76 kilometers

12 A school is planning a field trip for 288 students. Each school bus holds 36 students. How many buses will the school need?

F 6

G 8

H 10

J 12

K NH

UNIT 11 • TABLE OF CONTENTS

Algebra: Variables and Coordinate Graphing

Dear Family,

During the next few weeks, our math class will be learning about variables and coordinate graphing.

You can expect to see homework that provides practice using words to describe relationships. Here is a sample you may want to keep handy to give help if needed.

Finding a Rule

A table can be used to show the relationship between the number of automobiles and the number of wheels.

automobiles (*a*)	wheels (*w*)
1	4
2	8
3	12
4	16

In words, the relationship can be described as: *Four times the number of automobiles is the number of wheels.*

The algebraic rule that describes this relationship is: $4 \times a = w$.

A table can be used to show the relationship between the number of pounds and the number of ounces.

pounds (*p*)	ounces (*o*)
1	16
2	32
3	48
4	64

In words, this relationship can be described as: *Sixteen times the number of pounds is the number of ounces.*

The algebraic rule that describes this relationship is: $16 \times p = o$.

During this unit, students will need to continue practicing finding rules and relationships as well as working with variables.

Sincerely,

The word phrase "three more than Nancy's age" can be written as an arithmetic phrase or **expression.**

□ + 3

unknown number

An unknown number can also be represented by a letter.

A letter that represents an unknown number is called a variable.

n + 3

variable

This phrase is called an **algebraic expression.** An algebraic expression is a math phrase that contains at least one number, variable, and operation.

Name the variable in the algebraic expression.

1. $5 + w$ _____ $p - 8$ _____ $16 \div r$ _____

2. $(11 + x) \div 3$ _____ $7 \times (r + 2)$ _____ $(9 - h) + 5$ _____

3. $7 \times y$ _____ $(4 + n) \times 2$ _____ $(3 - j) \times 6$ _____

Match the word phrase with an algebraic expression.

4. _____ *r* subtract 7   A. $4 + w$

5. _____ 8 divided by *x*   B. $y + 9$

6. _____ the sum of **4** and *w*   C. $p \times 5$

7. _____ **6** less than *h*   D. $r - 7$

8. _____ **9** greater than *y*   E. $7 - r$

9. _____ *p* times **5**   F. $8 \div x$

10. _____ **7** decreased by *r*   G. $h - 6$

**Choose a letter to represent the unknown number.
Then write an algebraic expression for the word phrase.**

Word Phrase	Variable	Algebraic Expression
11. 6 less than a number	_____	_____
12. the product of **8** and a number	_____	_____
13. a boy's age divided by **7**	_____	_____
14. 5 more than a number	_____	_____
15. the sum of **11** and a number	_____	_____
16. double a number	_____	_____

**Problem Solving
Reasoning**   Solve.

17. Bryan is **8** years older than Tracey.

   a. Write an algebraic expression to represent Bryan's age.

      Use *t* as the variable. _____

   b. If Tracey is **12** years old, how old is Bryan? _____

   c. If Bryan is **10** years old, how old is Tracey? _____

18. Cory is *twice* Mai's age.

   a. Write an algebraic expression to represent Cory's age.

      Use *m* as the variable. _____

   b. If Mai is **14** years old, how old is Cory? _____

   c. If Cory is **18** years old, how old is Mai? _____

Test Prep ★ Mixed Review

19 Lisa can jump rope 109 times a
minute. At this rate, how many jumps
would she make in 11 minutes?

   A 399

   B 1,130

   C 1,199

   D 1,356

20 Which of the following is a prime
number?

   F 21

   G 27

   H 29

   J 33

Meaning of Equations

A mathematical sentence with an equals sign (=) is called an **equation**.

4 + 2 = 6

An equation is balanced when the value on one side of the equals sign is the same as the value on the other side.

You can think of a balance scale.

4 + 2 marbles on the left side → 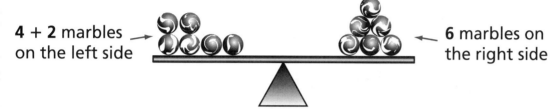 ← 6 marbles on the right side

4 + 2 = 6 is a balanced equation.

If you add the same number to both sides of a balanced equation, the equation stays balanced.
Add **3** to both sides of **4 + 2 = 6.**

(4 + 2) + 3 or **9** marbles on the left side → 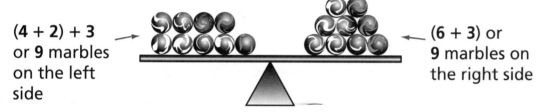 ← (6 + 3) or **9** marbles on the right side

4 + 2 + 3 = 6 + 3 is a balanced equation.

A balanced equation is a number sentence that is true.

Write *Yes* if the equation is balanced. Write *No* if it is not balanced.

1. 6 + 4 = 10 _____   6 + 4 + 2 = 10 + 2 _____

2. 2 + 5 + 7 = 6 + 7 _____   3 + 4 + 8 = 7 + 4 _____

3. 3 + 8 = 12 _____   3 + 8 + 4 = 11 + 4 _____

Complete the equation so that it is balanced.

4. 4 + 5 + 2 = 9 + ___   3 + 1 + 7 = ___ + 7   8 + 5 + 9 = 8 + ___

5. 7 + ___ + 1 = 10 + 1   11 + 4 + ___ = 15 + 6   ___ + 8 + 11 = 13 + 11

6. 10 + ___ + 5 = 16 + 5   8 + 2 + 9 = 8 + ___   ___ + 16 + 1 = 23 + 17

7. 34 + 15 + 7 = 49 + ___   37 + 11 + 8 = ___ + 8   68 + 5 + 19 = 73 + ___

8. 80 + ___ + 16 = 100 + 16   10 + 90 + 18 = ___ + 18   23 + 18 + 12 = 23 + ___

A balanced equation stays balanced if you multiply both sides by the same number.

This is a balanced equation:
$3 + 1 = 4$

Now multiply both sides by **2**.

$(3 + 1) \times 2$ →
8 marbles on the left side

← 4×2
8 marbles on the right side

$(3 + 1) \times 2 = 4 \times 2$ is a balanced equation.

Write *Yes* if the equation is balanced. Write *No* if it is not balanced.

9. $(5 + 4) \times 2 = 9 \times 2$ _____

$(6 + 6) \times 2 = (6 + 5) \times 2$ _____

10. $(1 + 5) \times 2 = 6$ _____

$(2 + 3) \times 2 = 5 \times 2$ _____

Complete the equation so that it is balanced.

11. $(4 + 3) \times 2 = $ _____ $\times 2$

$(8 + 1) \times 7 = $ _____ $\times 7$

12. $(5 + 6) \times 2 = 11 \times$ _____

$(7 + 5) \times 2 = 12 \times$ _____

Problem Solving Reasoning Solve.

13. Lyle has **4** red and **6** green marbles. Jane has **10** blue marbles. If they each doubled the number of marbles they have, who would have the greater number?

Explain. _____

_____

Test Prep ★ Mixed Review

14 Which shows all the factors of 34?

A 2, 4, 9, 18   C 1, 6, 9

B 2, 17   D 1, 2, 17, 34

15 A boat is sailing a distance of 3,315 miles. If the boat sails 65 miles a day, how many days will the trip take?

F 49   H 51

G 50   J 53

Name _____   **Equations and Sentences**

The word sentence, "The length of a rug decreased by **12** feet is **32** feet.", can be written as an **algebraic equation.**

$$y - 12 = 32$$

An algebraic equation contains an equals sign and at least one variable, number, and operation.

Write the letter of the algebraic equation that matches the word sentence.

1. _____ If a number is decreased by **5**, it is **10**.   A. $n - 6 = 13$

2. _____ If a number is increased by **5**, it is **10**.   B. $n \div 2 = 10$

3. _____ Six more than a number is **13**.   C. $n + 6 = 13$

4. _____ Six less than a number is **13**.   D. $n - 5 = 10$

5. _____ A number divided by **2** is **10**.   E. $10 \div n = 2$

6. _____ Ten divided by a number is **2**.   F. $n + 5 = 10$

Write an algebraic equation for the word sentence. Use n for the variable.

7. Tim's age doubled is **24**.

_____

8. Twelve less than the number of rocks is **14**.

_____

9. Thirteen dollars less than the price of a baseball bat is **$8**.

_____

10. The length of a rug increased by 5 meters is **15** meters.

_____

To solve an equation, you need to find a value for the variable that balances the equation.

$4 + n = 6$

$4 + n$ marbles on the left side. → **6** marbles on the right side.

The value of n must be **2**.
Replace n with **2** in the equation.
$4 + 2 = 6$
The equation is balanced.

Circle the value for the variable that makes the equation balanced.

11. $8 - t = 3$ 2   4   5

12. $y + 7 = 15$ 6   8   10

13. $5 \times n = 45$ 6   9   11

14. $16 - r = 11$ 5   8   9

Find the value of the variable that makes the equation balanced.

15. $p + 7 = 18$, $p = $ _____

16. $r + 10 = 23$, $r = $ _____

17. $t \times 8 = 48$, $t = $ _____

18. $2 + m = 44$, $m = $ _____

19. $j \div 7 = 8$, $j = $ _____

20. $64 \div 8 = k$, $k = $ _____

 Quick Check

Write an algebraic expression for the word phrase.

21. 7 more than a number

22. 6 less than a number

_____   _____

Complete the equation so it is balanced.

23. $2 + 3 + 6 = 7 +$ ☐

24. $(2 + 7) \times 2 = 9 \times$ ☐

Write an algebraic equation for the word sentence. Use n for the variable.

25. 10 less than the number of students is 25. _____

26. Triple Ellen's age is 33. _____

Problem Solving Strategy: Writing an Equation

In this lesson, you will write equations to solve word problems.

You will use a variable in the equation to represent the number you want to find in order to solve the problem.

Problem

Stephanie wants to buy some red nail polish. Nail Glo costs twice as much as Supershine. Nail Glo costs $6. How much does Supershine cost?

1 Understand As you reread, ask yourself questions.

- What information do you have?

  Nail Glo costs _____ as much as Supershine.

  Nail Glo costs _____.

- What do you need to find out?

  _____

2 Decide Choose a method for solving.

Try the strategy Write an Equation.

- Draw a circle around the equation that could be used to represent the problem.

  $2 \times 6 = s$ $2 \times s = 6$

3 Solve Solve the equation.

- Use a related equation.

  $6 \div 2 = s$ is the related equation.

  The solution of $6 \div 2 = 3$ so, $s = 3$.

- Check. $2 \times s = 6$ $2 \times$ _____ $= 6$ True.

4 Look back Check your answer. Write the answer below.

Answer _____

Read the problem again. Check your answer.

- Why was it important to go back and reread the problem to check your answer?

  _____

  _____

Solve. Use the Write an Equation strategy or any other strategy you have learned.

1. Mr. Vesprini bought **6** dozen muffins. How many muffins was that?

   Think: Circle the equation that can help you solve the problem.

   $6 \times 12 = m$ $6 \times m = 12$

   Answer _____

2. The total cost of a hot dog and a carton of orange juice is **$3.25**. The hot dog cost **$1.75**. How much was the orange juice?

   Think: Circle the equation that can help you solve the problem.

   $\$1.75 + j = \$3.25$ $\$3.25 + \$1.75 = j$

   Answer _____

3. The area of a rectangular hallway is **24** square feet. The width of the hallway is **3** feet. What is the length of the hallway?

   _____

4. You need $\frac{3}{4}$ cup of corn meal to make one pan of cornbread. How many cups of corn meal would you need to make **3** pans of cornbread?

   _____

5. A restaurant has four pizza toppings: pepperoni, sausage, green pepper, and mushrooms. How many different two-topping pizzas can be made?

   _____

6. The perimeter of a rectangle is **16** feet. The area of the rectangle is **15** square feet. The length is greater than the width. What are the length and width?

   _____

7. There is a bus stop in front of Luann's house. A bus arrives at the stop every **45** minutes and goes into town. The first bus comes at **7:15** A.M. If the bus trip takes **12** minutes, what is the latest bus Luann can take in order to get to town by **1:00** P.M.?

   _____

8. Rachel is **50** inches tall. Alyssa is **2** inches shorter than Rachel. Benjamin is **3** inches taller than Alyssa. Spencer is **5** inches taller than Benjamin. How much taller is Spencer than Alyssa?

   _____

9. A square kitchen has an area of **100** square feet. What is the kitchen's perimeter?

   _____

10. Jenny has some money in her pocket. Sharon gave her **$13** more. Then Jenny had **$15**. How much money did Jenny start with?

    _____

Name _____

You can use a table to show the relationship between the number of tricycles and the number of wheels.

tricycles (t)	wheels (w)
1	3
2	6
3	9
4	w

← **1** tricycle has **3** wheels.
← **2** tricycles have **6** wheels.
← **3** tricycles have **9** wheels.
← **4** tricycles have w wheels.

Look for a pattern in the table above.
Describe the pattern as a rule.

Three times the number of tricycles is the number of wheels.

You can write the rule as an algebraic equation. $3 \times t = w$

Use the algebraic equation to find how many wheels **4** tricycles have.

Replace t with **4**. $3 \times 4 = w$
Find the product. $12 = w$

There are **12** wheels when there are **4** tricycles.

_____

Describe the rule using words. Then complete the tables.

1. _____   _____

_____   _____

bicycles (b)	wheels (w)
1	2
2	4
3	6
4	

cups (c)	ounces (n)
1	8
2	16
3	
4	

2. _____   _____

length (l)	width (w)
5	8
6	9
7	
8	

side (s)	perimeter (p)
1	4
2	8
3	
4	

Describe the rule using words. Complete the table.
Then write the rule as an algebraic equation using the variables given.

3. _____
_____

plants (*p*)	flowers (*f*)
1	6
2	12
3	18
4	

Algebraic equation: _____

4. _____
_____

clarinets (*c*)	trumpets (*t*)
3	6
6	9
9	
12	

Algebraic equation: _____

5. _____
_____

feet (*f*)	inches (*i*)
2	24
4	48
6	
8	

Algebraic equation: _____

6. _____
_____

yards (*y*)	feet (*f*)
1	3
2	6
3	
4	

Algebraic equation: _____

7. _____
_____

x	*y*
2	1
4	3
6	
8	

Algebraic equation: _____

8. _____
_____

x	*y*
11	12
12	13
13	
14	

Algebraic equation: _____

Test Prep ★ Mixed Review

9 A clothing company is shipping an order for 246 sweaters in boxes. If each box holds 12 sweaters, how many boxes will be needed?

A 22   **C** 20

B 21   **D** 18

10 What number could go in the ☐ to make the equation true?

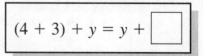

$$(4 + 3) + y = y + \boxed{}$$

F 3   **H** 6

G 4   **J** 7

Name _____

You can use ordered pairs and a **coordinate grid** to locate points.

A coordinate grid has a horizontal line, called the *x*-axis, and a vertical line, called the *y*-axis.

Each axis is labeled like a number line. The point where the *x*-axis and *y*-axis meet is called the origin.

Ordered pairs are used to locate points on the grid. The origin is at point **(0, 0).**

In an ordered pair

- the first number tells how far to move right along the *x*-axis. It is called the *x*-coordinate.

- the second number tells how far to move up the *y*-axis. It is called the *y*-coordinate.

Locate the point **(4, 5)**

1. Start at the origin.

2. Move **4** units right, along the *x*-axis.

3. Move **5** units up, along the *y*-axis.

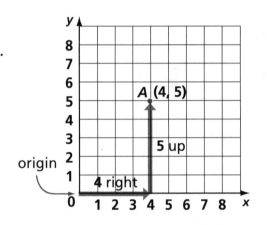

Complete the set of directions that describes the location of each ordered pair.

1. (2, 6) move _____ 2, move _____ 6

2. (7, 1) move _____ _____, move _____ _____

Locate and label each point.

3. A (8, 4)   B (8, 3)   C (7, 2)

D (6, 1)   E (5, 2)   F (4, 3)

G (4, 4)   H (4, 5)   I (5, 6)

J (6, 7)   K (7, 6)   L (8, 5)

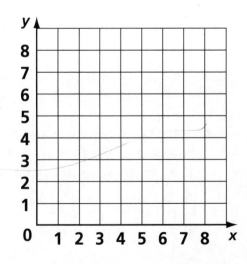

4. Using line segments, connect the points from exercise **3** in alphabetical order. What figure is formed?

_____

Name all the sums for 5 using the given equation. Write the addends as ordered pairs. Then graph the ordered pairs.

Addends $x + y = 5$	Ordered pairs (x, y)	Graph the ordered pairs on this grid.

5. $0 + \underline{\hphantom{000}} = 5$ $(0, \underline{\hphantom{00}})$

6. $\underline{\hphantom{000}} + 4 = 5$ $(\underline{\hphantom{00}}, 4)$

7. $\underline{\hphantom{000}} + \underline{\hphantom{000}} = 5$ $(\underline{\hphantom{00}}, \underline{\hphantom{00}})$

8. $\underline{\hphantom{000}} + \underline{\hphantom{000}} = 5$ $(\underline{\hphantom{00}}, \underline{\hphantom{00}})$

9. $\underline{\hphantom{000}} + \underline{\hphantom{000}} = 5$ $(\underline{\hphantom{00}}, \underline{\hphantom{00}})$

10. $\underline{\hphantom{000}} + \underline{\hphantom{000}} = 5$ $(\underline{\hphantom{00}}, \underline{\hphantom{00}})$

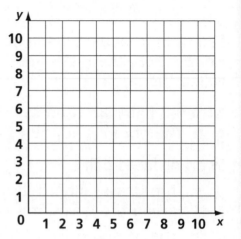

11. Connect the points on the graph. What do you have?

_____

| Problem Solving |
| Reasoning |

Solve.

12. Laura graphed the points **(2, 4)**, **(2, 6)** and **(5, 4)**. She needs one more point to make a rectangle. What point should she graph?

_____

13. Write *True* or *False*. The length of the rectangle is **3** units. Then, the length of the rectangle is the difference of the *x*-coordinates. _____

14. Explain how you could find the width of the rectangle. Then find it.

_____

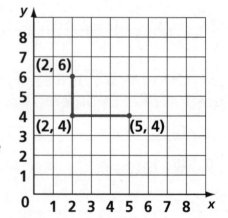

Test Prep ★ Mixed Review

15 A movie theater has 141 seats. Each row except the first row has 9 seats. How many seats are in the first row?

 A 8   **C** 4

 B 6   **D** 2

16 Carlos hiked 8,648 yards in 4 hours. What is the average number of yards he hiked each hour?

 F 216   **H** 2,262

 G 2,162   **J** 22,312

Name _____

You can use words or symbols to write a rule about the numbers in an ordered pair.

$$(3, 5)$$

Words: Add **2** to the first number to get the second number.

Symbols: $x + 2 = y$

Use the rule to write more ordered pairs. The table shows different numbers for **x**. It also shows how to get numbers for **y** using the rule.

Write the ordered pairs from the table.

(1, 3)   (2, 4)   (3, 5)   (4, 6)   (5, 7)

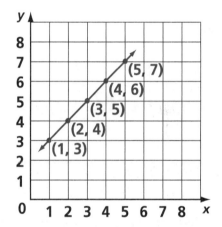

first number x	rule x + 2	second number y
1	1 + 2	3
2	2 + 2	4
3	3 + 2	5
4	4 + 2	6
5	5 + 2	7

Use the coordinate grid to graph the ordered pairs.

The graph of these ordered pairs forms a straight line.

Complete the table. Write the ordered pairs. Then graph and connect the points on the grid.

1.

x	x − 1	y
1	1 − 1	
2	2 − 1	
3	3 − 1	
4	4 − 1	
5	5 − 1	

Ordered Pairs

(1, _____)

(2, _____)

(3, _____)

(4, _____)

(5, _____)

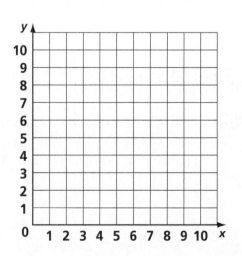

Complete the function table. Write the ordered pairs. Then graph and connect the ordered pairs on the grid.

2.

x	x + 1	y
1	1 + 1	
2		
3		
4		
5		

Ordered Pairs

(_____ , _____)

(_____ , _____)

(_____ , _____)

(_____ , _____)

(_____ , _____)

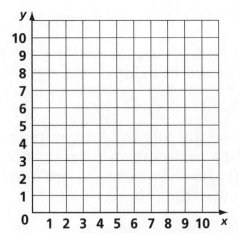

3.

x	x × 2	y
1	1 × 2	2
2	× 2	
3	× 2	
4	× 2	
5	× 2	

Ordered Pairs

(_____ , _____)

(_____ , _____)

(_____ , _____)

(_____ , _____)

(_____ , _____)

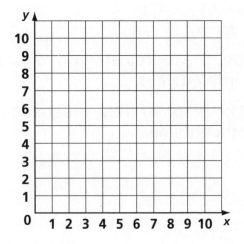

4.

x	x × 1	y
2		
3		
5		
6		
8		

Ordered Pairs

(_____ , _____)

(_____ , _____)

(_____ , _____)

(_____ , _____)

(_____ , _____)

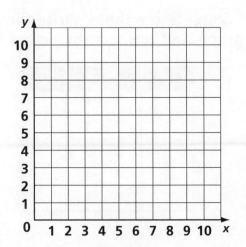

Name _____

Complete a function table for the rule and the
given values of *x*. Write the ordered pairs. Then
graph and connect them on the grid.

5. *x* − 5 = *y*   *x* = 5, 6, 7, and 8

_____
_____
_____
_____

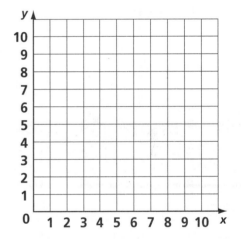

6. *x* + 7 = *y*   *x* = 0, 1, 2, and 3

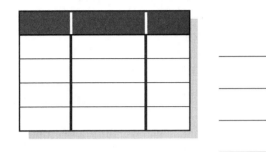

_____
_____
_____
_____

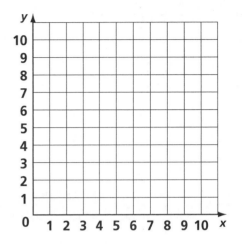

7. (*x* × 2) − 6 = *y*   *x* = 3, 5, 7, and 8

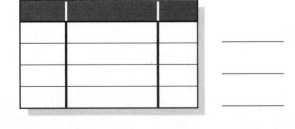

_____
_____
_____
_____

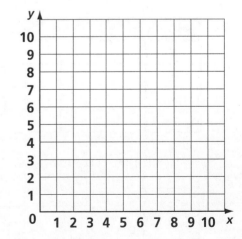

Solve.

8. Write *True* or *False*. The length of the line that connects the points **(3, 2)** and **(3, 9)** is the difference of the *y*-coordinates: **9 − 2**

   or **7** units. _____

9. Explain how you could find the length of the line that connects the points **(0, 4)** and **(9, 4)**.

   _____

   _____

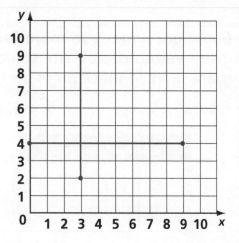

✓ Quick Check

10. Name all the sums for 4 using the given equation. Write the addends as ordered pairs. Then graph and connect the ordered pairs.

    Work Space.

    x + y = 4   **(x, y)**

    0 + _____ = 4   (0, _____)

    1 + _____ = 4   (1, _____)

    2 + _____ = 4   (2, _____)

    3 + _____ = 4   (3, _____)

    4 + _____ = 4   (4, _____)

    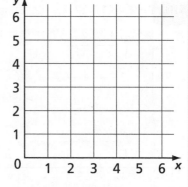

11. Complete the function table. Write the ordered pairs. Then graph the ordered pairs on the grid.

x	x + 2	y
1		
2		
3		
4		

(_____)

(_____)

(_____)

(_____)

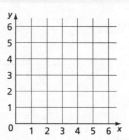

Some problems give more facts than you need. You need to decide which facts are necessary.

Some problems do not give enough facts. In this lesson, you may need to tell what fact or facts you need to solve a problem.

Tips to Remember:

1. Understand	2. Decide	3. Solve	4. Look back

- Read each problem more than once. Circle the important words and numbers. Cross out the words and numbers that you don't need.
- Try to remember a real-life situation like the one described in the problem. What do you remember that might help you find a solution?
- When you can, make a prediction about the answer. Then compare your answer and your prediction.

Cross out the extra information. Then solve the problem. If information is missing, name the fact or facts needed on the answer lines.

1. The Barker family drove to Orlando, Florida. They drove the total distance, **1044** miles, in **3** days. Their average speed was **51** miles per hour. What was the average number of miles they traveled per day?

Think: How does the question help you decide what facts are needed?

_____

_____

Answer _____

_____

2. When they arrived in Orlando, the Barkers stayed at a large hotel. There were **350** guest rooms and **2** restaurants. Their room cost **$85** (tax included) per night. What was their total room bill?

Think: What information do you need to find the total room bill?

_____

_____

Answer _____

_____

Cross out the extra information. Then solve the problem. If information is missing, name the fact or facts that you need.

3. Yosemite National Park is **300** miles north of Los Angeles and **200** miles east of San Francisco. The Chin family drove to Yosemite. They drove at an average speed of **50** miles per hour. How many hours did the trip take?

_____

_____

4. There is an observatory on the **86**th floor of the Empire State Building. On a clear day, you can see for **80** miles. A ticket to go up to the observatory costs **$3.75**. How much will **3** tickets cost?

_____

5. Elevator ticket prices at the Eiffel Tower vary. To go to the first level (**188** feet), the cost is **$3.50**. To go to the second level (**380** feet), the cost is **$7.30**. To go to the highest level (**1,060** feet), the cost is **$9.90**. What is the difference in price between the highest level and the first level?

_____

6. About **3** million people visit the Statue of Liberty each year. The statue weighs **225** tons and is **151** feet high. The Dori family climbed up from the ground level to the crown and then climbed down. It took them a total of **3** hours and **20** minutes. How many steps did they climb altogether?

_____

_____

Extend Your Thinking

7. Go back to problem 4. Complete the graph below to show the cost of tickets to the observatory.

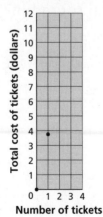

Number of tickets

Do all the points lie on a line?

_____

8. Go back to problem 5. Use the information in the problem to complete the graph below.

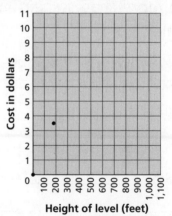

Height of level (feet)

Do all the points lie on a line?

_____

Choose a variable for each unknown number.
Then write an algebraic expression for the
word phrase.

Word Phrase	Variable	Algebraic Expression
1. 4 more than a number	_____	_____
2. the product of **6** and a number	_____	_____
3. a person's height doubled	_____	_____

Complete the equation so that it is balanced.

4. $4 + 5 + 4 = 9 +$ _____

5. $11 + 8 + 3 =$ _____ $+ 3$

6. $(7 + 5) \times 2 =$ _____ $\times 2$

7. $(6 + 5) \times 3 = 11 \times$ _____

Circle the value for the variable that makes the
equation balanced.

8. $12 - t = 7$ 2   4   5

9. $y + 6 = 14$ 6   8   10

10. $8 \times n = 48$ 6   9   11

11. $21 - r = 9$ 30   14   12

Solve the equation.

12. $j \times 7 = 70$ $j =$ _____

13. $y + 13 = 53$ $y =$ _____

Write an algebraic equation for the word sentence.
Then find the solution. Use *n* for the variable.

14. Five more than some number is **18**. What is the
number?

_____

15. The sum of Rick's test score and **15** is **100**. What was
Rick's score?

_____

16. A number divided by **6** is **4**. What is the number?

_____

Complete the table. Describe the rule using words. Then write the rule as an algebraic equation using the variables given.

m	n
4	8
6	12
17. 8	
18. 10	

19. Words: _____

_____

20. Algebraic rule: _____

_____

Complete the function table for the rule and the values of x listed. Write the ordered pairs. Then graph and connect them on the grid.

x	x – 4	y
4	4 – 4	0
21. 5		
22. 6		
23. 7		

Ordered Pairs

(4, 0)

_____

_____

_____

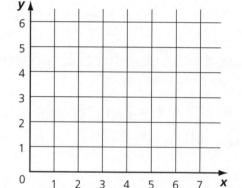

24. If you connected the points on the graph, what would you draw?

_____

Solve.

25. Luke is **12** years old and **4** years older than his sister Erica. What number sentence could be used to find Erica's age? How old is Erica?

_____

Cross out the extra information. Then solve the problem.

26. A museum was visited by **1,290** people on Friday, **3,615** people on Saturday, and **2,753** people on Sunday. How many people did not visit the museum on Friday?

_____

1 The line graph shows the high temperature each day for a week. How much warmer was the temperature on Friday than on Thursday?

High Temperatures for a Week

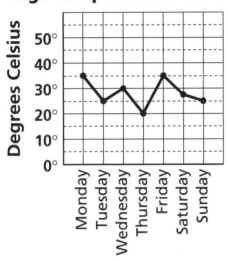

Day of the Week

A 15° C   C 7° C

B 10° C   D 5° C

2 Find the rule for the function table shown below. Choose the algebraic expression that states the rule.

p	n
5	25
8	40
11	55
13	65

F $p + 20$ H $p + 32$

G $p \div 5$ J $p \times 5$

3 Plot the points (3, 6) and (6, 6) on the coordinate grid. Draw lines to connect these points to the other points shown. What shape did you make?

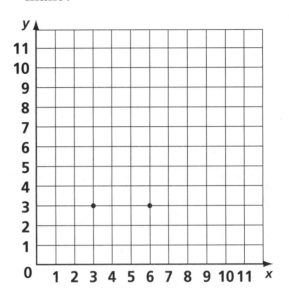

A Triangle   C Square

B Circle   D Hexagon

4 Students recorded the number of people in their families. They displayed the results on a line plot.

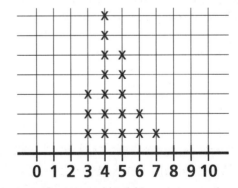

What is the median number of people in these families?

F 4   H 6

G 5   J 18

5 Choose the shape that answers this riddle.

I have exactly 2 sides that are parallel. What shape am I?

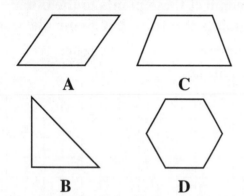

A

C

B

D

6 At a sports arena, there are 122 seats in every row. There are 93 rows. How many seats are in the stadium all together?

F 1,244   **H** 10,246   **K** NH

G 1,464   **J** 11,346

7 What is line segment z?

A Diameter   **C** Ray

B Radius   **D** Chord

8 What number could go in the ☐ to make the equation true?

$$15 + x = (\boxed{} + 8) + x$$

F 6   **H** 8

G 7   **J** 9

9 Find the rule for the function table shown below. Choose the algebraic expression that states the rule.

x	y
37	43
18	24
48	54
13	

A $x + 6$ **C** $y \div 3$

B $x \times 7$ **D** $x + 8$

10 Mr. O'Connell's driveway is 45 yards long. What is the length of his driveway in feet?

F 540   **H** 270

G 450   **J** 135

11 A rectangle has a perimeter of 26 feet. Which of the following could be the measurement of its area?

A 42 square feet

B 32 square feet

C 26 square feet

D 18 square feet

Tables of Measures

Metric System

Prefixes

kilo (k)	=	1,000
hecto (h)	=	100
deka (da)	=	10
deci (d)	=	$\frac{1}{10}$
centi (c)	=	$\frac{1}{100}$
milli (m)	=	$\frac{1}{1,000}$

Length

1 kilometer (km)	=	1,000 meters (m)
1 meter	=	10 decimeters (dm)
1 decimeter	=	10 centimeters (cm)
1 meter	=	100 centimeters (cm)
1 centimeter	=	10 millimeters (mm)
1 meter	=	1,000 millimeters

Capacity and Mass

1 liter	=	1,000 milliliters (mL)
1 kilogram	=	1,000 grams (g)
1 gram	=	1,000 milligrams (mg)

Customary System

Length

1 foot (ft)	=	12 inches (in.)
1 yard (yd)	=	3 feet
1 yard	=	36 inches
1 mile (mi)	=	5,280 feet
1 mile	=	1,760 yards

Capacity

1 cup (c)	=	8 fluid ounces (fl oz)
1 pint (pt)	=	2 cups
1 quart (qt)	=	2 pints
1 gallon (gal)	=	4 quarts

Weight

1 pound (lb)	=	16 ounces (oz)
1 ton (T)	=	2,000 pounds

Other Measures

Time

1 minute (min)	=	60 seconds (s)
1 hour (h)	=	60 minutes
1 day	=	24 hours
1 week (wk)	=	7 days
1 month (mo)	≈	4 weeks
1 year (yr)	=	12 months
1 year	=	52 weeks
1 year	=	365 days
1 leap year	=	366 days
1 decade	=	10 years
1 century	=	100 years

Counting

1 dozen (doz)	=	12 things
1 score	=	20 things
1 gross (gro)	=	12 dozen
1 gross	=	144 things

Geometric Formulas

Rectangle	**Square**	**Rectangular Prism**	**Cube**
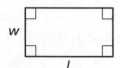	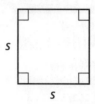	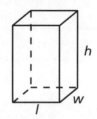	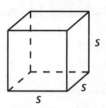
Perimeter: $P = 2 \times (l + w)$	Perimeter: $P = 4 \times s$	Surface Area: $SA = 2 \times (l \times w) +$ $(w \times h) + (l \times h)$	Surface Area: $SA = 6 \times (s \times s)$
Area: $A = l \times w$	Area: $A = s \times s$	Volume: $V = l \times w \times h$	Volume: $V = s \times (s \times s)$

Glossary

A

acute angle An angle whose measure is less than 90°.

addend A number to be added in an addition expression.

adding zero property Adding zero to any number does not change the number.
Examples:
$7 + 0 = 7; n + 0 = n$

A.M. A symbol used for times from midnight to noon.

angle A geometric figure formed by two rays with a common endpoint.

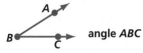

angle *ABC*

area A measure of the number of square units in a region. The area of the region shown below is 6 square centimeters.

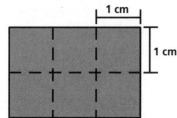

associative property of addition (also called the *grouping property of addition*) Changing the grouping of the addends does not change the sum.
Example:
$(7 + 5) + 6 = 7 + (5 + 6)$

associative property of multiplication (also called the *grouping property of multiplication*) Changing the grouping of the factors does not change the product.
Example:
$(7 \times 5) \times 2 = 7 \times (5 \times 2)$

average (or mean) The sum of given numbers, divided by the number of addends used in finding the sum.
Example: The average of 4, 5, and 9 is 6.

axis (see *x*-axis, *y*-axis) A reference line on a coordinate grid or graph.

B

bar graph A pictorial representation of data that uses lengths of bars to show the information.

base A side or face in a plane or space figure.

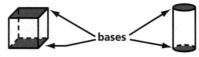

bases

C

capacity The maximum amount of liquid that a container can hold.

Celsius temperature scale (°C) The temperature scale in the metric system in which the freezing temperature of water is 0°C and the boiling temperature of water is 100°C.

circle A plane figure that has all of its points the same distance from a given point called the *center*.

center

circle graph A pictorial representation of data that uses sections of a circle to show the information.

common factor A number that is a factor of two or more whole numbers.
Example: 1, 2, 3, and 6 are common factors of 12 and 18.

common multiple A number that is a multiple of two or more whole numbers.
Example: Common multiples of 3 and 4 are 12, 24, 36, . . .

commutative property of addition (also called the *order property of addition*) Changing the order of the addends does not change the sum.
Example: $3 + 4 = 4 + 3$

commutative property of multiplication (also called the *order property of multiplication*) Changing the order of the factors does not change the product.
Example:
$3 \times 5 = 5 \times 3$

compatible numbers Numbers used to make estimates. They are easy to work with mentally and are close to the given numbers.

composite number A number that has more than two factors.
Example: 9 is composite, because its factors are 1, 3, and 9.

cone A space figure with one flat, circular surface and one curved surface.

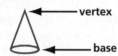

congruent figures Figures that have exactly the same size and shape.

coordinates An ordered pair of numbers that locate a point on a coordinate grid. The first number represents how many units to move across. The second number represents how many units to move up.

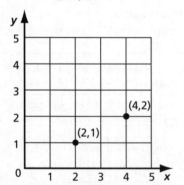

coordinate grid A grid with number lines used to locate points in a plane.

cube A rectangular prism whose faces are all congruent squares.

customary system The system of measurement that uses units such as foot, quart, pound, and degrees Fahrenheit.

cylinder A space figure with two congruent circular bases joined by a single curved surface.

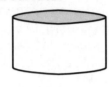

D

data Numerical information.

decimal A number that uses place value to indicate parts of a whole. The decimal point separates the whole number digits from the digits representing parts of a whole.
Examples: 1.6, 3.67

decimal point A symbol used to separate tenths and hundredths from whole numbers. It is also used to separate dollars and cents.
Example:

3.67 $5.10
decimal points

degree A unit of measure of temperature or of an angle.

denominator The digit written below the fraction bar in a fraction. It tells how many parts are in the whole.
Example:
$\frac{1}{5}$ ← denominator

diameter A line segment passing through the center and joining any two points on a circle.

diameter

difference The answer to a subtraction problem.

digit Any of the symbols 1, 2, 3, 4, 5, 6, 7, 8, 9, and 0.

distance The length of a path between two points.

distributive property The product of a number and the sum of two numbers is equal to the sum of the two products.
Example:
$3 \times (20 + 7) =$
$(3 \times 20) + (3 \times 7)$

dividend The number that is divided in a division problem.

divisible When a number can be divided by another number without a remainder.
Example: 4, 16, and 64 are all divisible by 4.

divisor The number by which the dividend is divided in a division problem.

E

edge A line segment where two faces of a space figure meet.

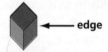
edge

elapsed time The time that passes between the beginning and end of an event.
Example: The elapsed time between 9:30 A.M. and 2:15 P.M. is 4 hours 45 minutes.

endpoint A point at the end of a line segment or ray.

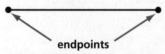
endpoints

equation A number sentence in which an equal sign is used.
Example: 3 + 7 = 10
             3 + n = 10

equilateral triangle A triangle with three congruent sides.

equilateral triangle

equivalent fractions Two or more fractions that represent the same number.
Example:
$$\frac{1}{2} \rightarrow \frac{2}{4} \rightarrow \frac{3}{6} \rightarrow \frac{4}{8}$$

equivalent measures Two or more measures that represent the same amount.
Example: 2 gal = 8 qt

estimate To find an approximate solution by using rounded numbers.

even number A whole number that is divisible by 2.

event Any outcome or set of outcomes of an experiment.

expanded form A number written as the sum of the value of its digits.
Example: The expanded form of 2,316 is 2,000 + 300 + 10 + 6.

expression A combination of numbers and symbols that represent a quantity.
Examples:
(7 + 3) ÷ 5 or 6 × *n*

F

face A flat surface that is a side of a space figure.

face

factor A number to be multiplied in a multiplication expression.

factor (of a number) A number that divides exactly into another number.
Example: The numbers 1, 2, 3, 4, 6, and 12 are all factors of 12.

Fahrenheit temperature scale (°F) The temperature scale in the customary system in which the freezing temperature of water is 32°F and the boiling temperature of water is 212°F.

---

formula An equation that expresses a mathematical relationship.
Example: A formula for area *A* of a rectangle with length *l* and width *w* is
$A = l \times w$

fraction A number that names a part of a region or set.
Examples: $\frac{1}{2}$ or $\frac{3}{4}$

H

hexagon A polygon that has six sides.

horizontal line A straight line on a grid that goes across, rather than up.

I

impossible event In probability, an event that cannot take place. The probability of an impossible event is expressed as 0.

inequality A number sentence that states that two numbers or expressions are greater than (>), less than (<), or not equal to (≠) each other.
Examples: 3 + 6 < 10
5 + 7 ≠ 10

intersecting lines Line segments that cross each other.

inverse operation An operation that undoes the results of another operation.
Example: 3 × 8 = 24
24 ÷ 3 = 8

isosceles triangle A triangle with at least two congruent sides.

K

key (of a pictograph) A part of a pictograph that tells what each symbol on the graph represents.

L

line A set of points that extends endlessly in two opposite directions.

line *AB* or $\overleftrightarrow{AB}$

line graph A pictorial representation of data that uses line segments to show changes over time.

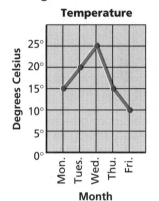

line plot A pictorial representation of data along a number line.

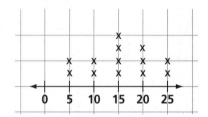

line segment A part of a line that has two endpoints.
A ●———————● *Z*

line symmetry A figure has line symmetry when it can be folded to make two parts that match exactly.

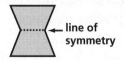
line of symmetry

M

mass The amount of matter in an object. Some units of mass are gram and kilogram.

mean *See* average.

median The middle point of a set of data, arranged from least to greatest.
Example: The median of 2, 4, 5, 6, 7 is 5.

metric system An international system of measurement that uses the meter, liter, gram, and degrees Celsius as the basic units of measure.

mixed number A number, such as $2\frac{2}{3}$ that is made up of a whole number and a fraction less than one.

mode The number (or numbers) that occurs most often in a set of data. If every number occurs only once, the data has no mode.
Example: The mode of 2, 4, 5, 5 is 5.

multiple The product of the number and any whole number.
Example: The multiples of 4 are 0, 4, 8, 12, 16, . . .

multiplying by 1 property Multiplying any number by 1 is equal to that number.
Example: $8 \times 1 = 8$

multiplying by 0 property Multiplying any number by 0 is equal to 0.
Example: $8 \times 0 = 0$

N

negative number A number that is less than zero.
Example:

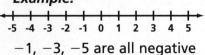

-1, -3, -5 are all negative numbers.

net A flat pattern that folds into a space figure.

number line A line that has its points labeled with numbers.

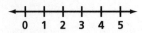

number sentence A statement showing how numbers in an operation are related.
Example: $9 \times 3 = 27$

numerator The number written above the bar in a fraction. It tells how many parts of the whole.
Example:
 numerator

O

obtuse angle An angle whose measure is greater than 90° and less than 180°.

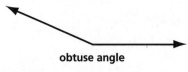
obtuse angle

octagon A polygon that has 8 sides.

odd number A whole number that is not divisible by 2.

open sentence A number sentence that contains a variable.
Example: $10 + n = 17$

order of operations The rules that define the order in which the operations in an expression are to be evaluated.

Order of Operations

1. Do operations in parentheses first.
2. Multiply and divide from left to right.
3. Add and subtract from left to right.

---

outcome A result in a probability experiment.

outlier An item of data that is significantly greater or less than the other items of data.

P

parallel lines Two lines in the same plane that do not intersect.

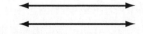

parallelogram A quadrilateral in which both pairs of opposite sides are parallel.

parentheses Symbols used in number sentences to show what part of a problem to solve first.
Example:
$(7 \times 3) \times 2 = 21 \times 2$

pentagon A polygon with five sides.

perimeter The distance around a polygon. It is found by adding the lengths of all the sides.

period Each group of three digits seen in a number written in standard form.
Example: In 306,789,245, the millions period is 306, the thousands period is 789, and 245 is the ones period.

perpendicular lines Two lines that intersect to form right angles.

pictograph A pictorial representation of data that uses symbols to represent quantities.

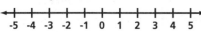

Class A	🎱 🎱 🎱 🎱
Class B	🎱 🎱
Key 🎱 = 5 votes	

place-value system A system of numeration in which the value of a digit depends on its position in the number.
Example: In 8,756, the digit 7 is in the hundreds place.

plane A flat surface that extends in all directions without end.

plane figure A figure whose points are all in the same plane.

point A location in space. It is represented by a dot.

polygon A plane figure composed of line segments that meet only at their endpoints. The segments must form a closed figure.

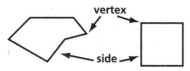

positive number A number that is greater than zero.
Example:

1, 3, and 5 are all positive numbers.

prediction In a probability experiment, a guess about an outcome that is based on earlier events.

prime number A whole number greater than 1 that has exactly two factors, itself and 1.
Example: 2 = 2 × 1

prism A space figure that is named for the shape of its two parallel bases.

triangular prism

probability The chance that an event will occur; probability is expressed using a number from 0 to 1.

product The answer to a multiplication problem.

pyramid A space figure whose base is a polygon and whose other faces are triangles that share a common vertex. A pyramid is named by the shape of its base.

Q

quadrilateral A polygon that has four sides.

quotient The answer in a division problem.

R

radius A segment from any point on a circle to its center; also the length of this segment.

radius

range The difference between the least and greatest number in a set of data.
Example: In the data set 2, 4, 5, 5 the range is 3 (5 − 2 = 3).

ray A part of a line that has one endpoint. When naming it, the endpoint is used first.

endpoint   *A*   *B*   ray *AB*

rectangle A parallelogram that has four right angles.

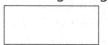

rectangular prism A space figure having six rectangular faces.

region The space inside a closed figure.

regular polygon A polygon that has all sides congruent and all angles congruent.

remainder The number that is left over in a division problem.

rhombus A parallelogram that has all of its sides congruent.

right angle An angle whose measure is 90°.

90°

rounding Changing a number up or down to the nearest 10, 100, 1,000, and so on.
Examples:
12,501 rounded to the nearest hundred is 12,500.
4.38 rounded to the nearest tenth is 4.3.

S

scalene triangle A triangle that has no congruent sides.

sequence Numbers arranged according to some pattern or rule.

side A line segment forming part of a figure.

simplest form A fraction whose numerator and denominator have no common factor greater than 1.
Example: $\frac{1}{2}$ is the simplest form of $\frac{5}{10}$.

space figure A figure that is not entirely in one plane such as a sphere, a rectangular prism, or a pyramid.

sphere A space figure that has all of its points the same distance from the center.

square A rectangle that has all its sides congruent.

standard form A number that is expressed using digits and a base 10 place-value system.
Example: 3,126 is the standard form of the number three thousand, one hundred twenty-six.

sum The answer to an addition problem.

surface area The total area of all the faces or surfaces of a space figure.

survey An approach to collecting data that involves asking many people the same question or questions.

Symmetric figure A figure that has one or more lines of symmetry.

T

trapezoid A quadrilateral that has exactly one pair of parallel sides.

tree diagram An organized way of listing all the possible outcomes of an experiment.

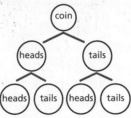

triangle A polygon that has three sides.

turn (rotation) The rotation of a figure around a point.

turn symmetry (rotational symmetry) When a figure still looks exactly the same after being rotated less than a full turn around a point.

U

unit A fixed quantity used as a standard for length, area, volume, weight, and so on.

unit price The cost of a single unit of an item.
Example: $3 for each pound of hamburger meat.

V

variable A letter that is used to represent one or more numbers.

vertical line A straight line on a grid that goes up and down, rather than across.

vertex (plural: vertices) The common point where two sides or edges meet.

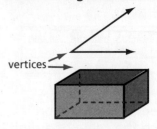

vertices

volume A measure of the space within a closed figure in space.

W

whole number Any of the numbers 0, 1, 2, 3, . . .

X

x-axis The horizontal number line on a coordinate grid.

Y

y-axis The vertical number line on a coordinate grid.

Symbols

=	is equal to
≠	is not equal to
<	is less than
>	is greater than
$n,$	placeholders
+	add
−	subtract
×	multiply
÷	divide
$\overline{)}$	divide
∠	angle
$\overline{AB}$	line segment AB
$\overrightarrow{AB}$	ray AB
$\overleftrightarrow{AB}$	line AB